Positive Psychology

Positive Psychology

Exploring the Best in People

Volume 4

Pursuing Human Flourishing

Edited by

Shane J. Lopez

Foreword by

Sonja Lyubomirsky

Praeger Perspectives

Westport, Connecticut
London

Library of Congress Cataloging-in-Publication Data

Positive psychology : exploring the best in people / edited by Shane J. Lopez ; foreword by Sonja Lyubomirsky.
    p. cm.—(Praeger perspectives)
    Includes bibliographical references and index.
    ISBN 978-0-275-99350-4 ((set) : alk. paper) — ISBN 978-0-275-99351-1 ((vol. 1) : alk. paper) — ISBN 978-0-275-99352-8 ((vol. 2) : alk. paper) — ISBN 978-0-275-99353-5 ((vol. 3) : alk. paper) — ISBN 978-0-275-99354-2 ((vol. 4) : alk. paper)
    1. Positive psychology. I. Lopez, Shane J.
    BF204.6.P66 2008
    150.19'8—dc22   2008010558

British Library Cataloguing in Publication Data is available.

Library of Congress Catalog Card Number: 2008010558
ISBN: 978-0-275-99350-4 (set)
        978-0-275-99351-1 (vol. 1)
        978-0-275-99352-8 (vol. 2)
        978-0-275-99353-5 (vol. 3)
        978-0-275-99354-2 (vol. 4)

First published in 2008

Praeger Publishers, 88 Post Road West, Westport, CT 06881
An imprint of Greenwood Publishing Group, Inc.
www.praeger.com

Printed in the United States of America

The paper used in this book complies with the Permanent Paper Standard issued by the National Information Standards Organization (Z39.48–1984).

10 9 8 7 6 5 4 3 2 1

To three experts in giving positive psychology away
Chip Anderson (1942–2005)
Don Clifton (1924–2003)
C. R. Snyder (1944–2006)

Contents

Foreword

In 1980, David Burns published the phenomenal best-seller, *Feeling Good: The New Mood Therapy*, in which he outlined the cognitive–behavioral techniques scientifically established to lift depression and anxiety. *Feeling Good* became the most frequently recommended book for depressed individuals by U.S. mental health professionals, and over four million readers purchased it. The book gave people suffering from depression, anxiety, and low self-esteem the tools to *feel better*. Indeed, studies showed that 70% of the book's readers markedly improved in their symptoms and maintained those improvements for a period of 3 years—essentially moving from a −8 on a general mood scale to a 0, or a perhaps even to a +2.

Times have changed. The goals of today's psychologists are loftier and more ambitious. During the last decade or so, researchers in the growing field of positive psychology have made tremendous advances in knowledge about not only how to lift people from feeling dreadful to *feeling good*, but how to elevate them to *feeling great*—to living flourishing lives, to developing their strengths, gifts, and capacities to the fullest. In a nutshell, positive psychology is the psychology of what makes life worth living. It represents a commitment on the part of research psychologists to focus attention on the sources of psychological wellness—for example, on positive emotions, positive experiences, and positive environments, on human strengths and virtues. The label is rooted in the principle that empowering individuals to build a positive state of mind—to live the most rewarding, fruitful, and happiest lives they can—is just as critical as psychology's conventional focus on mending their defects and healing their ailments and pathologies.

Positive psychology's focus on character, flourishing, and fulfilment may seem like a wise and obvious shift, yet psychology from mid-20th century on had been fixated on disease, disorder, and the dark side of life. Fortunately, we're in a new era, each month bringing us hot-off-the-presses scientific articles about how to achieve and sustain happiness, how to make life more productive and more enjoyable, and how to build character and learn resilience. These key findings, however, are generally only published in technical scholarly journals subscribed by universities and thus they lie beyond the reach of the student or nonexpert. The body of work produced by positive psychology has yet to be brought together and elucidated in an accessible, comprehensive and comprehensible volume. Until now. This four-volume Praeger Perspectives set has assembled and translated for the first time the discoveries about how to become happier and more fulfilled, about how to define and develop human strengths, about how people rise to the occasion during the worst of times and about much more.

Yet I would wager that you have already been offered answers to many of these questions in self-help books, Dr. So-So's radio and TV programs, and in countless newspaper articles, magazine pieces, and blogs. Why then is this four-volume set from Praeger Perspectives needed? Because the answers, explanations, and prescriptions proposed by self-help gurus, and interpreted and often misinterpreted by the media, generally have limited grounding in scientific theory and even less empirical confirmation. In contrast to the information you generally find in today's media, every statement, claim, and recommendation in this set is backed up by cutting-edge scientific research. You will find few conclusions in these chapters purely based on the authors' life experiences or that of their grandmother or neighbors or depressed clients or random people they have interviewed. Empirical research holds multiple advantages over such anecdotal or clinical observations. By using the scientific method, researchers are able to untangle causes from effects and to study a phenomenon systematically and without bias. Of course, science is imperfect and has its own set of limitations, but we can be much more confident in its conclusions than those of a single person tendering advice based on his or her assumptions, prejudices, and narrow collection of experiences.

One of my all-time favorite letters to the editor was by this newspaper reader, who wrote on the subject of science:

> There are questions of faith, such as "Does God exist?" There are questions of opinion, such as "Who is the greatest baseball player of all time?" There are debate questions, such as "Should abortion be legal?" And then there are questions that can be answered to a degree of certainty by the application of the scientific method, which are called empirical questions—in other words, those that can be largely settled by the evidence. (Ivins, 2000)

Questions about human strengths, the benefits of positive emotions, growth in the face of stress and trauma, and the pursuit of happiness and flourishing turn out to be just such empirical questions. Scientific advances in the field of positive psychology are now solid enough to interpret and translate into descriptions, explanations, and recommendations for the nonscientist. These four volumes about the best in people promises to be a landmark set, representing the most rigorous research and the current state of knowledge about positive psychology. Yet it is written in an accessible and uplifting style, such that you may come away from reading the chapters with a new perspective on yourself, on human nature, and perhaps even with a clear sense of how to change your life.

Sonja Lyubomirsky

REFERENCE

Ivins, M. (2000, September 22). The manufactured public schools crisis. *The Fort Worth Star Telegram.*

Preface

On my first bus ride to a new school I watched smiling kids hop on and interact with friends. As the new kid, I sat back quietly and watched people play, laugh, and bounce around. The happiest of the lot was a girl named Deana; her whole face smiled. Deana fascinated me; she was so comfortable and joyful. I assumed that she was a very popular kid who knew all the others on the bus; I was so wrong. She was also a new kid. And, unlike me, who had lived in the neighborhood for years but was switching to a different school, Deana was new to the town ... and to the state. How did Deana learn how to walk into a strange situation with confidence, and to beam? That is the kind of psychology that grabbed me. Decades later, that brand of psychology came to be known as positive psychology. That is what this set of books is about.

During my 10 years in college, I learned valuable knowledge and skills needed to relieve human suffering. I have found great satisfaction in my work with people who are struggling with psychological disorders. I learned little about positive psychology, little about what cultivates the best in people. I learned little about the Deanas of the world. I wanted your educational experience to be different, more balanced, focusing on the suffering and the flourishing of all people. In this four-volume set for Praeger Perspectives, *Positive Psychology: Exploring the Best in People*, you will meet many Deanas and you will learn about positive psychology, the best in people, how they use their strengths and emotions to make good lives for themselves and those around them.

As editor, I asked some of the world's best positive psychology scholars and practitioners to tell the story of their research and ideas about the best in people. I encouraged each to write a chapter that his or her neighbors would want to read, rather than a chapter that colleagues down the hall would consider "scholarly." The contributors did an amazing job of condensing their life's work into accessible descriptions and explanations of how people are strong, happy, and buoyant in good times and in bad. As a team, we comment on the major discoveries of positive psychology, that strengths are real and potent and positive emotions are extremely valuable to human development, and demystify how people overcome adversity and become the best people they can be. We share the story of positive psychology research and practice in four distinct yet related volumes:

Volume 1: *Discovering Human Strengths*
Volume 2: *Capitalizing on Emotional Experiences*
Volume 3: *Growing in the Face of Adversity*
Volume 4: *Pursuing Human Flourishing*

The real-world implications of positive psychology are communicated via anecdotes and case studies. At the end of each chapter, personal mini-experiments encourage you to put positive psychological principles to the test in daily life.

In Volume 1 (*Discovering Human Strengths*), we explore how human strengths are discovered, developed, and parlayed into successes in all domains of life. In this volume, educators, psychologists, and philosophers discuss how we work to bring out the best in ourselves and in others. In Volume 2 (*Capitalizing on Emotional Experiences*), contributors tell the story of some of the major psychology findings of the late 20th century, stemming from the study of positive emotions and how to make the most of them. While you will recognize many of the concepts presented in this volume, such as gratitude and emotional intelligence, these chapters will take you beyond a basic knowledge of positive emotional experiences and help you learn how to capitalize on them. Volume 3 (*Growing in the Face of Adversity*) focuses on resilience, which has been attributed to the ordinary magic of the human spirit. In this volume you will be struck by a consistent theme, individual growth during the hard times is a very social process. Finally, in Volume 4 (*Pursuing Human Flourishing*) school psychologists, family experts, college administrators, and business gurus review new work on how we can become successful and develop well-being at home, work, and school.

Positive psychology, the study of what is right with people, is reshaping the scholarly and public views of the science and practice of psychology and is shining a spotlight on the good in us all. I believe that *Positive Psychology: Exploring the Best in People* provides a comprehensive yet brief summary of this area of scholarship and practice and an abundance of exercises that we hope will pique your interest in strengths, positive emotions, resilience, and flourishing.

The experience of compiling and editing these chapters allowed me to discover the best in colleagues who contributed to this set. I thank them wholeheartedly, and I am especially grateful to Jeff Rettew (managing editor), Rhea Owens (assistant to the editor), Allison Rose Lopez (special editor), Neil Salkind (Studio B), and Elizabeth Potenza (Praeger) who gave life to this project.

VOLUME 1: DISCOVERING HUMAN STRENGTHS

What would happen if we study the best in people? Donald Clifton, psychology professor and former chairperson of Gallup, posed this question and it has become incorporated into the mission of many positive psychologists. Scholars' responses to this question have led to the development of two measures of strengths that have been completed by over 2 million people and, as a result, strengths development programs are becoming commonplace in businesses, schools, and places of worship. No doubt you will be asked to take a strengths measure as part of a school or work experience within 5 years of reading this volume.

In this volume we introduce you to the two measures of human strengths, the Clifton StrengthsFinder and the Values in Action Inventory of Strengths, that have stood the test of psychometricians and laypersons. Rettew, Lopez, Bowers, and Cantwell make personal, philosophical, and evidence-based cases for why strengths matter. Sparks and Baumeister extend their classic work on "bad is stronger than good" by considering why we should focus on strengths to balance our weaknesses.

Three chapters in this volume explore the many benefits of specific strengths, wisdom (Ardelt), courage (Pury), and optimism (Rasmussen and Wallio). The chapters on wisdom and courage suggest that these strengths, among others, can be learned. The optimism chapter summarizes an extensive body of work which indicates that positive expectations for the future and health go hand in hand.

The strengths of a historical figure, Martin Luther King Jr., are examined via his writings. Rice's chapter teaches us how to shine a light on the strengths of the inspirational figures in our lives.

Finally, one of the most eminent psychologists in the 20th century, Albert Bandura, describes how we can give positive psychology away to the world.

VOLUME 2: CAPITALIZING ON EMOTIONAL EXPERIENCES

Most people don't *know* how to respond to positive emotional experiences; they just do what feels natural. Until recently, social scientists and mental health practitioners knew much about managing negative emotions (e.g., anger, fear) and little about the how to make the most of positive emotions (e.g., joy, contentment). Now, positive psychologists are beginning to demystify how people respond to emotional experiences in productive ways. In this volume, we focus on the intrapersonal and interpersonal processing of positive emotions, the positive moral emotion of gratitude, the practice of giving, emotional intelligence, the new science of allophilia, and a new view of masculinity.

In the first chapter, Kok and colleagues explain the Broaden and Build Theory of Positive Emotions. In short, positive emotions expand our personal views of self and the world, help generate personal resources, and create an upward spiral of growth. The findings reviewed in this chapter have enhanced much of our thinking about personal growth and human flourishing.

Danner and colleagues highlight some of the findings from landmark research known as the Nun Study. To pique your interest, the upshot is that positive emotions, as reflected in autobiographical essays of young women entering the convent, are related to living longer. Another example of a thin slice of personal data about positive emotions is shared by Impett and Gordon, close relationship researchers, who teach us how to capitalize on positive experiences in the interpersonal context.

Benefits of thanking (Tsang and colleagues; Froh and Bono), giving (Dillard and colleagues), and being emotionally intelligent (David and Ebrahimi) are described across four chapters. Little did we know that thanking others and doing good could be so good for us.

Finally, two groups of researchers cover some brand new ground. Pittinsky and Maruskin introduce us to a new word, "allophilia," and a new science of interpersonal relations. Wong and Rochlen discuss the emotional side of men and how attending to emotional experiences can transform men and their relationships.

VOLUME 3: GROWING IN THE FACE OF ADVERSITY

Growing up in southern Louisiana you learn to respect the water and the weather. In 2005, water and the weather joined forces in the form of two of the biggest and most destructive hurricanes ever, Katrina and Rita. Now, you have heard of Katrina; it nearly wiped out New Orleans. You may not remember Katrina's not so little sister, Rita, which hammered my homeland, Acadiana. Two days after the storm, I was heading back home to help my mother, who lost her house in the storm. I wasn't prepared for what I would experience, the worst and the best in people. And, I wasn't surprised by how quickly people were bouncing back. Rebuilding of homes and lives was happening on every corner. Two observations I made during my time down there are supported by the chapters in this volume. First, people can bounce back from just about anything, and they do so by being determined and hopeful. Second, bouncing back is a social phenomenon; we rarely, if ever, do it alone.

In this volume, Fazio and colleagues tell compelling stories about their own growth through loss and adversity. They then provide a framework to help us think about how we move forward in our lives after experiencing the worst of times.

Two chapters (Berman and colleagues; Zacchilli and colleagues) explain how we deal with things we will all experience: romantic conflict and relationship loss. Most folks will wish they had read the work of these close relationship researchers before they started dating—I wish I had. Forgiveness (according to Holter and colleagues), a matter of choice, could be incorporated into attempts to deal with relationship struggles even at young ages.

A series of chapters address specific struggles and means for overcoming them. Specifically, Wehmeyer and Shogren discuss how students with mild cognitive disabilities become self-determined learners. Aronson and Rogers describe the repercussions of stereotype threats and how to prevent or overcome them. Then, Ebberwein identifies a set of adaptive skills that will make workers more flexible across the career span.

The final chapter, by Greenberg, taps into one of the oldest forms of making meaning out of bad times—storytelling. The robust positive effects of emotional storytelling are described in compelling detail.

VOLUME 4: PURSUING HUMAN FLOURISHING

Imagine a ladder standing before you. The bottom rung is zero and the top rung is ten. On which step of the ladder do you stand today? On which step will you stand in 5 years?

Your responses to these questions, which have been used by pollsters and researchers for 50 years, tell us a great deal about your level of hope and well-being. The mental image conjured up when thinking about your life in 5 years probably involves flourishing, or living a good life. Flourishing is the focus of this volume.

The first chapter, by Ambler, defines human flourishing as complete mental health. In the presence of positive emotions and in the absence of symptoms of mental illness and distress, we move toward the top rung of the life ladder.

Two of the chapters (Kurtz and Lyubomirsky; Myers) consider the contributors to and sustainability of happiness. You may be surprised to learn that genetics and money are part of the complex story about human happiness. Vansteenkiste and colleagues add to the discussion of pathways to well-being by examining the negative role of materialism in achieving that state.

Next, three chapters (Gilman and colleagues; Harter; Eagle) describe how exemplars do well (very well) in school and at work and are part of families that work, and one chapter (Kerr and Larson) tells the story of how smart girls develop into talented, high achieving women.

Finally, the last three chapters show how we can actively seek optimal human functioning by becoming leaders (Avolio and Wernsing), cultivating civic engagement (Sherrod and Lauckhardt), and overcoming the depressive symptoms (Rashid) that may be burdening us.

CHAPTER 1

Who Flourishes? The Criteria of Complete Mental Health

Virginia Miller Ambler

They were a peculiar lot—the hospitable Coast Guard officer, the college student in the middle of her undergraduate career, the brilliant young physicist working on his second master's degree, the aspiring musician living in an apartment near his parents, the Catholic nun, and my mom. For two years in the early 1990s this unconventional group of six met with a medical researcher in Massachusetts who listened as they reflected on what it was like to live with bipolar disorder. Indeed, each of the six had been diagnosed with the serious psychiatric condition characterized by dramatic disturbances in mood, most commonly experienced as alternating episodes of mania and depression. Many of them had entertained suicidal thoughts. Most had been hospitalized at one time or another. All of them were undergoing treatment for their mental illness.

Although the group members never did see each other again after the research project was complete, the experience was a profound one for my mother who came to appreciate that her bipolar life was qualitatively different from the others' lives. While her five companions in the group were only in their 20s, Mom's illness had not manifested itself until she was 40 years old. "You are so lucky," the others told her with a hint of longing. "You've been able to establish a life. You have a degree from Berkeley, a wonderful marriage, and you've raised three grown daughters with whom you are very close." They recognized and reflected back to my mother the many ways in which her experiences exemplified a "life well-lived" (Keyes & Haidt, 2003, p. 6). In light of what Ryff and Singer (2003) have called "challenged thriving," her positive functioning was most remarkable because it was evident in the context of significant life challenge and adversity (p. 15).

Now in her 60s, my mother's life remains rich—she is active in her church, volunteers as she is able, travels to spend time with her children and grandchildren, and enjoys regular dates with her husband of 43 years. Even as she manages her chronic illness, she expresses profound gratitude for the full life she is living. While none of us can know when or if another manic episode will come, her story reinforces the underlying reason for my own interest in positive psychology's approach to mental health—we need to think about illness and health in ways that go beyond the presence or absence of a clinical diagnosis (Peterson, 2006).

This chapter will describe first how the study of mental health proceeds from and reflects the broader themes of positive psychology. Then, following a discussion of Corey L.M. Keyes's (2002, 2005, 2007) criteria for measuring mental health, I will share the results of my doctoral research, which applied the concept of "flourishing as mental health" to the educational experiences of traditionally aged undergraduate college students. Finally, since the "philosophical underpinnings of positive psychology demand an experiential component to solidify learning" (Peterson, 2006, p. 21), the personal mini-experiments at the end of this chapter will encourage you to explore dimensions of your own emotional, psychological, and social well-being, as well as the quality of your relationships—relationships that may be critically important to your mental health.

MENTAL HEALTH AS A FOCUS OF POSITIVE PSYCHOLOGY

Martin Seligman (1998a) argued that the building of human strength has been psychology's forgotten mission. He and like-minded colleagues agreed that "since the end of World War II, psychology has moved too far from its original roots, which were to make the lives of all people more fulfilling and productive, and too much toward the important, but not all important, area of curing mental illness" (¶3). The field of positive psychology attempts to extend the spectrum of inquiry, arguing that the study of mental *health* is distinct from and complementary to the well-established interest in mental illness (Keyes & Lopez, 2002).

Unfortunately, the study of "mental health" has often translated to the study of "mental illness." Consider, for example, the stated mission of the National Institute of Mental Health (2004): "The mission of the National Institute of Mental Health (NIMH) is to understand mind, brain and behavior, and thereby reduce the burden of mental illness through research" (¶1). Happily, in the several decades since NIMH was first established, much has indeed been learned about mental illness—"a persistent and substantial deviation from normal functioning that impairs an individual's ability to execute their [sic] social roles ... and generates suffering" (Spitzer & Wilson, 1975 as cited in Keyes, 2003). It is disappointing that far less is known about positive emotions, states, and traits. Peterson and Park (2003) highlighted the problem with psychology's having focused so disproportionately on mental illness:

We have studied depression by using a standardized depression inventory in which the best one can do is score zero, indicating the absence of depressive symptoms. However, not all zero scores are equal. There is a world of difference between people who are not suicidal, not lethargic, and not self-deprecating versus those who bound out of bed in the morning with shiny faces and twinkling eyes. (p. 146)

The prevailing assumption reflected in research and in national practice seems to have been that mental health is appropriately defined by the absence of mental illness. Yet, if the positive were just the absence of the negative, positive psychology would be irrelevant, requiring only "a psychology of relieving negative states" (Seligman & Pawelski, 2003, p. 159). A more comprehensive definition is that of the World Health Organization (2004), which considers mental health as "a state of well-being in which the individual realizes his or her own abilities, can cope with the normal stresses of life, can work productively and fruitfully, and is able to make a contribution to his or her community" (p. 12). This definition affirms a belief that positive psychologists embrace—that mental health is not just the absence of mental illness, but the presence of something positive (Jahoda, 1958; Keyes, 2002, 2007).

Keyes' Definition of Mental Health as Flourishing

In an effort to empirically assess the nature and incidence of mental *health* as opposed to mental illness, Keyes (2002) introduced his concept of "flourishing" in what has been called "the first balanced framework for understanding and promoting mental health" (C. R. Snyder, 2003, p. 702). Not unlike mental illness, mental health according to Keyes' model is defined as "an emergent condition based on the concept of a syndrome" (Keyes, 2002, p. 208). In other words, a state of *health* is indicated when a set of symptoms at a specific level are exhibited for a period of time that coincides with distinctive cognitive and social functioning. Those symptoms Keyes (2002) considered in determining mental health are symptoms of an individual's *subjective well-being*—including emotional well-being (positive feelings) and *functional well-being* (both psychological and social).

Subjective Well-Being as Symptoms of Mental Health

According to Keyes, Shmotkin, and Ryff (2002), subjective well-being emerged in the late 1950s as a relevant index for measuring people's quality of life through individuals' own perceptions of their lives. Broadly defined, subjective well-being consists of "an individual's cognitive evaluation of life, the presence of positive or pleasant emotions, and the absence of negative or unpleasant emotions" (Emmons, 2003, p. 109). One strength of this definition is the assumption that people have diverse values, goals, and strengths (Diener, Sapyta, & Suh, 1998). Thus, by allowing people to define well-being for themselves, such subjective measures accurately reflect whether a person's life is satisfying based on his or her own values, goals, and life circumstances. Conceptually and empirically, subjective well-being includes an assessment of one's own affective states (e.g., happiness, satisfaction), one's psychological functioning (e.g., personal growth, sense of purpose, autonomy), and one's social functioning (e.g., social acceptance, sense of community, belonging; Keyes, 2002; Keyes, Hysom, & Lupo, 2000; Keyes & Waterman, 2003).

Subjective well-being, as Keyes (2002, 2003, 2005) explained is the critical psychological construct for understanding mental health. *Emotional well-being* is defined as a cluster of symptoms reflecting the presence or absence of positive feelings about one's life. Such symptoms are ascertained from individuals' responses to structured scales measuring the presence of positive affect and the absence of negative affect. However, Ryff (1989) has argued that well-being is more than just happiness with life. Therefore, subjective well-being also includes measures of positive functioning—both psychological and social. According to Keyes (2003), *psychological well-being* represents more private and personal criteria for evaluation—criteria that have been measured reliably and with validity by a six dimensional scale that includes: "self acceptance, positive relations with others, personal growth, purpose in life, environmental mastery, and autonomy" (p. 300). Keyes further asserted (1998), that positive functioning in life must include *social well-being* as well, and that individuals are mentally healthy when they view social life as meaningful and understandable, when they see society as possessing potential for growth, when they feel they belong in their communities, are able to accept all parts of society, and when they see their lives as contributing to society.

The Mental Health Continuum: From Languishing to Flourishing

The assertion that healthiness is 'more than the absence of illness' may not be novel to many who study physiological and psychological health (Jahoda, 1958). At the same time, there has been little significant progress over the last 50 years reflecting this view in either the scientific or practical realms (Ryff & Singer, 1998). Having recognized empirically that mental health and mental illness are not opposite dimensions of a single construct, Keyes' (2002) introduced the mental health continuum. His model defines mental health as a syndrome of symptoms of positive feelings and positive functioning in life. According to Keyes (2002):

> The mental health continuum consists of complete and incomplete mental health. Adults with complete mental health are *flourishing* in life with high levels of well-being. To be flourishing, then is to be filled with positive emotions and to be functioning well psychologically and socially. Adults with incomplete mental health are *languishing* in life with low well-being. Thus, languishing may be conceived of as emptiness and stagnation, constituting a life of quiet despair (p. 210).

The diagnostic scheme for Keyes' (2002) understanding of mental health actually parallels the scheme used by the American Psychiatric

Association (2000) to diagnose major depression—individuals are diagnosed with the disorder when they exhibit just over half of the total symptoms measured. Thus, in terms of the mental health continuum, to be *languishing* in life, individuals must exhibit a low level on measures of emotional and functional well-being. Such individuals have incomplete mental health, yet they may or may not ever experience clinical depression. Similarly, individuals who are *flourishing* in life must exhibit high levels of well-being as measured by emotional and functional well-being scales. These individuals are "mentally healthy because they ... fit the diagnostic criteria for the presence of mental health" (Keyes, 2003, p. 302). Adults who are *moderately mentally healthy* are neither languishing nor flourishing.

The "Complete Health" Approach to Mental Health

In 2002, Keyes applied the mental health continuum model to data from the 1995 Midlife in the United States study of 3,032 adults between the ages of 25 and 74. Findings from that study revealed that most adults studied (89.5%) had not experienced a depressive episode in the previous 12 months, yet only 17.2% of those nondepressed cases fit the criteria for flourishing in life. More than half the sample (58.7%) had moderate mental health, and nearly 20% of adults fit the criteria for languishing in life (Keyes, 2003). Results of this study clearly illustrated that although many individuals remain free of mental illness each year, and indeed over their lifetimes, the absence of mental illness infrequently reflected genuine mental health, or flourishing.

It is important, therefore, to assess not only the presence of mental illness but also the level of an individual's mental health as well. In fact, there are grave reasons, Keyes (2002, 2003) noted, to be as concerned about pure languishing in life (the absence of both mental health and mental illness) as about diagnosed depression. Languishing individuals experienced substantial functional impairment at levels comparable to people experiencing pure episodes of major depression. Moreover, languishing was also found to be as *prevalent* as pure episodes of major depression. In contrast, functioning markedly improved among moderately mentally healthy adults and flourishing adults. Adults who were diagnosed as completely mentally healthy—that is, free from mental illness *and* flourishing—functioned superior to all others both in terms of physical activities (e.g. work attendance, daily life activities), and in a variety of psychological/social areas (e.g. having personal goals, feeling close to friends and family).

Mental health must be understood as a complete state that takes into account assessments of both mental health and mental illness (Keyes, 2007). Table 1.1 highlights the diagnostic categories of the Complete Mental Health Model.

Within the framework of these diagnostic categories, empirical evidence affirms that the absence of mental illness does not imply the presence of mental health, and the presence of mental illness does not imply the absence of mental health (Keyes, 2007)—just as my mother's diagnosis of

Table 1.1
Diagnostic Categories of the Complete Mental Health Model

Mental illness diagnosis (last 12 months)	Mental health diagnosis		
	Languishing	Moderately mentally healthy	Flourishing
No	Languishing	Moderate mental health	Flourishing: Complete mental health
Yes	Mental illness and languishing	Mental illness and moderate mental health	Mental illness and flourishing

Source: Based on the American Psychiatric Association's (2000) *Diagnostic and Statistical Manual of Mental Disorders.*

bipolar disorder does not preclude her living a life of emotional and functional well-being. As scholars and practitioners continue to examine the importance of understanding mental health, Keyes (2003) argued that the promotion of flourishing must become the objective, not merely the treatment and prevention of mental illness. "In sum, it is time to truly pursue the study and promotion of mental health, and this can be achieved with a more positive psychology" (p. 309).

WHO FLOURISHES IN COLLEGE? APPLYING THE COMPLETE MENTAL HEALTH MODEL TO UNDERGRADUATE STUDENTS

Psychological illness among college students is on the rise and represents a significant concern for today's college and university campuses. Certainly the popular press reflects a profound concern about issues of depression, suicide, alcoholism, eating disorders, and other serious psychological diagnoses on college campuses (Crouse, 2003; Ellen, 2002; Franey, 2002; Hallett, 2003; Kelly, 2001; Knight, Wechsler, Kuo, Seibring, Weitzman, & Schuckit, 2002; Lamas, 2004; Lite, 2003; Marano, 2002; O'Connor, 2001; K. S. Peterson, 2002; Rimer, 2004; Schwartz, 2003; Shy, 2001), with the April 16, 2007, shooting rampage of a mentally ill student at Virginia Tech being the most horrific of recent examples (Shapira & Jackman, 2007). Empirically, the results of a 13-year longitudinal study affirm that students today are presenting themselves to college counseling centers more frequently and with a greater complexity of problems than ever before (Benton, Robertson, Tseng, Newton, & Benton, 2003). As a student affairs administrator, I am aware that my colleagues across the country have identified student mental health issues as being among the most critical challenges facing the contemporary college campus (Kadison & DiGeronimo, 2004; M. B. Snyder, 2004), and higher education is surely feeling the pressure—for "increasingly, colleges are [seen as] the first best hope for rescuing the minds of America's future" (Marano, 2002, ¶16).

While the promotion of students' mental health and positive personal growth have long been significant priorities for those of us who work in student affairs, practitioners and scholars alike have focused attention primarily on the incidence and nature of psychopathology among students, the strategies for managing the demand for counseling, treatment options for the mentally ill, and systematic approaches to preventing the most tragic of consequences (e.g., suicide, self-abuse, addiction). Current research on student mental health actually has done little to shed light on those students who are mentally *healthy*, those who exhibit high levels of well-being and functioning and who are flourishing on our campuses.

Positive Psychology and Research on College Students

The noted gap in our understanding of mental *health* on campus reflects the more pervasive void in the broader field of psychology that the positive psychology movement strives to fill. In an effort to promote better mental health on campus, is it enough to focus our research and attention primarily on the trends and treatment of those who are psychologically ill or those who struggle with intense personal or adjustment issues? Positive psychologists argue that there is much to be learned about mental health by studying those who exhibit positive, healthy, adaptive features of human functioning (Csikszentmihalyi, 2003; Diener, 2003; Harvey & Pauwels, 2003; Keyes, 2002, 2003; Keyes & Haidt, 2003; Keyes & Lopez, 2002; King, 2003; Lyubomirsky & Abbe, 2003; C. Peterson & Park, 2003; Ryff, 2003; Seligman, 1998a, 1998b, Seligman & Pawelski, 2003; C. R. Snyder & Lopez, 2002). Rather than allowing student affairs research to be driven solely by what some have described as a therapeutic culture gone too far (Rimer, 2004; Seligman, 1998a, 1998b), positive psychologists would urge higher education scholars to complement the existing studies on psychopathology with empirical research investigating those factors that distinguish individual students and student communities who thrive, flourish, and otherwise function in an optimal way from those with more limited functioning (Lyubomirsky & Abbe, 2003). Using positive psychology as a disciplinary foundation, my doctoral research was an attempt to do just that.

ANNA'S STORY: PLACING MY RESEARCH IN A REAL LIFE CONTEXT

As an undergraduate, Anna was a phenomenal leader on our campus—working on William and Mary's national-award-winning Bone Marrow Drive for four years and chairing it during her senior year, serving on the Undergraduate Honor Council and the Judicial Appeals Committee, helping to organize and raise the funds to bring the art exhibit, The Century Project, to campus this year and twice serving as the student chair of Family Weekend. She was a strong student who worked tirelessly to write a senior honors thesis in English. Anna was also a phenomenal friend—to her peers, and also to me.

What most people didn't know about Anna is that in her junior year, after returning from a summer doing volunteer work in Africa, she began to lose weight and often felt weak and exhausted. Visits to the doctor left more questions than answers. Her life as an undergraduate was made difficult by a disease that eluded diagnosis, even by national medical experts. Swelling and pain in her joints often made walking or even sitting difficult activities for Anna. And she endured a host of other symptoms and many treatments which, in themselves, were sometimes debilitating. After an extended leave from campus for a series of medical consults and for some rest at her home far from Williamsburg, Virginia, Anna and her family contacted our student affairs office to see what kind of arrangements could be made to help Anna move back to Williamsburg and continue, as best she could, with her life at the College. She and her parents were absolutely convinced that she should resume as active—as "engaged"—an experience as she was capable of sustaining. Why? What was it about the campus environment that led her and her family to believe it was important to her subjective sense of well-being?

Introduction to the Study

For college faculty and staff who work daily with some of the most able and engaged women and men in the nation, the idea of learning more about "nurturing genius" (Seligman as cited in Keyes & Haidt, 2003) is surely consistent with the highest of professional aspirations. How might students' experiences in their higher educational institutions encourage or hinder their thriving? After all, positive psychology is not only the study of positive feeling but also the study of positive institutions (Seligman & Pawelski, 2003). In advocating a new vision for psychology as a discipline, positive psychology also resonates with the core commitments and values of student affairs as a profession. As the American College Personnel Association's *Principles of Good Practice* (1996) statement affirmed, student affairs practice is rooted in "our conviction that higher education has a duty to help students reach their full potential" (¶7). It is within this intersection of the comparable missions of positive psychology and higher education and student affairs that my dissertation research was undertaken.

Student Development in Higher Education: Echoes of Positive Psychology

Positive psychologist Carol Ryff (2003) suggested that "it is only from particular vantage points, such as clinical or abnormal psychology, that the positive focus constitutes a novelty. For other subfields, especially life-span developmental and personality psychology, there has always been concern for healthy, optimal human functioning" (p. 157). Indeed, Ryff's claim is supported by a review of the literature that forms the foundation of student development as a field of study for professionals in higher education (Evans, Forney, & Guido-DiBrito, 1998). In the 1960s particularly, social scientists—largely from psychology and sociology—began to theorize about how students change and grow in college. Both in theory and in practice, student affairs professionals in higher education have had a sustained interest in how students develop in college and in how institutional structures, programs, and services promote students' optimal functioning. While formal theories on student development are relatively new in the context of American higher education, the developmental focus is not new:

> From the paternalistic faculty authority figure who supervised Harvard students in 1636 to the contemporary student affairs professional who uses developmental theory to examine students' human potential, student development has existed in some configuration ... since the beginning (Evans, Forney, & Guido-DiBrito, 1998, p. 3).

The Impact of College on Students

A host of scholars have studied how college affects student outcomes (e.g., Astin, 1993; Pascarella & Terenzini, 1991, 2005), including learning, moral reasoning, identity development, and cognitive growth. Research has shown that college does indeed have an impact—that students do grow and change during their years in higher education (Boyer, 1987; Hernandez, Hogan, Hathaway, & Lovell, 1999; Hood, 1984; Kuh et al., 1991; Moore, Lovell, McGann, & Wyrick, 1998; Pascarella & Terenzini, 1991, 2005). Compared with theories built around psychosocial frameworks, the foundation of college impact models is the *origin* of change (as opposed to the *process* of change), such as institutional programs, policies, and specific student experiences within the higher education environment.

According to *Involvement Theory*, "students learn by becoming involved" (Astin, 1985, p. 133), and involvement itself is "the amount of physical and psychological energy that the student devotes to the academic experience" (Astin, 1984, p. 297); A highly involved student, therefore, likely devotes considerable energy to studying, spends much time on campus, participates actively in student organizations, and interacts frequently with faculty members and other students. In contrast, a typical uninvolved student neglects studies, spends little time on campus, abstains from extracurricular activities, and has infrequent contact with faculty members or other students (Astin, 1984). While Astin (1984) acknowledged that motivation is an ever-present factor in human behavior, he also emphasized that involvement theory is concerned with the behavioral aspects of the student experience. What a student actually does is more critical to defining involvement, according to the theory, than what the individual thinks or feels.

Measuring Student Involvement

Within the last several years, the National Survey of Student Engagement (NSSE) was established with a grant from the Pew Charitable Trusts in an effort to assess the extent to which students are involved in empirically derived good educational practices (Kuh, 2002). Its primary activity is an annual survey of college students, the results of which document dimensions of quality in undergraduate education and assist colleges, universities, and other organizations to improve student learning. NSSE, and its instrument, *The College Student Report*, reflect the abundance of research on college student development that shows that the time and energy students devote to educationally purposeful activities is the single best predictor of their learning and personal development. For that reason, *The College Student Report* was selected to measure student involvement for this study.

The NSSE (2005) results fall into five key clusters of activity and involvement variables that research has shown to be linked to desired outcomes of college:

- **Level of Academic Challenge**—Challenging intellectual and creative work is central to student learning and collegiate quality. The importance of academic effort and the setting of high expectations for student performance are emphasized.
- **Student Interactions with Faculty Members**—Students learn firsthand by interacting with faculty members inside and outside the classroom. Teachers are role models, mentors, and guides for life-long learning.
- **Active and Collaborative Learning**—Students are intensely involved in their education and are asked to think about and apply what they are learning in different settings.
- **Enriching Educational Experiences**—Academic programs are augmented by complementary learning opportunities inside and outside the classroom. Experiencing diversity, using technology, and participating in activities help students integrate and apply knowledge.
- **Supportive Campus Environment**—The college is committed to students' success and cultivates positive relationships among different groups on campus.

Purpose of My Research

As the Study Group on the Conditions of Excellence in American Higher Education (Schroeder, 1996) reported:

> There is now a great deal of research evidence to suggest that the more time and effort students invest in the learning process and the more intensely they engage in their own education, the greater will be their growth and achievement, their satisfaction with their educational experiences, and their persistence in college (p. 17).

Because involvement significantly predicts other positive college outcomes, my research project explored the extent to which student involvement might also predict students' mental health as defined by Keyes' (2002, 2005) mental health continuum. In other words, I wanted to know who flourishes on college campuses.

Collecting Data

Specifically, the study examined the mental health, involvement, and achievement of traditionally aged undergraduate students (18–23) at a mid-sized, selective, public university in the mid-Atlantic region of the United States (State College). Using Keyes' (2002, 2005) mental health continuum model, the study identified students who are flourishing and distinguished them from students who are moderately mentally healthy or languishing. In addition to examining the prevalence of these three levels of mental health (i.e., flourishing, moderately mentally healthy, and languishing), it also explored the extent to which individual involvement—as defined by Astin (1984, 1985, 1993) and as measured by the National Survey of Student Engagement's *College Student Report* (NSSE, 2005)—predicts mental health. Inspired by my relationship with Anna, I wanted to know more about the relationship between the way students engage in their college education and their mental health.

Data were collected from 534 undergraduate juniors (44% of the 1206 students who were invited to participate in the study), 68.4% of whom were female and 31.6% of whom were male. Based on Keyes' (2002, 2005) mental health continuum model, more than two-thirds of the respondents were classified as being moderately mentally healthy (67.2%), with the remainder being classified on the two extremes of the continuum—flourishing (15.4%) and languishing (17.4%). In addition to looking at gender differences, data analysis also took into account students' socioeconomic status and their level of academic achievement (as indicated by grade point average). Race and ethnicity was not considered due to the homogenous nature of the respondents—nearly 83% were Caucasian. Details of the data analysis, including all requisite tables and statistical measures, are laid out in great detail in Chapter 4 of my dissertation (Ambler, 2006). For the purposes of this essay, I highlight the following significant findings.

- Mental health category (languishing, moderate mental health, languishing) was *not* related to students' gender. Thus, the proportion of men and women in each of the three mental health categories did not differ significantly.
- Students' mental health category was *not* related to their socioeconomic status. Thus the proportion of those classified as high/middle and low socioeconomic status in each of the three mental health categories did not differ significantly.
- Students' mental health category was *not* related to their level of academic achievement. Thus, there were no significant differences in grade point average among those who are flourishing, moderately mentally healthy, and languishing.
- Among the most compelling results are comparisons of student involvement measures by mental health category. For all five involvement variables—Academic Challenge, Active/Collaborative Learning, Student/Faculty Interaction, Enriching Educational Experiences, and Supportive Campus Environment—the average involvement scores of those who are "flourishing" were significantly higher than the average scores of the "moderately mentally healthy," whose average scores were significantly higher than those who were "languishing."

- For both male and female students, one of the five involvement variables—Supportive Campus Environment—was by far the most predictive of their mental health and well-being.
- A more in-depth analysis of the role of a Supportive Campus Environment revealed that having *supportive interpersonal relationships* was most predictive of mental health score for *all* students. For male students, relationships with supportive faculty were most significant, followed by relationships with peers, while supportive peer relationships were most significant for female students, followed by relationships with college administrators.

Implications for the College Campus

Who flourishes in college? The benchmarks for education practice (NSSE, 2005) which most significantly predicted mental health in this study—Academic Challenge, Active/Collaborative Learning, Enriching Educational Experiences, and Supportive Campus Environment—provide a useful framework for interpreting these results.

Increasing Level of Academic Challenge

Students who flourish (compared with those who are moderately mentally healthy or languishing) are more likely to report having worked harder than they thought they would to meet faculty expectations; they are regularly prepared for class, they are challenged beyond memorization to analyze, synthesize, evaluate, and apply ideas and experiences; and they experience a campus environment that emphasizes the importance of studying and academics. For them, challenging intellectual and creative work is central to student learning (NSSE, 2005). This finding reflects Boyer's (1990) first dimension of the ideal campus community—purposefulness. In an educationally purposeful campus community, he asserts, "learning is pervasive" (p. 16). Moreover, the cognitive experiences reported by flourishing students in this study are those at the highest levels of Bloom's (1956) taxonomy of educational objectives, which are application, analysis, synthesis, and evaluation.

Engaging in Active/Collaborative Learning

Students who flourish are more likely to be actively engaged in the classroom by asking questions and contributing to class discussions. They are more involved in making presentations, working on projects with classmates, and integrating service with their academics by tutoring others, or taking part in community-based projects as part of their course work. In addition, they often discuss ideas from readings or class with people outside of the course. Students who flourish work collaboratively with others and "are asked to think about and apply what they are learning in different settings" (NSSE, 2005). The advantages of such engagement are also consistent with Baxter-Magolda (1992) who found that optimal learning for students is a relational activity, including opportunities for critical thinking and peer collaboration, for connecting learning to real life, and for engaging actively in the classroom (Evans, Fornery, & Guido-DiBrito, 1998).

Enriching Educational Experiences

Students who flourish report seeking and experiencing learning opportunities inside and outside the classroom (NSSE, 2005). They use technology to facilitate learning, and they are more likely to have taken advantage of opportunities such as internships, community service, study abroad, independent study, and co-curricular activities. Such enriching activities contribute to a student's broader educational experience by "situating learning in the student's own experience" (Baxter-Magolda, 1992, p. 378). The findings are also consistent with the student affairs profession's focus on the development of the *whole* student, and the foundational belief that student learning takes place both in and outside the classroom (Astin, 1984, 1993; Chickering & Reisser, 1993; Komives & Woodward, 1996; Kuh, Schuh, Whitt, et al., 1991; Pascarella & Terenzini, 1991, 2005).

In addition, students who flourish are more likely to report engaging with people who are different from themselves—in terms of background, religion, politics, and so on. They experience their institutional climate as one that "encourages contact among students of different economic, social, and racial or ethnic backgrounds" (NSSE, 2005). Gurin (1999) found that students (both White and non-White) who experience the most diversity in classroom settings and in informal interactions with peers show the greatest engagement in active thinking processes and growth in intellectual and academic skills. The current study affirms that optimal mental health is another benefit significantly related to diversity in the college setting.

Experiencing a Supportive Campus Environment

More than any other involvement variable, this one is most significantly related to mental health for all students in the study. Male students who are flourishing report having quality relationships with faculty members who are "available, helpful, and sympathetic" (NSSE, 2005, p 2). Also significantly related to male mental health is having relationships with peers that are "friendly, supportive, and [who promote] a sense of belonging" (NSSE, 2005, p. 2). The relationships most significant for female students in this study were those with supportive and friendly peers, as well as administrators whom they found to be helpful (NSSE, 2005). Students who flourish—male and female alike—are more likely than moderately mentally healthy or languishing students to experience the campus environment as being supportive of their success, both within and outside the classroom.

Limitations of the Study

The focus of this study was the relationship between mental health and student involvement. Although the results indicate that students' mental health is indeed significantly related to their level of engagement in the educational process, this research cannot show causality. In other words, it is not possible to know from these results if traditionally aged students flourish as a result of their involvement, or if students who flourish are the ones who choose to be more actively involved.

My study was also limited by the nature of the participants and their institution. Results from the study do not address mental health differences by race or ethnicity, for example, because the sample itself was not sufficiently diverse. Moreover, students at State College—a selective, academically rigorous, and highly residential public institution—may exhibit different patterns of involvement or levels of mental health than would traditionally aged students attending other kinds of institutions.

Research Conclusions

Astin (1985) argues, "The effectiveness of any educational policy or practice is directly related to the capacity of that policy or practice to increase student involvement" (p. 136). Given the results of this study, it is at least possible, that an increase in student involvement might result in an enhanced sense of students' well-being, or mental *health*. Certainly higher education literature is replete with studies affirming the benefits of students' active engagement—their involvement—in educational experiences (Astin, 1984, 1993; Chickering & Reisser, 1993; Goodsell, Maher, & Tinto, 1992; Kuh, Schuh, Whitt, et al., 1991; Pascarella & Terenzini, 1991, 2005; Sorcinelli, 1991; Tinto, 1993). At the same time, the concept of mental *health* as distinct and separate from mental *illness* is relatively new (Keyes, 2002, 2005, 2007; Keyes & Haidt, 2003) for which there is a limited literature base, particularly with regard to individuals aged 18-23. This study brought together in a unique way (a) foundational constructs in our understandings of undergraduates and the impact of college on students, with (b) a newly proposed model of mental health, one that has never been applied to a college population and that reflects an emerging academic discipline—positive psychology (Fish, 2005; Goldberg, 2006; Seligman, Steen, Park, & Peterson, 2005).

That such significant relationships were found between students' mental health and the extent to which they are engaged in their broad educational experience is indeed noteworthy—and especially so, as these relationships exist regardless of students' gender, their socioeconomic status, and their level of academic achievement. The results of this study suggest that students who flourish may be those most likely to be involved, or perhaps that students actually flourish *because* of their involvement and engagement in the educational experience. Further research should examine more closely those factors which are related to and which could better promote optimal mental health among students on our campuses.

ANNA—THE REST OF THE STORY

Together, Anna and her mother were invited to move into the President's Cottage, a small colonial out-building beside the President's house on the historic William and Mary campus. She continued with her classes, provided inspiring leadership for her organizations (even if committee meetings were sometimes held in the cottage while she rested). Though she decided not to complete her honors thesis, she nevertheless graduated with an impressive grade point average and received one of our most prestigious student awards at Commencement that year. Anna experienced powerful support in the midst of a challenging ordeal—making it possible for her to complete a most fulfilling undergraduate career. Although her illness remains yet a mystery, she encounters fewer debilitating episodes. In the fall of 2007 she began a Physician's Assistant program at an Ivy League institution, pursuing her dream to become a medical practitioner for underserved populations. She continues to flourish.

PERSONAL MINI-EXPERIMENTS

Four Pathways to Flourishing

In this chapter, we have discussed the criteria for complete mental health, or *flourishing*. According to Keyes (2002), one's mental health is best reflected by a combined measure of emotional well-being, psychological well-being, and social well-being. In addition, recent research on college students (Ambler, 2006) affirms what Peterson (2006) offers as his three-word summary of positive psychology, "other people matter" (p. 249). We encourage you to examine your own subjective sense of well-being and to explore ways of enhancing positive interpersonal relationships in your life.

Emotional Well-Being: Some strategies for enhancing our ability to savor positive experiences in our lives include (a) talking about our positive experience with others; (b) taking time to congratulate ourselves and feel pride in our individual accomplishments; and (c) sharpening our perceptions to focus on specific meaningful elements of a positive experience as it is happening. (Peterson, 2006; Pleasure and Positive Experience, pp. 69–72).

Psychological Well-Being: One way to give attention to your psychological well-being might be to focus on your personal goal-setting. Try your hand at exploring the following topics through some reflective writing: (a) Write about a time when you achieved a goal you had set for yourself. Describe the situation and your approach to it. What helped or hindered you on the road to achieving that goal? How did you feel when your goal was finally reached? (b) Imagine you have a close friend who is struggling in his/her attempt to reach a personal goal. Write an encouraging letter to that friend with your best advice on setting and achieving a goal. Include examples from your own experiences.

Social Well-Being: One natural way to enhance social well-being might be to take on a new volunteer or service activity. On behalf of a cause or organization in your community, commit to getting involved and making a difference. There is ample scholarly evidence (Piliavin, 2003) that "on many levels—psychologically, socially, and even physically—one indeed does 'do well by doing good'" (p. 243).

Other People Matter: John Gottman suggested that the "ratio of the explicitly positive to the explicitly negative during actual interactions must exceed 5:1" (cited in Peterson, 2006, p. 270). In others words for every complaint or criticism that one partner voices, there need to be at least five compliments. Choose an important relationship in your life and focus for one week on meeting or exceeding that 5:1 ratio when it comes to your own positive to negative responses and comments.

REFERENCES

Ambler, V. M. (2006). *Who flourishes in college? Using positive psychology and student involvement theory to explore mental health among traditionally aged undergraduates.* Ph.D. dissertation, The College of William and Mary, Williamsburg, Virginia.

American College Personnel Association. (1996). *Principles of good practice.* Alexandria, VA: Author.

American Psychiatric Association. (2000). *Diagnostic and statistical manual of mental disorders.* (4th ed., text rev.). Washington, DC: Author.

Astin, A. W. (1984). Student involvement: A developmental theory for higher education. *Journal of College Student Personnel, 25,* 297–308.

Astin, A. W. (1985). *Achieving educational excellence.* San Francisco: Jossey-Bass.

Astin, A. W. (1993). *What matters in college: Four critical years revisited.* San Francisco: Jossey-Bass.

Baxter-Magolda, M. B. (1992). *Knowing and reasoning in college: Gender-related patterns in students' intellectual development.* San Francisco: Jossey-Bass.

Benton, S.A., Robertson, J. M., Tseng, W. C., Newton, F. B., & Benton, S. L. (2003). Changes in counseling center client problems across 13 years. *Professional psychology: Research and Practice, 34,* 66–72.

Bloom B. S. (1956). *Taxonomy of educational objectives, handbook. I: The cognitive domain.* New York: McKay.

Boyer, E. L. (1987). *College: The undergraduate experience in America.* New York: Harper and Row.

Chickering A. W., & Reisser, L. (1993) *Education and identity* (2nd ed). San Francisco: Jossey-Bass.

Crouse, J. S. (2003, February 5). Psychological problems skyrocket among college students. Retrieved April 14, 2004, from http://www.cwfa.org/articles/3241/BLI/reports.

Csikszentmihalyi, M. (2003). Legs or wings? A reply to R. S. Lazarus. *Psychological Inquiry, 14,* 113–115.

Diener, E. (2003). What is positive about positive psychology: The curmudgeon and Pollyanna. *Psychological Inquiry, 14,* 115–120.

Diener, E., Sapyta, J. J., & Suh, E. (1998). Subjective well-being is essential to well-being. *Psychological Inquiry, 9,* 33–37.

Ellen, E. F. (2002, August). Identifying and treating suicidal college students. *Psychiatric Times, 19.* Retrieved April 14, 2004, from http://www.psychiatric-times.com/p020801.html.

Emmons, R. A. (2003). Personal goals, life meaning, and virtue: Wellsprings of a positive life. In Keyes and Haidt (Eds.) *Flourishing: Positive psychology and the life well-lived*. Washington, DC: American Psychological Association.

Evans, N. J., Forney, D. S. & Guido-DiBrito, F. (1998). *Student development in college: Theory, research, and practice*. San Francisco: Jossey-Bass.

Fish, T. (2005, July 4). A positive first: Master's program in positive psychology. *Science and theology news*. Retrieved April 13, 2006, from http://www.stnews.org/news-1009.htm.

Franey, L. (2002, November 27). Colleges try to help mentally ill students. *The Northerner*. Retrieved April 14, 2004, from http://www.thenortherner.com/global_user_elements/printpage.cfm?storyid=333883.

Goldberg, C. (2006). Harvard's crowded course to happiness: Positive psychology draws student in droves. [Electronic version] *The Boston Globe*. Retrieved April 13, 2006, from http://www.boston.com/news/education/higher/articles/2006/03/10/harvards_crowded_course_to_happiness.

Goodsell, A. H., Maher, M., Tinto, V. (Eds.) (1992). *Collaborative learning: A sourcebook for higher education*. University Park: National Center on Post-Secondary Teaching, Learning, and Assessment, The Pennsylvania State University.

Gurin, P. (1999). The compelling need for diversity in higher education. Expert reports in defense of the University of Michigan. *Equity and Excellence in Education, 32*, 36–62.

Hallett, V. (2003, August 22). When to say "help!" [Electronic version] *U.S. News and World Report*. Retrieved April 14, 2004 from http://www.usnews.com/usnews/edu/college/articles/brief/04mental_brief.php.

Harvey, J. H., & Pauwels, B. G. (2003). The ironies of positive psychology. *Psychological Inquiry, 14*, 125–128.

Hernandez, K., Hogan, S., Hathaway, C., & Lovell, C. D. (1999). Analysis of the literature on the impact of student involvement on student development and learning: More questions than answers. *NASPA Journal, 36*, 184–197.

Hood, A. B. (1984). *Student development: Does participation affect growth?* Bloomington: Association of College Unions International.

Jahoda, M. (1958). *Current concepts of positive mental health*. New York: Basic Books.

Kadison, R., & DiGeronimo, T. F. (2004). *College of the overwhelmed: The campus mental health crisis and what to do about it*. San Francisco: Jossey-Bass.

Kelly, K. (2001, January 15). Lost on the campus. *Time Reports: Understanding Psychology*. Retrieved April 14, 2004, from http://www.time.com/time/classroom/psych/unit6_article5.html.

Keyes, C. L. M. (1998). Social well-being. *Social Psychology Quarterly, 61*, 121–140.

Keyes, C. L. M. (2002). The mental health continuum: From languishing to flourishing in life. *Journal of Health and Social Behavior, 43*, 207–222.

Keyes, C. L. M. (2003). Complete mental health: An agenda for the 21st century. In Keyes and Haidt (Eds.) *Flourishing: Positive psychology and the life well-lived* (pp. 293–312). Washington, DC: American Psychological Association.

Keyes, C. L. M. (2005). Mental illness and/or complete mental health? Investigating axioms of the complete state model of health. *Journal of Consulting and Clinical Psychology, 73*, 539–548.

Keyes, C. L. M. (2007). Promoting and protecting mental health as flourishing: A complementary strategy for improving national mental health. *American Psychologist, 62*, 95–108.

Keyes, C. L. M., & Haidt, J., (Eds.). (2003). *Flourishing: Positive psychology and the life well-lived.* Washington, DC: American Psychological Association.

Keyes, C. L. M., Hysom, S. J., & Lupo. (2000). The positive organization: Leadership legitimacy, employee well-being, and the bottom line. *The Psychologist Manager, 4,* 143–153.

Keyes, C. L. M., & Lopez, S. J. (2002). Toward a science of mental health. In C. R. Snyder and S. J. Lopez (Eds.), *Handbook of Positive Psychology* (pp. 45–59). New York: Oxford University Press.

Keyes, C. L. M., Schmotkin, D. and Ryff, C. D. (2002). Optimizing well-being: The empirical encounter of two traditions. *Journal of Personality and Social Psychology, 82,* 1007–1022.

Keyes, C. L. M., & Waterman, M. B. (2003). Dimensions of well-being and mental health in adulthood. In M. Bornstein, L. Davidson, C. L. M. Keyes, & K. A. Moore (Eds.), *Well-being: Positive development through the life course* (pp. 481–501). Mahwah, NJ: Erlbaum.

King, L. A. (2003). Some truth behind the trombones. *Psychological Inquiry, 14,* 128–131.

Knight, J. R., Wechsler, H., Kuo, M., Seibring, M., Weitzman, E. R., & Schuckit, M. A. (2002). Alcohol abuse and dependence among U.S. college students. *Journal of Studies on Alcohol, 63,* 263–270.

Komives S. R. & Woodward D. B. (1996). *Student services: A handbook for the profession.* San Francisco: Jossey-Bass.

Kuh, G. D. (2002). The National Survey of Student Engagement: Conceptual Framework and Overview of Psychometric Properties. Retrieved April 1, 2004, from http://www.iub.edu/~nsse/html/psychometric_framework_2002.htm.

Kuh, G. D., Schuh, J. H., Whitt, E. J., Andreas, R. E, Lyons, J. W., Strange, C. C., et al. (1991). Involving colleges: Successful approaches to student learning and development outside the classroom. San Francisco: Jossey-Bass.

Lamas, D. (2004, January 5). The dark side of college life: Students cope with academic pressure, depression and suicide. *Columbia Chronicle.* Retrieved April 14, 2004, from http://www.ccchronicle.com/back/2004-01-05/campus7.html.

Lite, J. (2003, September 22). Lifeline for those who need one. *Wired News.* Retrieved April 14, 2004, from http://www.wired.com/news/print/0,1294,60418,00.html.

Lyubomirsky, S. & Abbe, A. (2003). Positive psychology's legs. *Psychological Inquiry, 14,* 132–136.

Marano, H. E. (2002, May). Crisis on the campus. [Electronic version]. *Psychology Today.* Retrieved April 17, 2004, from http://www.psychologytoday.com/htdocs/prod/ptoarticle/pto-20030501-C93505.asp.

Moore, J., Lovell, C. D., McGann, T., & Wyrick, J. (1998). Why involvement matters: A review of research on student involvement in the collegiate setting. *College Student Affairs Journal, 17,* 4–17.

National Institute of Mental Health (2004). *Mission Statement.* Retrieved April 18, 2004, from http://www.nih.gov/about/almanac/organization/NIMH.htm.

National Survey of Student Engagement. (2005). Exploring Different Dimensions of Student Engagement: 2005 Annual Survey Results. Retrieved November 13, 2005, from http://nsse.iub.edu/pdf/NSSE2005_annual_report.pdf.

O'Connor, E. M. (2001). Student mental health: Secondary education no more. [Electronic version]. *Monitor on Psychology, 32.*

Pascarella, E. T., & Terenzini, P. T. (1991). *How college affects students.* San Francisco: Jossey-Bass.

Pascarella, E. T., & Terenzini, P. T. (2005) *How college affects students: A third decade of research.* San Francisco: Jossey-Bass.

Peterson, C. (2006). *A Primer in Positive Psychology.* New York: Oxford University Press.

Peterson, C., & Park, N. (2003). Positive psychology as the evenhanded positive psychologist views it. *Psychological Inquiry, 14,* 141–146.

Peterson, K. S. (2002, May 21). Depression among college students rising. [Electronic version]. *USA Today.* Retrieved April 14, 2004, from http://www.usatoday.com/news/health/mental/2002-05-22-college-depression.htm.

Piliavin, J. A. (2003). Doing well by doing good: Benefits for the benefactor. In C. L. M. Keyes and J. Haidt, (Eds.), *Flourishing: Positive Psychology and the Life Well-Lived.* Washington DC: American Psychological Association.

Rimer, S. (2004, April 6). Today's lesson for college students: Lighten up. *The New York Times,* p. A1.

Ryff, C. D. (1989). Happiness is everything, or is it? Explorations on the meaning of psychological well-being. *Journal of Personality and Social Psychology, 57.* 1069–1081.

Ryff, C. D. (2003). Corners of myopia in the positive psychology parade. *Psychological Inquiry, 14,* 153–159.

Ryff, C. D., & Singer, B. (1998). The contours of positive human health. *Psychological Inquiry, 9,* 1–28.

Ryff, C. D., & Singer, B. (2003). Flourishing under fire: Resilience as a prototype of challenged thriving. In C. L. M. Keyes and J. Haidt (Eds.) *Flourishing: Positive psychology and the life well-lived* (pp. 15–36). Washington, DC: American Psychological Association.

Schroeder, C. C. (Ed.) (1996). The student learning imperative. [Special issue]. *Journal of College Student Development, 37(2).*

Schwartz, K. (2003, May 27). Handling stress on campus. *The Christian Science Monitor.* Retrieved April 14, 2004, from http://www.csmonitor.com/2003/0527/p20s01-lehl.html.

Seligman, M. E. P. (1998a). President's address from the American Psychological Association's annual report. Retrieved on November 5, 2003, from http://www.psych.upenn.edu/seligman/aparep98.htm.

Seligman, M. E. P. (1998b). Positive psychology network concept paper. Retrieved on November 5, 2003, from http://www.psych.upenn.edu/seligman/aparep98.htm.

Seligman, M. E. P., & Pawelski, J. O. (2003). Positive psychology: FAQs. *Psychological Inquiry, 14,* 159–163.

Seligman, M. E. P., Steen, T. A., Park, N., & Peterson, C. (2005). Positive psychology progress: Empirical validation of interventions. *American Psychologist, 60,* 410–421.

Shapira, I., and Jackman, T. (2007). Gunman kills 32 at Virginia Tech in deadliest shooting in U.S. history. Retrieved July 11, 2007, from http://www.washingtonpost.com/wp-dyn/content/article/2007/04/16/AR2007041600533.html.

Shy, L. (2001, September 11). Psychological illnesses rise among freshmen. Retrieved April 14, 2004, from http://www.dailyillini.com/sep01/sep11/news/stories/campus02.shtml.

Snyder, C. R. (2003). [Review of the book *Flourishing: Positive psychology and the life well-lived*]. *Journal of Social and Personal Relationships, 20,* 702–703.

Snyder, C. R., & Lopez, S. J., Eds. (2002). *Handbook of positive psychology.* New York: Oxford University Press.

Snyder, M. B. (2004, March). *Senior student affairs officer round table: Hottest topics in student affairs.* Session held at the annual meeting of the National Association of Student Personnel Administrators, Denver, Colorado.

Sorcinelli, M. D. (1991). Research findings on the seven principles. In A. W. Chickering & Z. F. Gamson (Eds.), *Applying the seven principles for good practice in undergraduate education: New directions for teaching and learning* (pp. 13–25). San Francisco: Jossey-Bass.

Tinto, V. (1993). *Leaving college: Rethinking the causes and cures of student attrition* (2nd ed.). Chicago: University of Chicago Press.

World Health Organization. (2004). *Promoting mental health: Concepts, emerging evidence, practice* (Summary report). Geneva: Author.

CHAPTER 2

Toward a Durable Happiness

Jaime L. Kurtz and Sonja Lyubomirsky

When trying to envision a happy day, or a happy life, what images come to mind? For some people, it might be sharing a meal with good friends and family members while laughing together, telling stories, and feeling loved. For others, happiness may come from accomplishing an important goal and basking in the glory of a job well done. And for others still, happiness may be the byproduct of doing good deeds, helping others, and believing that the world is a better place because of it. Although people may vary a good deal in what they think will make them happy, an overwhelming majority of U.S. residents place "finding happiness" very high on their list of major life goals (Diener, Suh, Smith, & Shao, 1995).

How exactly *do* you "find happiness?" This question has been posed for thousands of years, and although many self-help books have attempted to offer answers, their authors have often based their conclusions, however well meaning, on their own personal, idiosyncratic experiences. Only recently has *scientific* evidence emerged to suggest a possible path to lasting happiness that is effective for the majority of people. By scientific, we mean that researchers have conducted rigorous experiments to determine whether particular strategies for increasing happiness actually work. The present chapter reviews this evidence and provides practical suggestions that you can use to create long-term, or sustainable, changes in your level of well-being.

IS HAPPINESS A WORTHWHILE GOAL?

Before we offer you suggestions on how to become a happier person, it is important to establish whether happiness is a desirable goal. Of course, everyone knows that happiness feels good to the person who is experiencing it. But some may argue that happy people are prone to be lazy, shallow, or unmotivated. However, recent evidence suggests quite the opposite. Rather than being simple and complacent, happy people are energetic, creative, and productive in the workplace, cooperative, and motivated to help others. In the social realm, happy individuals have more friends, more satisfying social interactions, and a lower likelihood of divorce. And in terms of physical and mental health, happy people have stronger immune systems, cope more effectively with stress, and, most strikingly, even live longer (Fredrickson, 2001; Lyubomirsky, King, & Diener, 2005). In sum, happiness doesn't merely "feel good." It carries a wide variety of benefits for the individual, as well as for families, workplaces, and communities.

DEFINING HAPPINESS

When we talk about how happiness can be increased, we aren't just talking about creating the sorts of momentary bursts you may get when your favorite team wins an important game or when you find a dollar on the street. Psychologists are quite good at boosting people's moods over short periods of time. Techniques like giving people a piece of candy, playing pleasant music, or providing positive feedback all produce momentary increases in positive affect (Schwarz & Strack, 1999). The problem is that these increases don't last. As we'll explain below, people's moods respond to and fluctuate along with changes in their environments. When something wonderful happens, they report feeling happier. When something unfortunate happens, they feel sad. However, these changes are often short-lived, and people return to their baseline level of happiness fairly quickly (Brickman & Campbell, 1971). The purpose of the research described in this chapter is to create lasting, sustainable changes in people's *dispositional* level of happiness. This can be thought of as how happy a person feels, on average, over a fairly long period of time.

Most researchers define happiness as consisting of three components: frequent instances of positive affect, infrequent instances of negative affect, and a high level of life satisfaction (Diener et al., 1995). Positive and negative affect are simply experiences of good feelings (e.g., excited, joyful, pleased) and bad feelings (e.g., irritable, sad, tense), respectively. Life satisfaction, by contrast, is a more global, cognitive evaluation of how content a person is with the state of his or her life. Those with a high level of life satisfaction would agree with statements such as, "The conditions of my life are excellent" (Diener, Emmons, Larsen, & Griffin, 1985).

It's important to add to our description of what we mean by happiness that it is thought of as a *subjective* state, meaning that self-reports are the standard way of determining how happy an individual is. Although a few researchers have assessed happiness by asking friends and family to give their impressions of how happy a particular person is (e.g., Sandvik, Diener, & Seidlitz, 1993), ultimately the final judge is "whoever lives inside [the] person's skin" (Myers & Diener, 1995, p. 11). Therefore, the term

"subjective well-being" (or simply "well-being") is often used as a syno-
nym for happiness, as it will be throughout this chapter.

CAN HAPPINESS BE INCREASED? REASONS FOR PESSIMISM

Is it possible to actually become happier? You may be surprised to learn
that, until fairly recently, there was very little scientific data to tell us
whether or not people can lastingly boost their happiness. In fact, in previous years, researchers were doubtful about the possibility of becoming happier. Two reasons underlie their pessimism—first, happiness is partially
determined by genetics, and, second, people tend to adapt (or get used to)
most positive life experiences, and what initially brought them great pleasure gradually ceases to do so. Therefore, some say, any attempts to increase
happiness would be futile, because people would simply return to their genetically determined happiness "baseline" following a pleasant experience.
We describe the evidence for this perspective below.

The Roles of Heredity and Personality

The baseline level of happiness, or set point, is higher for some people
than for others. In other words, some of you are naturally, or disposition-
ally, happier than others. Years of research on fraternal and identical twins
has led psychologists to conclude that this baseline is determined by genetics (Lykken & Tellegen, 1996). In other words, if you had an identical
twin, he or she would share your height, intelligence, and predisposition to
hypertension, and your level of happiness as well.

The fact that happiness has a high heritability is also consistent with
the finding that a person's level of happiness is strongly related to his
or her standing on several personality traits (Diener & Lucas, 1999).
For example, people who are highly neurotic tend to be less happy, and
extraverts are inclined to be happier than introverts. Traits such as these
are relatively fixed, meaning that, throughout the life span, people generally do not change much in where they stand on extraversion, neuroti-
cism, and so forth (McCrae & Costa, 1994). Some researchers have used
these findings to argue that happiness is yet another personality trait—
stable and resistant to any kind of meaningful change (Costa, McCrae, &
Zonderman, 1987).

Hedonic Adaptation

The theory of hedonic adaptation provides another source of pessimism
about the possibility of lastingly increasing happiness. Simply put, this is
the tendency for the emotional impact of both positive and negative events
to diminish over time (Brickman & Campbell, 1971; Diener, Lucas, &
Napa Scollon, 2006). To illustrate, think about a time in your life when
something extremely good happened to you. It may be something you had
daydreamed about and strove for, such as getting accepted into the college

of your choice, winning an important race in a track meet, or successfully asking your crush out on a date. How did you feel immediately after? Most likely, you felt exuberant. You probably thought about the event constantly, replaying it in your mind, telling your friends and family all about it, and feeling certain that the joy you were experiencing would last forever.

Of course, your joy did not last forever. Although thinking about your new life as a college student, your athletic prowess, or your upcoming date may have provided a burst of pleasure, later thoughts of the event gradually failed to reproduce the initial joy you felt. This is due to the process of *hedonic adaptation*, in which events that were initially laden with emotion gradually lose their intensity (Brickman & Campbell, 1971). From the life altering to the mundane, there is a wealth of evidence that people adapt to a variety of events. For example, people adapt to the outcome of a presidential election or a sporting event, the end of a romantic relationship, failing to receive a job promotion, being insulted, winning the lottery, becoming paralyzed, losing a loved one, being diagnosed with a serious illness, and so on (Brickman, Coates, & Janoff-Bulman, 1978; Gilbert, Pinel, Wilson, Blumberg, & Wheatley, 1997; Sieff, Dawes, & Loewenstein, 1999; Wortman, Silver, & Kessler, 1993).

To further illustrate, researchers Suh, Diener, and Fujita (1996) asked college students to report their level of subjective well-being and the number of positive and negative life experiences that they had experienced over the past 4 years. Although many students experienced major life events, such as the death of a family member, the beginning or end of a romantic relationship, becoming engaged or married, gaining admission to graduate school, and finding a job, there was no relationship between the number of recalled positive and negative events and students' reports of happiness, if the events had occurred more than 6 months in the past. These studies suggest that, despite the elation or heartbreak that an event may initially bring, the duration of these emotional reactions is often surprisingly short-lived. In other words, trying to become happier by changing the circumstances of your life—such as your relationship, job, health, or schooling—is not a strategy that is likely to succeed in the long-term.

Happiness Cannot Be Consciously Pursued

Finally, when people have the overt, conscious goal of making themselves happier, it sometimes backfires. Research by Schooler, Ariely, and Loewenstein (2003) has found that instructing people to try and feel as happy as they possibly could actually led to a decrease in momentary happy mood, relative to those who were not asked to try to be happy. Constantly assessing and monitoring happiness levels was similarly counterproductive. It seems that happiness is very often the byproduct of an enjoyable experience, but perhaps it cannot be a deliberate goal in and of itself. Or, as Nathaniel Hawthorne eloquently put it, "Happiness is as a butterfly which, when pursued, is always beyond our grasp, but which if you will sit down quietly, may alight upon you."

REASONS FOR OPTIMISM: THE SUSTAINABLE HAPPINESS MODEL

Some researchers have used the findings we have just described to support the claim that the quest to improve happiness is a fruitless effort (Lykken & Tellegen, 1996). Fortunately, both the fact that happiness has a genetic component and the fact that we adapt to positive life events does not mean that it is impossible to become happier. New research suggests that a person's level of happiness is not set in stone, and that he or she can raise this level by taking advantage of certain intentional activities.

As explained below, the sustainable happiness model (Lyubomirsky, Sheldon, & Schkade, 2005) proposes that happiness is determined by three factors: The genetically determined set point, life circumstances, and intentional activities (see Figure 2.1). The implication of this model is that a large percentage of your happiness is determined by your own conscious, effortful activities and, thus, that increases in happiness *can* be successfully achieved.

The Set Point

The largest piece of the pie is known as the set point—quite literally, the point at which one's happiness level is set, or fixed. People tend to have a level of happiness that they gravitate back to following a significant event, and this set point is higher for some people than for others. In other words, some are born happier than others. You probably know people who always seem to be in good spirits and are habitually looking on the bright side. As the saying goes, when life gives them lemons, they make lemonade. On the other hand, you are likely also familiar with people who are generally unhappy. They see the glass as half empty, and find it hard to derive much pleasure from their daily lives. Psychologists would say that these two sets of people have different set points for well-being. Years of research from a field called "behavioral genetics" has led psychologists to conclude that this set point for happiness is determined by genetics (Lykken & Tellegen, 1996). For example, identical twins are extremely similar in how

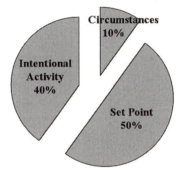

Figure 2.1. What Determines Happiness?

generally happy (or unhappy) they are, even when raised thousands of miles apart, but fraternal twins (whether raised together or apart) are no more similar to one another than regular siblings. Thus, willfully trying to raise your set point by altering your genes is currently impossible. Clearly, the key to lasting increased happiness lies elsewhere.

Circumstances

You may be surprised to learn that life circumstances account for a mere 10% of people's happiness (Argyle, 1999; Diener et al., 1999). By circumstances, we mean factors that constitute the background of your life. For example, if you were to write a brief autobiography, it would include a great deal of information about your life circumstances. Examples include your demographics (e.g., gender, ethnicity), personal experiences (e.g., past traumas and triumphs), life status variables (e.g., marital status, education level, health, and income), your physical appearance, and the physical setting where you live.

Researchers argue that altering your life circumstances is not a promising way of increasing happiness. Although you may feel that you'd be happier if you had more money, lived in a warmer climate, or were better looking, this is generally not the case. Studies show that people adapt quickly to changes in income and marital status, to name just a few (Diener & Oishi, 2000; Lucas, Clark, Georgellis, & Diener, 2003). Also, more attractive people are not happier (Diener, Wolsic, & Fujita, 1995), and—assuming basic needs are met—rich people are only slightly happier than their less wealthy counterparts (e.g., Diener, Horwitz, & Emmons, 1985). What accounts for these counterintuitive findings? Most likely, the reason that happiness is not strongly related to life circumstances is that such factors as income, beauty, and even marital status are particularly prone to adaptation and people generally don't dwell on them. Instead, these circumstantial factors tend to exist in the background of your emotional life.

This is actually good news. Imagine if the key to happiness *did* lie within the realm of your life circumstances. Because many of these circumstances are fairly constant and extremely difficult to change, successfully altering your happiness would be a very costly undertaking. Fortunately, you don't need to undergo plastic surgery, move to the beaches of California, promptly find a marital partner, or obtain a significant pay raise in order to be happier. As explained in the next section, the keys to lasting happiness are much less costly and much more accessible than you might imagine.

Intentional Activity

Even after accounting for the effects of heredity (i.e., the set point) and for the life circumstances that do not seem to make people happy for any significant period of time, a very large portion of the pie chart—40%, in fact—still remains. This portion of the sustainable happiness model, which constitutes people's intentional activities, is what gives researchers hope about the possibility of lastingly increasing well-being. Broadly defined, intentional activities are actions or exercises that a person chooses to engage in. More specifically, they can be thoughts (e.g., counting your blessings) or behaviors (e.g., doing a random act of kindness) that alter your perspective on yourself, your life, and the world in general. Psychologists have found that by electing to engage in certain intentional activities, people can actually make themselves lastingly happier. This is great news, because it tells you that you could be a whole lot happier, if you commit to performing activities that are likely to produce happiness. And, fortunately, a growing amount of psychological research indicates what kinds of activities work best. The following sections describe several activities that have been found to effectively produce sustainable increases in happiness.

EXPRESSING GRATITUDE

Cultivating a grateful mindset, which can be thought of as "a felt sense of wonder, thankfulness, and appreciation for life" (Emmons & Shelton, 2002, p. 460), turns out to be conducive to lasting happiness. However, in using gratitude as a strategy to increase happiness, it must involve more than reflexively saying "thank you." To reap the benefits gratitude brings, you must focus your attention on the positive things in your life and truly savor them.

Empirical Evidence

Several recent studies have shown that focusing attention on the positive things in life—essentially, "counting your blessings"—leads to increases in both physical health and happiness (Emmons & McCullough, 2003; Sheldon & Lyubomirsky, 2006). In one of the first studies on gratitude (Emmons & McCullough, 2003), one group of volunteers was asked to list five things for which they were thankful, once a week for 10 weeks in a row. Their "blessings" ranged from "my family" to "good health" to "The Rolling Stones." Other volunteers participated in two control groups—that is, instead of focusing on gratitude every week, these individuals were asked either to think about their five daily hassles or five major events that had occurred. Relative to these two groups, those who were asked to express gratitude felt more optimistic and more satisfied with their lives. Also, they reported fewer physical symptoms (such as headaches, coughing, or nausea) and more time spent exercising.

Subsequent studies have continued to examine the effect of expressing gratitude on happiness. Lyubomirsky, Sheldon, and Schkade (2005) had participants list their "blessings" in gratitude journals. One group was asked to write in their journals once a week, and a second group was asked to write in them three times a week. A different group of participants was assigned to a control condition, which did not require them to do any exercise. It is interesting to note that compared with controls, participants who expressed their gratitude did show increases in well-being over a 6-week time period, but only those who did the writing exercise only once a week. When writing three times a week, participants did not become lastingly happier, possibly because the exercise grew to be routine, frustrating, or boring.

Writing letters to express your appreciation is another way to create a grateful mind-set and thereby foster happiness. One study (Lyubomirsky, Dickerhoof, Boehm, & Sheldon, 2007) found that writing gratitude letters to specific people, for 15 minutes once a week over the course of 8 weeks, produced boosts in happiness that persisted over the course of the study and were still apparent as long as 9 months after the study was over. This was true even for those individuals who did not share or deliver their letters. However, in real life, many people have the desire to actually tell the objects of their gratitude how much they are appreciated. This is also an effective strategy for increasing happiness and for fostering good relationships. In an online study, Seligman, Steen, Park, and Peterson (2005) instructed a group of participants to think of a person to whom they were grateful but had never properly thanked. Then this group was asked not only to write a gratitude letter but also to deliver it to the recipient. As a result, relative to a control group, these participants reported increases in their happiness that persisted for a full month.

Why Does It Work?

Why does expressing gratitude increase happiness? There are several likely reasons. First, feeling grateful for what you have helps to undo the effects of adaptation mentioned above, thereby changing the way you regard your life. To illustrate, think for a moment about the pleasant but constant things you encounter in your daily life, such as a beautiful tree outside your window, a good-natured and helpful coworker, your favorite local restaurant, or your best friend. However pleasant these things are, people have a tendency to stop appreciating them over time, or as mentioned previously, to *adapt* to them (Brickman & Campbell, 1971). But when you are in a grateful mind-set, which may be brought on by telling your best friend or coworker how much they mean to you, writing a detailed account of all the positive attributes of your favorite restaurant, or simply making a list of several pleasant aspects of your immediate environment, you are bringing these things to the forefront of your attention, relishing them, and appreciating them more fully. In other words, these activities aid in savoring and create a positive focus on present experience.

The happiest people are those who report having strong social support and close relationships (Myers, 2000). Thus, another reason why expressing gratitude is beneficial is that it can help foster these important social bonds. Specifically, when you are feeling grateful for the people in your life, you may feel motivated to spend more time with them and to treat them well (Emmons & Shelton, 2002). A "gratitude visit" exercise, such as the one developed by Seligman and colleagues (2005), has obvious social bene-fits, strengthening the bonds between the writer of the letter and its recipi-ent. One student delivered a gratitude letter to her best friend. She remarked, "By the time she was done reading her letter, she was crying ... her reaction made me cry as well. She hugged me. I had obviously made my best friend's day ... whenever I would think about the incident it most definitely brought a smile to my face and even two days after when she and I would talk on the phone, she still mentioned it."

VISUALIZING YOUR BEST POSSIBLE SELF

A second activity for increasing happiness works by creating a sense of optimism. It involves thinking about your life in the future and visualizing living it as your "best possible self" (BPS; King, 2001). For example, a college-aged woman might envision her ideal life 10 years down the road and write about having great success as a journalist, being married to a devoted and intelligent man, having two healthy children, living in a house in the country, owning horses, and traveling to exotic locations ev-ery summer.

It's important to point out that visualizing your BPS is more than a fan-tasy or a daydream and is it meant to be an exercise in self-deception. While it is vitally important to have goals and dreams, these should be attainable and feasible (Diener & Fujita, 1995). Otherwise, you may be setting your-self up for failure. For example, it would be rather improbable to conjure up a future as the next Bill Gates. And a man who is $5'4''$ probably should not visualize a successful career in the NBA. The purpose of the activity is to lay out your life goals and to think optimistically—not fancifully—about how they might be realized.

Empirical Evidence

In one study (King, 2001), participants spent 20 minutes a day, for 4 days, writing about how they want their life to be in the future. Compared with those who wrote about more neutral topics, people who wrote about their best possible future selves experienced increases in positive mood both immediately after the writing exercises and several weeks later.

This study was recently replicated to examine the effects of engaging in this activity over a longer period of time—either 4 weeks (Sheldon & Lyu-bomirsky, 2006) or 8 weeks (Lyubomirsky et al., 2007). For example, in the 4-week study, participants in the BPS condition were instructed to write about desirable images of their future selves, whereas those in a con-trol condition were asked to recall daily events. As predicted, over the 4-week time period, those in the BPS condition reported experiencing increases in positive emotions after doing the writing exercises, compared with the control participants (see also Lyubomirsky et al., 2007). There-fore, visualizing your best possible self on a regular basis seems to be another effective means of increasing happiness.

Why Does It Work?

Essentially, the BPS activity is fostering an optimistic mindset, because it involves assuming that you will achieve your most cherished future goals, thereby creating a positive image of your future self and an enhanced sense of efficacy, purpose, and meaning. To illustrate, as she completes the writing exercise, the hypothetical college-aged woman described above may be having thoughts like, "Hey! I *am* a good writer. My journalism professor tells me I have the talent and drive to succeed, and I *can* make my career goals happen!" The writing exercise reveals her goals as being more attainable, and this may foster a sense of self-determination and motivation.

Indeed, optimistic people are more likely to persist in the face of challenges, because they maintain the belief that their goals are within reach. Also, if a person truly believes that his or her long-term goals are realizable, which this exercise encourages, they may be better equipped to cope with minor setbacks (Scheier & Carver, 1993). After failing to secure a coveted journalism internship, for instance, the woman above would certainly be disappointed, but she has the newfound perspective to think of it as only a minor setback and to maintain the confidence that, if she keeps persisting, she will secure a similar opportunity down the road.

In addition, this exercise allows people to articulate and solidify their life goals *in writing*. The act of physically writing down your dreams for the future helps you structure and logically formulate the story, whereas simply thinking about your future life in your head may trigger a more nebulous, unstructured flow of ideas (Lyubomirsky, Sousa, & Dickerhoof, 2006; Pennebaker & Graybeal, 2001). When your ideal future is laid out with a sense of structure and coherence, the steps you need to take to achieve it may appear to be clearer and more under your control.

PERFORMING ACTS OF KINDNESS

A third strategy that produces lasting changes in well-being involves doing acts of kindness. This may be surprising, because helpful (or "prosocial") behavior can easily be construed as a self-sacrifice. Whether it is done on an individual basis, or through a formal volunteer organization, helping others is often thought of as time-consuming, tiring, and thankless. However, mounting evidence suggests that prosocial behavior actually has positive outcomes for both the recipient (the person who is benefiting from a kind act) *and* for the benefactor (the person doing the kind act; Piliavin, 2003).

Empirical Evidence

Recent research (Tkach, 2005) systematically examined the effects of doing acts of kindness over the course of several weeks. In one study, participants chose such acts as doing a roommate's dishes, helping a classmate with homework, or holding the door open for a stranger. In general, doing these acts increased participants' happiness, relative to controls. But it wasn't quite that simple. Researchers also varied (a) the frequency with which participants practiced acts of kindness (either three or nine times each week) and (b) the variety with which participants practiced acts of kindness (either varying their kind acts or repeating the same acts weekly). By contrast, a control group simply listed neutral life events from the past week and were not instructed to engage in any prosocial behavior.

Results showed that the frequency of doing kind acts did not impact well-being. However, the *variety* of kind acts that were done did have an effect, such that those who were asked to perform a range of kind acts showed a noticeable increase in happiness, even at a 1-month follow-up. Those who did not vary the types of acts they were doing actually showed a slight decrease in well-being at one point in the study, only to rebound to their original baseline by the end. The effect of variety on subsequent well-being can be partially explained by the idea of hedonic adaptation mentioned above. Imagine that you are doing the same kind act—opening the door for the person behind you—for several weeks. Initially, it might delight you to see people's surprised and grateful reactions to this behavior, but over time, these reactions may become predictable and dull, and the act may quickly become viewed as nothing more than a chore. If this is the case, it makes sense that this activity would cease to bring you happiness. By varying your kind acts, however, you ensure that each one brings you a burst of happiness as you commit it and witness the recipients' novel and unpredictable reactions.

Why Does It Work?

Presumably, performing acts of kindness works as a happiness-enhancing strategy because it changes your self-perception, allowing you to see yourself as a helpful, kind, and capable person (Bem, 1972). For instance, after volunteering to be a math tutor on the weekend, you may cease to think of yourself as a person who sleeps until noon on a Saturday, and begin to see yourself as one who willingly gets out of bed on a chilly weekend morning to help a struggling math student. This is a far more positive self-view.

Also, doing acts of kindness may help you learn about or capitalize on your personal strengths or talents (Seligman, 2002). The math tutor may learn that he is especially skilled at simplifying and explaining abstract concepts. A Habitat for Humanity volunteer may discover that she is good at working with her hands. As noted by Seligman (2002), making the most of strengths and skills creates a feeling of authenticity that is closely related to well-being.

Also, it simply feels good to observe the effects of your generosity. Seeing your math student vastly improve due to your help or receiving a heartfelt "thank you!" after serving someone at soup kitchen can be a genuine mood booster. But more than that, doing acts of kindness may help build strong social relationships and foster an "upward spiral" of social benefits. As noted by Algoe and Haidt (2005), the recipient of a kind act often feels a bolstered sense of positive feelings and connectedness to his or her benefactor, which strengthens their relationship. Moreover, doing things for others is socially engaging. It often requires direct interaction with people you may never meet or get to know well. Volunteers at a nursing home may learn the often-remarkable life histories of the patients. A math tutor may come to appreciate that his student is actually hard-working, but that he excels in the arts, rather than at math. Working at a homeless shelter may make you aware of the particular challenges faced by people living all around you. In this way, prosocial behavior can create a sense of empathy for the recipients. Therefore, it is no surprise that people who volunteer report feeling greater ties to the community (Putnam, 2000).

CHOOSING A HAPPINESS-INCREASING ACTIVITY

Right now you may be feeling quite motivated to try out some of these exercises in your own life. We offer some specific instructions on how to do this in the Personal Mini-Experiments at the end of the chapter. In addition, this section provides some helpful advice on how to make these happiness activities work best for you.

To reiterate and summarize what was mentioned above, too much of a good thing with regard to these activities is possible. It is important to keep them fresh, meaningful, and exciting, so we advise you to be mindful of the frequency with which you are doing them. Once a week seems like a good rule-of-thumb, and is consistent with the findings mentioned above (e.g., Lyubomirsky, Sheldon, et al., 2005). Performing the activities more frequently than this may inadvertently turn them into predictable, routine, or boring chores.

Also, consider ways that you might vary the activity you choose to engage in. For example, if your preferred activity is to express gratitude, think of how you could keep this feeling novel. One possibility is that you could focus in and expand on a different domain of life each week. For example, you might write about nature one week, your personal life the next, and your health the next. Ideally, each time you do this exercise, you will focus in on new things for which you can express gratitude, thereby finding more and more things that are worthy of your attention and appreciation.

As anyone who has achieved long-term weight loss, earned a college degree, or finished a marathon can attest, most meaningful successes in life do not come easily or quickly. In keeping with this notion, it is important to remember that improving your level of happiness requires committed effort. Research has found that those who have increased their happiness most successfully have been those individuals who have persisted with the intentional activities over the course of weeks or months (Lyubomirsky et al., 2007; Sheldon & Lyubomirsky, 2006). This means committing to both initiating and maintaining the happiness activities over a long period of time. As is the case with any goal, long-term commitment is required for success.

The activities described above do not work equally well for all. Accordingly, it is important to choose an activity that "fits" with your personality and goals. By fit, we mean that the activity feels natural and genuine to you. For example, in reading the above descriptions, one type of exercise may have jumped out at you, because it felt very feasible and authentic. Another one may have felt slightly unreasonable, hokey, or unnatural. This is because your personality, strengths, interests, and values will predispose you to enjoy and benefit from certain activities more than others. For example, very shy people might feel more comfortable writing in a gratitude journal rather than doing acts of kindness, which might require what they perceive as awkward interactions with strangers. In short, the happiness activities really only work when this sense of fit exists (Lyubomirsky, Sheldon, et al., 2005).

CONCLUSIONS

Despite research and theory to the contrary (Brickman & Campbell, 1971; Lykken & Tellegen, 1996), there is evidence, shown in the present chapter, that suggests that people can make long-term changes to their level of well-being. By engaging in certain intentional activities, such as expressing gratitude, visualizing one's best possible future self, and doing kind acts, individuals report increases in their happiness over periods of several weeks and even months. When implemented consistently and properly (meaning that the activity is well-timed, varied, and "fits" with the person doing it), these activities help change the way people think about and act in their daily lives. Surprising as it may be, we suggest that attaining lasting happiness does not require a large-scale overhaul of the conditions of one's life, but simply an effortful and habitual restructuring of daily behaviors and thoughts. In sum, recent research finds that the road to happiness is a lot closer than most people believe.

PERSONAL MINI-EXPERIMENTS

Start a Gratitude Journal

In this chapter, we discussed several activities that appear to create lasting improvements in people's levels of happiness. We describe these techniques in greater detail below, and hope that you will find one that works for you and will commit to using it regularly and habitually in your own life.

Choose a time of day when you have several minutes to "step outside" your life and thoughtfully reflect. It could be first thing in the morning, during lunch, or before bedtime. Think of three to five things for which you are currently grateful. These can range from minor events (the coworker who always smiles at you first thing in the morning, or the fact that your roommate took out the trash) to qualities of your life more broadly (your good health, a particular talent you have, or the positive qualities of your best friend). Do this task once a week to start. You may find that you would like to do it a little more often than that, and that is fine. The key is to tailor the activity to suit you best.

Having said that, research does show that people can get bored or weary of doing the exact same activity over and over, so our advice is to add some variety to the ways in which you express your gratitude. Some days, you may choose to simply list a few of your so-called "blessings." Other days, you may want to expand on them and write about *why* you are grateful for them. You could also vary the domain—one day writing about gratitude for people, the next day writing about gratitude for nature, and so on. Sometimes, you may prefer to actually tell someone in person how grateful you are to have him or her in your life.

Think About Your "Best Possible Self": "Think about your best possible self" means that you imagine yourself in the future, after everything has gone as well as it possibly could. You have worked hard and succeeded at accomplishing all of your life goals. Think of this as the realization of your life dreams, and of your own best potentials.

Set aside 20 minutes, once a week, and sit down to reflect upon your best possible future self. Write a detailed description of what your life might be like. Focus on aspects of both your personal and your professional life and vary the domains you consider each week, such as your romantic relationship, your career goals, and your health.

Perform Acts of Kindness: In our daily lives, we all perform acts of kindness for others. These acts may be large or small and the person for whom the act is performed may or may not be aware of the act. Examples include feeding a stranger's parking meter, donating blood, helping a friend with homework, visiting an elderly relative, or writing a thank-you letter. For this exercise, perform five acts of kindness each week and vary them as much as you want. Choose one day during the week (e.g., a Monday or a Saturday) in which to do all five kind acts. The acts do not need to be for the same person, and the act may or may not be similar to the acts listed above. Do not perform any acts that may place yourself or others in danger.

Keep a "kindness journal" in which you write down the details of performing your kind acts at the end of the day in which you did them. You may want to describe exactly what you did, who benefited from your kind act, and—if applicable—their reaction. Also, make a note of how you felt before, during, and after each act.

REFERENCES

Algoe, S., & Haidt, J. (2006). *Witnessing excellence in action: The "other-praising" emotions of elevation, gratitude, and admiration.* Manuscript submitted for publication.

Argyle, M. (1999). Causes and correlates of happiness. In D. Kahneman, E. Diener, & N. Schwarz. (Eds.), *Well-being: The foundations of hedonic psychology* (pp. 353–373). New York: Russell Sage Foundation.

Bem, D. J. (1972). Self-perception theory. In L. Berkowitz (Ed.), *Advances in experimental social psychology* (Vol. 6, pp. 1–62). New York: Academic Press.

Brickman, P., & Campbell D. T. (1971). Hedonic relativism and planning the good society. In M. H. Appley (Ed.), *Adaptation-level theory* (pp. 287–302). New York: Academic Press.

Brickman, P., Coates, D., & Janoff-Bulman, R. (1978). Lottery winners and accident victims: Is happiness relative? *Journal of Personality and Social Psychology, 36,* 917–927.

Costa, P. T., McCrae, R. R., & Zonderman, A. B. (1987). Environmental and dispositional influences on well-being: Longitudinal follow-up of an American national sample. *British Journal of Psychology, 78,* 299–306.

Diener, E., Emmons, R. A., Larsen, R. J., & Griffin, S. (1985). The satisfaction with life scale. *Journal of Personality Assessment, 49*, 71–75.

Diener, E., & Fujita, F. (1995). Resources, personal strivings, and subjective well-being: A nomothetic and idiographic approach. *Journal of Personality and Social Psychology, 68*, 926–935.

Diener, E., Horwitz, J., & Emmons, R. A. (1985). Happiness of the very wealthy. *Social Indicators Research, 16*, 263–274.

Diener, E., & Lucas, R. E. (1999). Personality and subjective well-being. In D. Kahneman, E. Diener, & N. Schwarz (Eds.), *Well-being: The foundations of hedonic psychology* (pp. 213–229). Cambridge, MA: MIT Press.

Diener, E., Lucas, R. E., & Napa Scollon, C. (2006). Beyond the hedonic treadmill: Revising the adaptation theory of well-being. *American Psychologist, 61*, 305–314.

Diener, E., & Oishi, S. (2000). Money and happiness: Income and subjective well-being across nations. In E. Diener, & E. Suh (Eds.), *Culture and subjective well-being* (pp. 185–218). Cambridge, MA: MIT Press.

Diener, E., Suh, E. M., Lucas, R. E., & Smith, H. L. (1999). Subjective well-being: Three decades of progress. *Psychological Bulletin, 125*, 276–302.

Diener, E., Suh, E. M., Smith, H., & Shao, L. (1995). National differences in reported well-being: Why do they occur? *Social Indicators Research, 34*, 7–32.

Diener, E., Wolsic, B., & Fujita, F. (1995). Physical attractiveness and subjective well-being. *Journal of Personality and Social Psychology, 69*, 120–129.

Emmons, R. A., & McCullough, M. E. (2003). Counting blessing versus burdens: An experimental investigation of gratitude and subjective well-being in daily life. *Journal of Personality and Social Psychology, 84*(2), 377–389.

Emmons, R. A., & Shelton, C. M. (2002). Gratitude and the science of positive psychology. In C. R. Snyder & S. J. Lopez (Eds.), *Handbook of positive psychology* (pp. 459–471). Oxford: Oxford University Press.

Fredrickson, B. L. (2001). The role of positive emotions in positive psychology: The broaden-and-build theory of positive emotions. *American Psychologist, 56*, 218–226.

Gilbert, D. T., Pinel, E. C., Wilson, T. D., Blumberg, S. J., & Wheatley, T. P. (1998). Immune neglect: A source of durability bias in affective forecasting. *Journal of Personality and Social Psychology, 75*(3), 617–638.

King, L. A. (2001). The health benefits of writing about life goals. *Personality and Social Psychology Bulletin, 27*, 798–807.

Lucas, R. E., Clark, A. E., Georgellis, Y., & Diener, E. (2003). Reexamining adaptation and the set point model of happiness: Reactions to changes in marital status. *Journal of Personality and Social Psychology, 84*, 527–539.

Lyubomirsky, S., Dickerhoof, R., Boehm, J. K., & Sheldon, K. M. (2007). *How and why do positive activities work to boost well-being?: Two experimental longitudinal investigations of regularly practicing optimism and gratitude.* Manuscript under review.

Lyubomirsky, S., King, L., & Diener, E. (2005). The benefits of frequent positive affect: Does happiness lead to success? *Psychological Bulletin, 131*, 803–855.

Lyubomirsky, S., Sheldon, K. M., & Schkade, D. (2005). Pursuing happiness: The architecture of sustainable change. *Review of General Psychology, 9*, 111–131.

Lyubomirsky, S., Sousa, L., & Dickerhoof, R. (2006). The costs and benefits of writing, talking, and thinking about life's triumphs and defeats. *Journal of Personality and Social Psychology, 90*, 692–708.

Lykken, D., & Tellegen, A. (1996). Happiness is a stochastic phenomenon. *Psychological Science, 7,* 186–189.

McCrae, R. R., & Costa, P. T. (1994). The stability of personality: Observations and evaluations. *Current Directions in Psychological Science, 3,* 173–175.

Myers, D. G. (2000). The funds, friends, and faith of happy people. *American Psychologist, 55,* 56–67.

Myers, D. G., & Diener, E. (1995). Who is happy? *Psychological Science, 6,* 10–19.

Pennebaker, J. W., & Graybeal, A. (2001). Patterns of natural language use: Disclosure, personality, and social integration. *Current Directions in Psychological Science, 10,* 90–93.

Piliavin, J. A. (2003). Doing well by doing good: Benefits for the benefactor. In C. L. M. Keyes & J. Haidt (Eds.), *Flourishing: Positive psychology and the life well-lived* (pp. 227–247). Washington, DC: American Psychological Association.

Putnam, R. D. (2000). *Bowling alone: The collapse and revival of American community.* New York: Simon & Schuster.

Sandvik, E., Diener, E., & Seidlitz, L. (1993). Subjective well-being: The convergence and stability of self-report and non-self-report measures. *Journal of Personality, 61,* 317–342.

Scheier, M. F., & Carver, C. S. (1993). On the power of positive thinking: The benefits of being optimistic. *Current Directions in Psychological Science, 2,* 26–30.

Schooler, J. W., Ariely, D. & Loewenstein, G. (2003). The pursuit and assessment of happiness can be self-defeating. In I. Brocas & J. D. Carrillo (Eds.), *The psychology of economic decisions. Vol. 1: Rationality and well being* (pp. 41–70). New York: Oxford University Press.

Schwarz, N., & Strack, F. (1999). Reports of subjective well-being: Judgment processes and their methodological implications. In D. Kahneman, E. Diener, & N. Schwarz (Eds.), *Well-being: The foundations of hedonic psychology* (pp. 61–84). New York: Russell Sage Foundation.

Seligman, M. E. P. (2002). *Authentic happiness: Using the new positive psychology to realize your potential for lasting fulfillment.* New York: Free Press.

Seligman, M. E. P., Steen, T. A., Park, N., & Peterson, C. (2005). Positive psychology progress: Empirical validation of interventions. *American Psychologist, 60,* 410–421.

Sheldon, K. M., & Lyubomirsky, S. (2006). How to increase and sustain positive emotion: The effects of expressing gratitude and visualizing best possible selves. *Journal of Positive Psychology, 1,* 73–82.

Sieff, E. M., Dawes, R. M. & Loewenstein, G. (1999). Anticipated versus actual reaction to HIV test results. *American Journal of Psychology, 112,* 297–311.

Suh, E., Diener, E., & Fujita, F. (1996). Events and subjective well-being: Only recent events matter. *Journal of Personality and Social Psychology, 70,* 1091–1102.

Tkach, C. (2005). *Unlocking the treasury of human kindness: Enduring improvements in mood, happiness, and self-evaluations.* Unpublished doctoral dissertation, University of California, Riverside.

Wortman, C. B., Silver, R. C., & Kessler, R. C. (1993). The meaning of loss and adjustment to bereavement. In M. S. Stroebe, W. Stroebe, & R. O. Hansson (Eds.), *Handbook of bereavement: Theory, research, and intervention* (pp. 349–366). New York: Cambridge University Press.

CHAPTER 3

Will Money Buy Happiness?

David G. Myers

Does fiscal fitness foster feeling fine? Does wealth promote well-being? Let's personalize this: Could money buy *you* happiness? If that sounds too crass, let's moderate the question: Would a *little* more money make you a *little* happier?

MONEY MATTERS

If only we had more money. A quarter century ago, when University of Michigan interviewers asked Americans what hampered their search for the good life, the most common answer was, "We're short of money" (A. Campbell, 1981, p. 41). What would improve their life quality? "More money" was the most frequent answer.

In 2006, such sentiments still prevailed when Gallup (Carroll, 2006) asked employed Americans, "Would you be happier if you made more money?" The answer, by a three to one margin: Yes. Indeed, the more the better. In an earlier Gallup Poll (Gallup & Newport, 1990), one in three women, two in three men, and four in five people earning more than $75,000 a year say they would like to be rich.

More evidence of the "greening of America" comes from the annual UCLA/American Council on Education survey of entering American collegians—more than 13 million between 1966 and 2007 (see Figure 3.1). From 1970 through the mid-1980s, students assigned decreasing importance to developing a meaningful philosophy of life and increasing importance to being very well off financially (which for most years of the last decade has remained the highest ranked of some 20 life goals, even

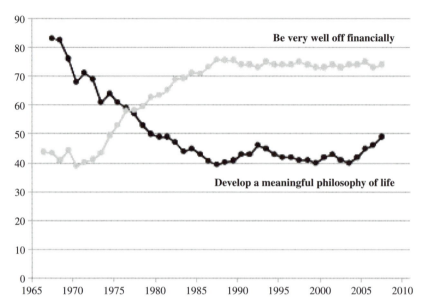

Figure 3.1. Percent of entering American collegians saying "very important or essential."

Source: Annual UCLA/American Council on Education surveys, reported in *The American Freshman.*

outranking "helping others who are in difficulty" and "raising a family"). It's today's American dream: Life, liberty, and the purchase of happiness.

Economist Thomas Naylor (1990) sensed this intense materialism during his 6 years of teaching corporate strategy courses at Duke University. After asking students to write their personal strategic plan, he observed that "With few exceptions, what they wanted fell into three categories: Money, power and things—very big things, including vacation homes, expensive foreign automobiles, yachts and even airplanes.... Their request to the faculty was: Teach me how to be a moneymaking machine." Few expressed concern for ethics, family, spirituality, or social responsibilities.

In *Luxury Fever*, the Cornell economist, Robert Frank (1999) reported that, at the 20th century's end, spending on luxury goods was outpacing the growth in overall spending four to one. Sales of luxury cars, private jets, cruise liners, and private mega yachts had soared. High-end Aspen hotel suites were booked months ahead. Malcolm Forbes, Jr., appealed to the modern ethos in marketing his magazine: "I want to make one thing very clear about FORBES, namely—*we are all about success and money*. Period."

Are Gallup's Americans, today's collegians, Thomas Naylor's business students, and *Forbes'* readers on to an important truth? Does being well off indeed produce—or at least correlate with—psychological well-being? Would people be happier if they could exchange their struggling middle class lives for palatial surroundings, Aspen ski vacations, and executive class travel? Would we be happier had we won the publishers' sweepstakes that allowed winners to choose a 40-foot yacht, a deluxe motor home, a designer wardrobe, a luxury car, and a private housekeeper? Would we be happier having the power and respect that accompanies affluence? "Whoever said money can't buy happiness isn't spending it right," proclaimed a Lexus ad.

WEALTH AND WELL-BEING

As people's money goes up does their misery go down? Does money enable "the good life"? We can triangulate on this by asking three focused questions:

- Are people happier in rich countries?
- In any given country, are richer people happier?
- Over time is economic growth accompanied by rising happiness?

Are Rich Countries Happy Countries?

In surveys of several hundred thousand people—from 16 nations in one 1980s study and from 82 nations in the most recent World Values Survey—there are striking national differences. In one 16-nation survey of 170,000 people, one in ten people in Portugal said they were "very happy," as did four in ten people in the Netherlands (Inglehart, 1990). These appear to be genuine national differences and not merely the result of translation differences. For example, regardless of whether they are German-, French-, or Italian-speaking, the Swiss reported greater well-being than their German, French, and Italian neighbors.

Comparing countries, we do see in Figure 3.2 (R. Inglehart, personal communication, April 13, 2006) a positive but curvilinear relationship between national wealth (indexed as Gross National Product per person) and well-being (a composite of self-rated happiness and life satisfaction). The curvilinear relationship replicates earlier World Values Survey data from 40 countries (Inglehart, 1997). In both data sets, the Scandinavians are generally prosperous and happy. Yet in both we also see a diminishing utility of increasing national wealth. As one moves from the very poor eastern European nations to the moderately well off countries, national well-being rises. Ronald Inglehart (1997, p. 64) explains: "The transition from a society of scarcity to a society of security brings a dramatic increase in subjective well-being."

But further increases in wealth pay few additional dividends. Inglehart (1997, p. 64) reasons that, "at this level starvation is no longer a real concern for most people. Survival begins to be taken for granted." And in both waves of the survey, there are curious reversals: The Irish, for example, have reported greater happiness and life satisfaction than the better off Germans. Moreover, the Latin American countries are "over achievers" (Inglehart, in press), with Puerto Rico and Mexico exhibiting the highest well-being among 82 countries in the latest available data.

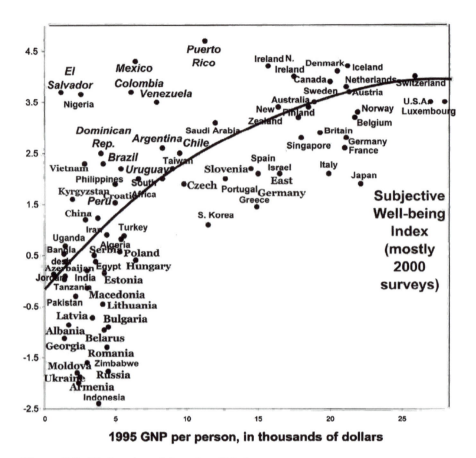

1995 GNP per person, in thousands of dollars

Figure 3.2. National wealth and well-being.
Source: Inglehart, in press.

Of course, national wealth is confounded with other happiness predictors, such as civil rights, literacy, and the number of continuous years of democracy. The Scandinavians and Swiss enjoy not just abundant wealth but also a history of stable freedom.

The bottom-line conclusion—that national poverty and insecurity demoralizes but that national wealth beyond a certain point implies no greater happiness—became real for me during the year in the mid-1980s that my family and I spent in St. Andrews, Scotland. To most Americans, Scottish life then would have seemed spartan. Incomes were about half those in the United States. Among families in our region, 44 percent did not own a car, and we never met a family that owned two. Central heating in this place not far south of Iceland was a luxury.

During our year there we enjoyed hundreds of conversations over daily morning coffees at my university department, in church groups, and over dinner or tea in many homes. Our repeated impression was that, despite their simpler living, the Scots appeared no less joyful than our American neighbors back home. We heard complaints about Margaret Thatcher, but never about being underpaid or unable to afford one's desires. There was less money and less consumption, but apparently no less satisfaction with living, no less warmth of spirit, no less pleasure in one another's company.

Within Countries, Are Rich People Happier?

We have seen that national wealth and well-being do correlate, up to a point. But the correlation is entangled with other happiness predictors, such as stable democracy and personal empowerment. So let's ask a second question: Within any country, are higher income people happier?

In historically poor countries, such as Bangladesh and India, being relatively well off has made for greater well-being (Argyle, 1999). In places where being relatively poor means living with unmet needs for food, clean water, secure rest, and warmth, relative affluence predicts happier lives.

In more economically developed Western countries, noted Inglehart (1990, p. 242), the income-happiness correlation is "surprisingly weak." As Figures 3.3 and 3.4 illustrate, happiness and life satisfaction are lower among the poor. But just as economic growth provides diminishing returns for national well-being, so, once comfortable, more money provides diminishing returns for individuals. The second $50,000, like the second piece of pie, seldom tastes as good as the first. To say that we "cannot live by bread alone" acknowledges that we do need bread, but that, having bread, other needs come to the fore (as Abraham Maslow recognized in his famous hierarchy of needs). Tell me someone's income and you haven't given me much clue as to their satisfaction with their marriage, their family, their friendships, or themselves—all of which do predict happiness. Thus, noted David Lykken (1999, p. 17) from his happiness studies, "People who go to work in their overalls … are just as happy, on average, as those in suits."

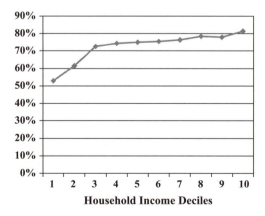

Figure 3.3. Personal income decile and life satisfaction in Australian Living Standards Survey, 1991–1992 (percent reporting high life satisfaction).

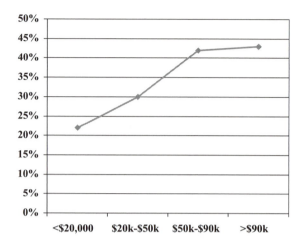

Figure 3.4. Personal income and happiness in National Opinion Research Center General Social Survey, 2004 (percent of Americans "very happy," by income).

Even in Calcutta and Pakistani slums, people "are more satisfied than one might expect" (Biswas-Diener & Diener, 2001; Suhail & Chaudhry, 2003). And though growing up poor puts children at risk for some social pathologies, growing up rich puts them at risk for other pathologies. Children of affluence are at elevated risk for substance abuse, eating disorders, anxiety, and depression (Luthar & Latendresse, 2005). And among nearly 1,000 American teens whose experience was periodically sampled by Mihaly Csikszentmihalyi (1999), those from upper middle-class backgrounds reported *less* happiness than those from the lowest socioeconomic class. One possible explanation, suggested Csikszentmihalyi, is that children of professional and executive parents tend to spend less time with their parents than do children of middle and working class parents.

Ergo, wealth is like health: Its utter absence can breed misery, yet having it is no guarantee of happiness. What matters more than money (assuming one can afford life's necessities with a sense of security) is how you feel about what you have. Those who live with a sense of gratitude—or who cultivate their gratitude by each day writing down what they are grateful for—enjoy greater happiness (McCullough, Tsang, Emmons, 2004; Watkins, 2004).

Even very rich people—the *Forbes'* 100 wealthiest Americans surveyed by Ed Diener and his colleagues (1985)—are only slightly happier than the average person. With net worths providing ample money to buy things they don't need and hardly care about, four in five of the 49 people responding to the survey agreed that "Money can increase OR decrease happiness, depending on how it is used." And some were indeed unhappy. One fabulously wealthy man said he could never remember being happy. One woman reported that money could not undo misery caused by her children's problems. When sailing on the *Titanic,* even first class cannot get you where you want to go.

Warren Buffett (1997) reported that Diener's findings are consistent with his own observation of billionaires. Indeed, examples of the wretched wealthy are not hard to come by: Howard Hughes, Christina Onassis, and J. Paul Getty and his heirs (Pearson, 1995). "If you were a jerk before, you'll be a bigger jerk with a billion dollars," added Buffett.

There is a progressive implication of the diminishing utility of income increases at high income levels, notes Robert Cummins (2006) from his analysis of Australian data. Beyond a certain point, further income loses its power to increase happiness. Said differently, more money will buy more happiness for the poor than for the rich. This implies that people's happiness could most effectively be raised "by providing additional financial resources to the lowest income groups" (p. 9).

At the other end of life's circumstances are many victims of disabling tragedies. Apart from prolonged grief over the loss of a loved one or lingering anxiety after a trauma (such as child abuse, rape, or the terrors of war), even tragedy usually is not permanently depressing. Learning that one is HIV-positive is devastating. But after 5 weeks of adapting to the grim news, those who tested positive felt less emotionally distraught than they had expected (Sieff, Dawes, & Loewenstein, 1999). Kidney dialysis patients recognize that their health is relatively poor, yet in their moment-to-moment experiences they report being just as happy as healthy nonpatients (Riis et al., 2005). People who become blind or paralyzed also usually recover near-normal levels of day-to-day happiness (Gerhart, Koziol-McLain, Loewenstein, & Whiteneck, 1994; Myers, 1993).

Among a sample of Germans incapacitated by ALS (amyotrophic lateral sclerosis or Lou Gehrig's disease, a progressive neurological disease that leads to paralysis), a striking 85 percent rated their quality of life as "satisfactory," "good," or "very good." Moreover, their ratings were not much affected by whether they were on ventilators or tube fed or not (Kübler, Winter, Ludolph, Hautzinger, & Birbaumer, 2005). "If you are a paraplegic," explains Daniel Kahneman (2005), "you will gradually start thinking of other things, and the more time you spend thinking of other things the less miserable you are going to be." Thus, most ALS patients, despite their tragic illness, gradually accommodate to their paralysis. Although somewhat less happy than the average person, they express considerably more happiness than able-bodied people with depression (Schwartz & Estrin, 2004).

These findings underlie an astonishing conclusion from the scientific pursuit of happiness. As the late New Zealand researcher Richard Kammann (1983) put it, "Objective life circumstances have a negligible role to play in a theory of happiness."

Over Time, Does Happiness Rise with Affluence?

Having compared rich with not-rich countries, and rich with not-rich individuals, we come to our third question: Over decades, does our happiness grow with our paychecks? For example, are Americans happier today than in 1940, when two out of five homes lacked a shower or bathtub, heat often meant hand-feeding a furnace, and more than a third of homes had no toilet? Or than in 1957, when economist John Galbraith was about to describe the United States as *The Affluent Society*?

Since 1957, our average per person income, expressed in inflation- and tax-adjusted dollars, has more than doubled, thanks partly to increased wages during the 15 or so years following 1957. Thus, compared with 1957, we now are the "doubly affluent society."

A caveat: The rising economic tide has lifted the yachts faster than the dinghies. In constant dollars, production workers' hourly earnings were no higher in 2006 than in 1973 (Bureau of Labor Statistics, 2007). Still, with increased nonwage income, increased working hours, and the doubling of married women's employment, most boats have risen. Compared to 1957, today's Americans have twice as many cars per person. We eat out two and a half times as often. We build vastly bigger houses. We are five times as likely to enjoy home air conditioning. And we (even many at lower income levels) relish the technology—the laptops, iPods, Playstations, and camera cell phones—that enriches our lives.

So, believing that more money would make us a little happier, and having seen our affluence ratchet upward little by little over the last half century, are we now happier? Now that we can dial pleasant room temperatures with our fingertips, eat fresh fruit in winter, sip skinny lattés, and travel by jet airliner with our handy suitcase on wheels, are we happier? Has our collective happiness floated upward with the rising economic tide and all the cool stuff it has given us?

It most definitely has not. Since 1957, when National Opinion Research Center interviewers first queried Americans, the number of "very happy" Americans has slightly declined, from 35 to 32 percent (see Figure 3.5).Twice as rich, and slightly less happy. In fact, between 1956 and 1988, the percentage of Americans saying they were "pretty well satisfied with your present financial situation" *dropped* from 42 to 30 percent (Niemi, Mueller, & Smith, 1989).

Meanwhile, various misery indexes were increasing during the third of a century after 1960, as the divorce rate doubled, the teen suicide rate more than doubled, and more people than ever (especially teens and young adults) became depressed (Myers, 2000a). Asked "Have you ever felt that you were going to have a nervous breakdown?" 17 percent of Americans said "yes" in 1957. This number rose to 24 percent in 1996 (Swindle, Heller, Bescosolido, & Kikuzawa, 2000). Similar increased depression has been observed in Canada, Sweden, Germany, and New Zealand (Klerman & Weissman, 1989; Cross-National Collaborative Group, 1992). At the very least, increased physical comfort has not been accompanied by increased psychological comfort.

We might call this soaring wealth and shrinking spirit "the American paradox." More than ever, we have big houses and broken homes, high incomes and low morale, more comfortable cars and more road rage. We excel at making a living but often fail at making a life. We celebrate our prosperity but yearn for purpose. We cherish our freedoms but long for connection. In an age of plenty, we feel spiritual hunger (Myers, 2000a).

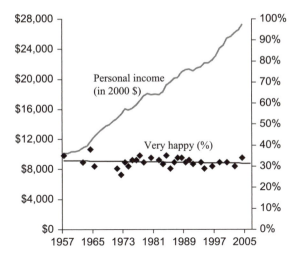

Figure 3.5. Economic growth and happiness. American's average buying power has almost tripled since the 1950s, while reported happiness has remained almost unchanged. (Happiness data from National Opinion Research Center General Social Survey; income data from *Historical Statistics of the United States* and *Economic Indicators*.)

It is hard to avoid a startling conclusion: Our becoming much better off over the last 5 decades has not been accompanied by one iota of increased subjective well-being. The same is true of the European countries, Australia, and Japan (Diener & Biswas-Diener, 2002; Easterlin, 1995; Eckersley, 2000). In these countries, people enjoy better nutrition, health care, education, and science, and they are somewhat happier than those in very poor countries. Yet their increasing real incomes have not produced increasing happiness. In Britain, for example, great increases in the percent of households with cars, central heating, and telephones have not been accompanied by increased well-being. And after a decade of extraordinary economic growth in China—from few owning a phone and 40 percent owning a color television to most people now having such things—Gallup surveys revealed a *decreasing* proportion of people satisfied "with the way things are going in your life today" (Burkholder, 2005).

The findings are startling because they challenge modern materialism: *Economic growth has provided no apparent boost to human morale.* Having been told over and again that "it's the economy, stupid," believing in the American version of "the good life," these results come as a shock. Yet in study after study and country after country we see much the same result: Once we have enough income to afford our needs and feel control over our lives, piling on more and more money and consumption entails thinning increases in our happiness. To modern materialists the conclusion may be shocking, but it is not original. Seneca (c. 4 B.C. to A.D. 65) observed nearly 2,000 years ago that

> Our forefathers ... lived every jot as well as we, when they provided and
> dressed their own meat with their own hands; lodged upon the ground, and
> were not as yet come to the vanity of gold and gems.... which may serve to
> show us, that it is the mind, and not the sum, that makes any person rich....
> No one can be poor that has enough, nor rich that covets more than he has.

Without romanticizing the struggles of oppression and poverty, Seneca
would say that to be rich is less an ample bank balance than a state of mind.
To be rich is to have wants that are simpler than our incomes can afford.

WHY RICHES, CONSUMPTION, AND MATERIALISM FAIL TO SATISFY

If his government achieves its 4 percent economic growth-rate goal,
noted Australian researcher Richard Eckersley (2001), its people will be
twice as rich in 20 years, "and 10 times richer than we were 100 years ago.
Can we be sure that this increasing wealth creation is beneficial to personal
and social well-being?" As we have seen, the psychological benefits will likely
be limited, especially for those already at higher income levels. Why is this?

Materialism

Materialism minimizes morale. This finding—that individuals who strive
most for wealth tend to live with lower well-being—"comes through very
strongly in every culture I've looked at," reports Richard Ryan (1999).
Seek extrinsic goals, such as wealth, beauty, and popularity, and you may
instead find anxiety, depression, and psychosomatic ills (Eckersley, 2005;
Sheldon, Ryan, Deci, & Kasser, 2004). Strive for intrinsic goals such as
"intimacy, personal growth, and contribution to the community" and you
likely will experience greater quality of life, notes Tim Kasser (2000, 2002).
Ryan and Kasser's research echoes an earlier finding by H. W. Perkins
(1991): Among 800 college alumni surveyed, those with "Yuppie values"—who preferred a high income and occupational success and prestige
to having very close friends and a close marriage—were twice as likely as
their former classmates to describe themselves as "fairly" or "very"
*un*happy.

Imagine yourself as a participant in a study by Sheldon, Elliot, Kim, and
Kasser (2001). Pause and think: "What were the most satisfying events that
you have experienced in the last month? And to what extent did those
events meet your desires for self-esteem, relatedness to others, and
autonomy? And your desires for money and luxury?" For most people, the
truly satisfying happenings in life less often involve money than feelings of
connection, control, and self-worth. In a study of university students, Ed
Diener and Martin Seligman (2002) confirmed that the best things in life
are not things; very happy university students are distinguished not by their
money but by their "rich and satisfying close relationships."

Moreover, materialists—people who identify themselves with expensive
possessions—experience fewer positive moods (Solberg, Diener, & Robinson,

2003). Materialists also report a relatively large gap between what they want and what they have, and they enjoy fewer close, fulfilling relationships. And for most of us, just thinking about money diminishes volunteerism, generosity, and feelings of connection. That's what Kathleen Vohs, Nicole Mead, and Miranda Goode (2006) observed when, in nine experiments, they primed people's thinking about money, as when asking them to unscramble phrases that were either about money ("high a salary paying") or not ("cold it outside is"). With money on their minds, university students became less willing to ask for help on a task, to help someone with dropped pencils, and to donate money.

Economist Robert Frank and his Cornell psychology colleagues Thomas Gilovich and Dennis Regan (1993) surveyed money-minded economics professors. Despite having relatively high salaries, economists were more than twice as likely as those in other disciplines to contribute no money to private charities. In responding to public television appeals, their median (and most common) gift was nothing. Moreover, in laboratory monetary games, students behave more selfishly after taking economics courses.

If, as research indicates (Myers, 1993, 2000b), happiness is mostly a matter of positive traits, close relationships, engaging work and leisure, and a faith that entails meaning, hope, and social support, then why is making more money so often our consuming passion? And why do yesterday's luxuries so quickly become today's necessities? Two principles drive this psychology of wealth and consumption.

Adaptation: Happiness and Prior Experience

Perhaps you have noticed. Bad events—an argument, a rejection, a setback—put you in the dumps. And good events—winning a big game, an A on a test, falling in love—trigger joy. But only for a while. "We are never happy for a thousand days, a flower never blooms for a hundred" says a Chinese proverb. Within a day or two, our moods settle back toward normal, with our ups and down reflecting the day's events.

Thus dejection and elation are both hard to sustain. When in a funk, we know we will rebound. Stung by criticism, we wallow in gloom, but not for long. Delighted by acclaim, we relish the success, but then discover that Seneca again was right: "No happiness lasts for long."

Our emotional resilience illustrates the "adaptation level" phenomenon, which is our tendency to adapt to any given experience and then notice variations from that level. Based on our experience we adjust our neutral levels—the points at which sounds seem neither loud not soft, temperatures neither hot nor cold, events neither pleasant nor unpleasant. We then notice and react to changes from these levels. Where I live in Michigan, a 50-degree morning feels distinctly cold in July and warm in January.

So, when our achievements rise (or when our income, prestige, or technology improves) we feel successful and satisfied. Before long, however, we adapt. What once felt good—that first color television, which I recall—comes to register as neutral, and what formerly was neutral (the black and white TV it replaced) now feels like deprivation. Having adapted upward, what once felt positive now feels negative. Satisfaction, as Richard Ryan (1999) has said, "has a short half-life." Or as Dutch psychologist Nic Frijda (1988) recognized, "Continued pleasures wear off.... Pleasure is always contingent upon change and disappears with continuous satisfaction."

Indeed, observed Donald Campbell (1975), a permanent social paradise on earth is impossible. If you awoke tomorrow to your utopia—no bills, no ills, basking in love—you would be ecstatic, for a time. But then you would begin recalibrating your adaptation level, and before long your emotions would again be a mix of gratification (when achievements surpass expectations) and frustration (when they fall below).

Richard Solomon (1980) documented a corollary "opponent-process" principle: Emotions trigger opposing emotions. Thus for many pleasures we pay a later price, and for much suffering we receive a later reward. For the euphoria of a drug high, we pay the price of craving and depression when the drug wears off. For enduring hard exercise or even the pain of childbirth, we afterward enjoy a well-earned glow.

As Solomon wisely noted, the opponent-process principle is bad news for hedonists. Those who seek artificial pleasures will pay for them later (and, as his experiments showed, repetition diminishes the pleasure's intensity). There is no free lunch. With every kick comes a kickback. "Take what you want," said God in an old Spanish proverb. "Take it and pay for it."

But the good news is that suffering or simplified living can lower our adaptation level, paving the way for an emotional rebound. Biblical wisdom anticipated the point. "Weeping may linger for the night, but joy comes with the morning" (Psalm 30:5). "Blessed are those who mourn, for they will be comforted" (Matthew 5:4). For pain endured and remembered, we gain a sweeter joy.

Our intuition tends to ignore the reality of adaptation. We assume a sequence: We want. We get. We are happy. In actuality, as Daniel Gilbert and Timothy Wilson (2000, p. 182) have shown, we often "miswant." Those who fantasize a desert island holiday with sun, surf, and sand may discover "how much they require daily structure, intellectual stimulation, or regular infusions of Pop Tarts." We are, they say, vulnerable to "impact bias"—overestimating the durability of emotions. In reality, our emotions are attached to elastic bands that pull us back from highs and lows.

Impact bias is important, say Wilson and Gilbert (2005) because our predictions of our future emotions influence our decisions. If we overestimate the intensity and duration of the pleasure we will gain from purchasing a new car or undergoing cosmetic surgery, then we make ill-advised investments in that new SUV or extreme makeover.

But then we can thank the adaptation-level phenomenon for fueling our ambition. Without it, we would dwell contentedly on our first plateau of success, feeling no further upward drive. Because every desirable experience, from passionate love to the pleasure of a new possession, is transitory, achievement breeds happiness only as new plateaus are followed by higher highs.

C. S. Lewis (1956/1984, p. 228) recognized this in his Narnia tales, which conclude as its creatures, with their world collapsing behind them, step into a joyous never-ending story. "All their life in this world and all their adventures in Narnia had only been the cover and the title page: Now at last they were beginning Chapter One of the Great Story which no one on earth has read: Which goes on forever: In which every chapter is better than the one before."

Social Comparison: Happiness and Others' Attainments

Happiness is relative not only to the past experiences to which we have adapted, but also to our observations of others' experiences. We compare ourselves and our outcomes with others. And we feel good or bad depending on whom we compare with. We feel agile when others seem clumsy, smart when others seem slow-witted, and rich when others seem poor. As Karl Marx wrote in *Wage-Labor and Capital* (1847/1976), "A house may be large or small; as long as the surrounding houses are equally small, it satisfies all social demands for a dwelling. But let a palace arise beside the little house, and it shrinks from a little house into a hut." In *Brother to a Dragonfly*, Will Campbell (1980) recalls experiencing the phenomenon: "Our poverty became a reality. Not because of our having less, but by our neighbors having more."

World War II Air Corps soldiers offered a classic example of such "relative deprivation"—the sense of being relatively worse off than one's comparisons. Although the Corps soldiers enjoyed a rapid rate of promotion, many were frustrated with their own promotion rates (Merton & Kitt, 1950). Seeing others promoted inflated their expectations. And when expectations fly above attainments, the result is frustration.

Further feeding our dissatisfaction is the tendency to compare upward. As we climb the success ladder, or gain affluence, we mostly compare with peers who are a rung or two above our current level. Bertrand Russell (1930/1985) saw no end to upward comparison: "Napolean envied Caesar, Caesar envied Alexander, and Alexander, I daresay, envied Hercules, who never existed. You cannot, therefore get away from envy by means of success alone, for there will always be in history or legend some person even more successful than you are."

Such social comparison finds a modern expression in today's reports of rich Silicon Valley entrepreneurs feeling envy for their super rich counterparts (Hafner, 2006). When a multimillionaire early executive of PayPal compares himself with the mega-millionaire YouTube creators, or when the wealthy founder of an Internet dating site compares himself with his best friend, who was a founder of PayPal, they feel wistful rather than wealthy.

Where inequality exists, comparisons are more likely to breed dissatisfaction. With the yachts rising faster than the dinghies over the last third of a century, American inequality has exacerbated. For example, the U.S. Census Bureau reports that the percentage of household income earned by the top fifth has increased from 43 percent to 50 percent. Across locations and over time, income inequality makes for more people who have rich neighbors, and thus more people at risk for diminished satisfaction with their own existence (Hagerty, 2000). Television's modeling of the lifestyles of the wealthy also serves to accentuate relative deprivation (Schor, 1998). Both these factors surely help explain why Chinese satisfaction has decreased since 1994 even while visible attainments have increased, though unequally so.

Managing our Adaptations and Comparisons in a Sustainable World

There is a bright side to the malleability of our happiness and life satisfaction. As increasing consumption and population combine to exceed the earth's carrying capacity and change the climate, we have the potential to respond not only with ecologically responsible technologies but also simplified living. With pricier petrol, Americans will follow Europeans by electing more fuel-efficient cars. Such simplification will at first cause dissatisfaction. But if the sacrifices are shared, we will adapt. And in time we will recover our normal mix of discontent, joy, and neutrality.

Positive psychology's contribution to a sustainable future will come from its consciousness-transforming insights into what makes for the genuinely good life. With echoes of the Old Testament prophet Isaiah (55:2), positive psychology invites us to consider: "Why do you spend your money for that which is not bread, and your labor for that which does not satisfy?" What's the point of accumulating stacks of unplayed CDs, closets full of seldom-worn clothes, three-car garages with luxury cars—all purchased in a vain quest for an elusive joy? And what's the point of leaving significant inherited wealth to one's heirs, as if it could bring them happiness, rather than applying it to a hurting world?

Ronald Inglehart, a social scientist who follows world values surveys, has discerned the beginnings of a subsiding of materialism and signs of a new generation maturing with increasing concern for personal relationships, the integrity of nature, and the meaning of life. Happily, those things that make for the genuinely good life—close relationships, a hope-filled faith, positive traits, engaging activity—are enduringly sustainable. As Jigme Singye Wangchuk, King of Bhutan (quoted by Mancall, 2004), has observed, "Gross national happiness is more important than gross national product."

Envisioning a new American dream need not romanticize poverty or destroy our market economy. But it will require our seasoning prosperity with purpose, capital with compassion, and enterprise with equity. Such a transformation in consciousness has happened before; today's thinking about race, gender, and the environment differs radically from a half century ago. If it is to happen again, as a new kind of satisfaction untethered from materialism, these practical principles may help.

Restrain Nostalgia-Fed Expectations

In Royal Institution lectures two centuries ago (later published as *Elementary Sketches of Moral Philosophy*) Sydney Smith advised that we "are always happier for having been happy; so that if you make them happy now, you make them happy twenty years hence, by the memory of it." Actually, despite our enjoyment of happy memories, dwelling on our past Camelot moments can make our present seem pedestrian. If we use our happiest memories, or our images of most ecstatic love, as our yardstick for assessing the present, we may doom ourselves to disappointment. In one German experiment, adults felt better about their present lives after recalling and writing down a significant low rather than high moment from their past (Strack, Schwarz, & Gschneidinger, 1985). Although magnificent memories are pleasant, nostalgia can breed discontent.

Indeed, noted Allen Parducci (1984), remembered ecstasies exact a price. Because the *range* of our prior experiences colors our assessments of our current experience, yesterday's highs often dull today's ordinary pleasures. Raise the top of your range—with an idyllic holiday from your everyday poverty, earning twice your previous high commission, sharing unbridled sexual passion—and you may discover, back in the real world, that your ordinary weekends, your regular commission, your routine lovemaking, now feel mundane.

Ed Diener and his colleagues (Diener, Colvin, Pavot, & Allman 1991; Smith, Diener, & Wedell, 1989) have confirmed the lesson: If super high points are rare, we're better off without them. Better *not* to expose ourselves to luxury, if its rarity only serves to diminish our daily quiet joys.

Experience Occasional Reminders of How Bad Things Can Be

Given time to fully recover, people report greater happiness after hospitalization for a health problem (Schwarz & Strack, 1990). Contrasts help define contentment. The pangs of hunger make food delicious. Tiredness makes the bed feel heavenly. Loneliness makes a friendship cherished.

In more routine ways we can give ourselves reminders of our blessings. The ground under the sleeping bag makes the bed, when back home, feel softer. The Lenten bowls of rice make the roast chicken tastier. The temporary separation from our loved one makes the union sweeter, the person less taken for granted. Such experiences help reframe our attitude and renew our gratitude.

Shelley Taylor (1989, pp. 167–168) illustrates the principle with a Jewish fable about a farmer who seeks a rabbi's counsel because his wife nags him, his children fight, and his surroundings are in chaos. The good rabbi tells him to go home and move the chickens into the house. "Into the house!" cries the farmer. "But what good will that do?" Nevertheless, he complies, and two days later returns, more frantic than before. "Now my wife nags me, the children fight, and the chickens are everywhere, laying eggs, dropping feathers, and eating our food. What am I to do?" The rabbi tells him to go home and bring the cow into the house. "The cow!" cries the distraught man. "That can only worsen things!" Again, the rabbi insists, the man complies, and then returns a few days later more harried than ever. "Nothing is helping. The chickens are into everything and the cow is knocking over the furniture. Rabbi, you have made things worse."

The rabbi sends the frantic man home to bring in the horse as well. The next day the man returns in despair. "Everything is knocked over. There is no room for my family. Our lives are in shambles. What shall we do?" Now the rabbi instructs, "Go home and take out the horse and cow and chickens." The man does so and returns the next day smiling. "Rabbi, our lives are now so calm and peaceful. With the animals gone, we are a family again. How can I thank you?" The rabbi smiles.

Choose Comparisons that Will Breed Gratitude

Two of my children work at the opposite ends of the economic spectrum. One provides personal technology services in the homes and yachts of one of the world's-mega billionaires. The other currently is living in South Africa, and doing volunteer work in impoverished townships. Although the second child is poorer, I wouldn't be surprised if she felt as rich as her sibling. As Abraham Maslow (1972, p. 108) noted, "All you have to do is to go to a hospital and hear all the simple blessings that people never before realized *were* blessings—being able to urinate, to sleep on your side, to be able to swallow, to scratch an itch, etc. Could *exercises* in deprivation educate us faster about all our blessings?"

Short of engaging the sick and the poor, even imagining others' misfortunes can trigger greater contentment with one's own fortune. Marshall Dermer, Cohen, Jacobson, and Anderson (1979) experimented with the phenomenon by inviting University of Wisconsin, Milwaukee, women to view grim depictions of Milwaukee life in 1900, with its sickening hygiene, hunger, unemployment, crime, and despair. Or they imagined and wrote about personal tragedies such as being burned and disfigured. After these experiences, the women expressed a greater sense of satisfaction with their own lives, which now seemed not so bad.

In another experiment, Jennifer Crocker and Lisa Gallo (1985) tested the wisdom of an old song, "Count your blessings, name them one by one." After five times completing the sentence, "I'm glad I'm not a ..." people felt relatively happy and satisfied with their lives. Those who instead counted their unfulfilled desires, by completing sentences beginning with "I wish I were a ..." then felt *worse* about their lives. "I cried because I had no shoes," says a Persian proverb, "until I met a man who had no feet."

PERSONAL MINI-EXPERIMENT

Thinking about Money Matters

In this chapter we have seen that national income correlates with national subjective well-being (but only to a point), that personal income correlates with personal well-being (but only to a point), and that economic growth over time has not been accompanied by increased well-being. We have also seen that the materialist values that prevail in modern America are not predictive of happiness. Two principles help explain why wealth and materialism fail to satisfy: The adaptation-level phenomenon and social comparison. As incomes and consumption rise, we at first feel good but then soon adapt. Comparing with others, we may even feel relatively deprived.

This being so, how would you—or will you in the future—answer these questions:

- What are your deeply felt aspirations? How important is it to make lots of money? If that is a significant goal for you, what motivates you—a desire for more possessions and comfort? For status? For the chance to leave a legacy?
- If you have or were to have significant wealth, what would you do with it while alive? Would you leave most of it to your heirs? If not, how would you distribute it?
- What sort of "ecological footprint" does your lifestyle demand? Is this what you intend?
- To influence consumption, would you favor changed incentives or regulations? For example, would you support or oppose higher fuel-efficiency requirements for cars and trucks? Higher fuel taxes to motivate smaller cars and fewer carbon dioxide emissions?

REFERENCES

Argyle, M. (1999). Causes and correlates of happiness. In D. Kahneman, E. Diener, & N. Schwarz (Eds.), *Well-being: The foundations of hedonic psychology*. New York: Russell Sage Foundation.

Biswas-Diener, R., & Diener, E. (2001). Making the best of a bad situation: Satisfaction in the slums of Calcutta. *Social Indicators Research, 55*, 329–352.

Buffett, W. (1997, April 21). Does money buy happiness? *Forbes*, 394.

Bureau of Labor Statistics (2007). Seasonally adjusted average hourly earnings, 1982 dollars. Retrieved April 10, 2007, from www.data.bls.gov.

Burkholder, R. (2005, January 11). Chinese far wealthier than a decade ago—but are they happier? *Gallup Poll News Service*. Retrieved August 7, 2006, from www.galluppoll.com.

Campbell, A. (1981). *The sense of well-being in America*. New York: McGraw-Hill.

Campbell, D. T. (1975). On the conflicts between biological and social evolution and between psychology and moral tradition. *American Psychologist, 30*, 1103–1126.

Campbell, W. (1980). *Brother to a dragonfly*. New York: Continuum.

Carroll, J. (2006, August 7). American workers would be happier in same job with higher pay. *Gallup Poll News Service*. Retrieved August 7, 2006, from www.galluppoll.com.

Crocker, J., & Gallo, L. (1985, August). The self-enhancing effect of downward comparison. Paper presented at the American Psychological Association Convention, Los Angeles, CA.

Cross-National Collaborative Group (1992). The changing rate of major depression. *Journal of the American Medical Association, 268*, 3098–3105.

Csikszentmihalyi, M. (1999). If we are so rich, why aren't we happy? *American Psychologist, 54*, 821–828.

Cummins, R. A. (2006, April 4). Australian unity wellbeing index Survey 14.1. Australian Centre on Quality of Life, Deakin University.

Dermer, M., Cohen, S. J., Jacobsen, E., & Anderson, E. A. (1979). Evaluative judgments of aspects of life as a function of vicarious exposure of hedonic extremes. *Journal of Personality and Social Psychology, 37,* 247–60.

Diener, E., & Biswas-Diener, R. (2002). Will money increase subjective well-being? A literature review and guide to needed research. *Social Indicators Research, 57,* 119–169.

Diener, E., Colvin, C. R., Pavot, W., & Allman, A. (1991). The psychic costs of intense positive affect. *Journal of Personality and Social Psychology, 61,* 492–503.

Diener, E., Horwitz, J., & Emmons, R. A. (1985). Happiness of the very wealthy. *Social Indicators, 16,* 263–274.

Diener, E., & Seligman, M. E. P. (2002). Very happy people. *Psychological Science, 13,* 81–84.

Easterlin, R. (1995). Will raising the incomes of all increase the happiness of all? *Journal of Economic Behavior and Organization, 27,* 35ff.

Eckersley, R. (2000). The mixed blessings of material progress: Diminishing returns in the pursuit of happiness. *Journal of Happiness Studies, 1,* 267–292.

Eckersley, R. (2001, March 23). Wealthier, but poorer for all that. *The Australian,* p. 13.

Eckersley, R. (2005). Is modern Western culture a health hazard? *International Journal of Epidemiology, 35,* 252–258.

Frank, R. H. (1999). *Luxury fever: Why money fails to satisfy in an era of excess.* New York: Free Press.

Frank, R. H., Gilovich, T., & Regan, D. T. (1993). Does studying economics inhibit cooperation? *Journal of Economic Perspectives, 7,* 159–171.

Frijda, N. H. (1988). The laws of emotion. *American Psychologist, 43,* 349–358.

Gallup, G., Jr., & Newport, F. (1990, July). Americans widely disagree on what constitutes 'rich.' *Gallup Poll Monthly,* 28–36.

Gerhart, K. A., Koziol-McLain, J., Lowenstein, S. R., & Whiteneck, G. G. (1994). Quality of life following spinal cord injury: Knowledge and attitudes of emergency care providers. *Annals of Emergency Medicine, 23,* 807–812.

Gilbert, D. T., & Wilson, T. D. (2000). Miswanting: Some problems in the forecasting of future affective states. In J. Forgas (Ed.), *Feeling and thinking: The role of affect in social cognition.* Cambridge: Cambridge University Press.

Hafner, K. (2006, November 21). In web world, rich now envy the superrich. *New York Times.* Retrieved November 21, 2006, from www.nytimes.com.

Hagerty, M. R. (2000). Social comparisons of income in one's community: Evidence from national surveys of income and happiness. *Journal of Personality and Social Psychology, 78,* 764–771.

Inglehart, R. (1990). *Culture shift in advanced industrial society.* Princeton: Princeton University Press.

Inglehart, R. (1997). *Modernization and postmodernization.* Princeton: Princeton University Press.

Inglehart, R. (in press). Cultural change and democracy in Latin America. In F. Hagopian (Ed.), *Contemporary Catholicism, religious pluralism, and democracy in Latin America.* South Bend, IN: Notre Dame University Press.

Kahneman, D. (2005, February 10). Are you happy now? *Gallup Management Journal.* Retrieved February 10, 2005, www.gmj.gallup.com.

Kammann, R. (1983). Objective circumstances, life satisfactions, and sense of well-being: Consistencies across time and place. *New Zealand Journal of Psychology, 12,* 14–22.

Kasser, T. (2000). Two versions of the American dream: Which goals and values make for a high quality of life? In E. Diener (Ed.), *Advances in quality of life theory and research*. Dordrecht, Netherlands: Kluwer.

Kasser, T. (2002). *The high price of materialism*. Cambridge, MA: MIT Press.

Klerman, G. L., & Weissman, M. M. (1989). Increasing rates of depression. *Journal of the American Medical Association, 261*, 2229–35.

Kübler, A., Winter, S., Ludolph, A. C., Hautzinger, M., & Birbaumer, N. (2005). Severity of depressive symptoms and quality of life in patients with amyotrophic lateral sclerosis. *Neurorehabilitation and Neural Repair, 19(3)*, 182–193.

Lewis, C. S. (1984). *The last battle*. New York: Collier Books. (Originally published 1956).

Luthar, S. S., & Latendresse, S. J. (2005). Children of the affluent: Challenges to well-being. *Current Directions in Psychological Science, 14*, 49–53.

Lykken, D. T. (1999). *Happiness*. New York: Golden Books.

Mancall, M. (2004). Gross national happiness and development: An essay. In K. Ura & K. Galay (Eds.), *Gross national happiness and development*. Thimphu, Bhutan: The Centre for Bhutan Studies.

Marx, K. (1976). *Wage-labour and capital and value, price and profit*. New York: International Publishers. (Originally published 1847)

Maslow, B. G. (1972). *Abraham H. Maslow: A memorial volume*. Monterey, CA: Brooks/Cole.

McCullough, M. E., Tsang, J-A., & Emmons, R. A. (2004). Gratitude in intermediate affective terrain: Links of grateful moods to individual differences and daily emotional experience. *Journal of Personality and Social Psychology, 86*, 295–309.

Merton, R. K., & Kitt, A. A. (1950). Contributions to the theory of reference group behavior. In R. K. Merton & P. F. Lazarsfeld (Eds.), *Continuities in social research: Studies in the scope and method of the American soldier*. Glencoe, IL: Free Press.

Myers, D. G. (1993). *The pursuit of happiness*. New York: Avon Books.

Myers, D. G. (2000a). *The American paradox: Spiritual hunger in an age of plenty*. New Haven: Yale University Press.

Myers, D. G. (2000b). The funds, friends, and faith of happy people. *American Psychologist, 55*, 56–67.

National Opinion Research Center (2004). General social survey. Accessed via sda. Berkeley.edu.

Naylor, T. H. (1990). Redefining corporate motivation, Swedish style. *Christian Century, 107*, 566–570.

Niemi, R. G., Mueller, J., & Smith, T. W. (1989). *Trends in public opinion: A compendium of survey data*. New York: Greenwood Press.

Parducci, A. (1984). Value judgments: Toward a *relational* theory of happiness. In J. R. Eiser (Ed.), *Attitudinal judgment*. New York: Springer-Verlag.

Pearson, J. (1995). *Painfully rich: The outrageous fortune and misfortunes of the heirs of J. Paul Getty*. New York: St. Martins.

Perkins, H. W. (1991). Religious commitment, Yuppie values, and well-being in post-collegiate life. *Review of Religious Research, 32*, 244–251.

Riis, J., Loewenstein, G., Baron, J., Jepson, C., Fagerlin, A., & Ubel, P. A. (2005). Ignorance of hedonic adaptation of hemodialysis: A study using ecological momentary assessment. *Journal of Experimental Psychology: General, 134*, 3–9.

Russell, B. (1985). *The conquest of happiness*. London: Unwin Paperbacks. (Originally published 1930).

Ryan, R. (1999, February 2). Quoted by Alfie Kohn. In pursuit of affluence, at a high price. *New York Times*. Retrieved February 2, 1999, from www.nytimes.com.

Schor, J. B. (1998). *The overworked American*. New York: Basic Books.

Schwartz, J., & Estrin, J. (2004, November 7). Living for today, locked in a paralyzed body. *New York Times*. Retrieved November 7, 2004, from www.nytimes.com.

Schwarz, N., & Strack, F. (1990). Evaluating one's life: A judgment model of subjective well-being. In F. Strack, M. Argyle, & N. Schwarz (Eds.), *The social psychology of well-being*. Oxford: Pergamon.

Seneca, L. A. (1928–1935). Morals of a happy life. In J. W. Basore (Trans.) *Moral essays* (Vol. 3). London: W. Heinemann.

Sheldon, K. M., Elliot, A. J., Kim, Y., & Kasser, T. (2001). What is satisfying about satisfying events? Testing 10 candidate psychological needs. *Journal of Personality and Social Psychology, 80,* 325–339.

Sheldon, K. M., Ryan, R. M., Deci, E. L., & Kasser, T. (2004). The independent effects of goal contents and motives on well-being: It's both what you pursue and why you pursue it. *Personality and Social Psychology Bulletin, 30,* 475–486.

Sieff, E. M., Dawes, R. M., & Loewenstein, G. (1999). Anticipated versus actual reaction to HIV test results. *The American Journal of Psychology, 112,* 297–313.

Smith, R. H., Diener, E., & Wedell, D. H. (1989). Intrapersonal and social comparison determinants of happiness: A range-frequency analysis. *Journal of Personality and Social Psychology, 56,* 317–325.

Solberg, E. C., Diener, E., & Robinson, M. D. (2003). Why are materialists less satisfied? In T. Kasser & A. D. Kanner (Eds.), *Psychology and consumer culture: The struggle for a good life in a materialistic world*. Washington, DC: American Psychological Association.

Solomon, R. L. (1980). The opponent-process theory of acquired motivation: The costs of pleasure and the benefits of pain. *American Psychologist, 35,* 691–712.

Strack, S., Schwarz, S., & Gschneidinger, E. (1985). Happiness and reminiscing: The role of time perspective, affect, and mode of thinking. *Journal of Personality and Social Psychology, 49,* 1460–1469.

Suhail, K., & Chaudhry, H. R. (2004). Predictors of subjective well-being in an eastern Muslim culture. *Journal of Social and Clinical Psychology, 23,* 359.

Swindle, R., Jr., Heller, K., Bescosolido, B., & Kikuzawa, S. (2000). Responses to nervous breakdowns in America over a 40-year period: Mental health policy implications. *American Psychologist, 55,* 740–749.

Taylor, S. E. (1989). *Positive illusions*. New York: Basic Books.

Vohs, K. D., Mead, N. L., & Goode, M. R. (2006). The psychological consequences of money. *Science, 314,* 1154–1156.

Watkins, P. C. (2004). Gratitude and subjective well-being. In R. A. Emmons and M. E. McCullough (Eds.), *The psychology of gratitude*. New York: Oxford University Press.

Wilson, T. D., & Gilbert, D. T. (2005). Affective forecasting: Knowing what to want. *Current Directions in Psychological Science, 14,* 131–134.

CHAPTER 4

Presenting a Positive Alternative to Strivings for Material Success and the Thin Ideal: Understanding the Effects of Extrinsic Relative to Intrinsic Goal Pursuits

Maarten Vansteenkiste, Bart Soenens, and Bart Duriez

Contemporary consumer culture offers a seemingly promising pathway to developing a satisfying and happy life. In numerous advertisements, we are told that the pursuit of a good life can be equated with a "goods life" (Kasser, 2002) or with the attainment of a "perfect body" (Dittmar, 2007). The mass media suggests that if we manage to garner the possessions that are presented to us on TV and in glossy magazines and if we are able to reach the idealized body images that role models exemplify, we are more likely to be satisfied with ourselves and with our lives in general. In bringing this message, the mass media creates a dream world in which wealth and the attainment of good looks are glorified as indicators of happiness and success (Kasser, Cohn, Kanner, & Ryan, 2007).

In line with the exponential growth of consumer culture over the past decades, psychologists have become increasingly interested in examining whether the promise of the "American Dream" (Kasser & Ryan, 1993) holds some truth or whether it represents a myth in which people might even get entrapped (Dittmar, 2007). The purpose of this chapter is to frame this discussion about consumerism and the good life within a well-grounded motivational theory, that is, Self-Determination Theory (SDT; Deci & Ryan, 2000; Ryan & Deci, 2000) and the qualitative distinction this theory makes between intrinsic goals (e.g., self-development, community contribution) and extrinsic goals (e.g., financial success, status). In doing so, we will not only focus on the implications of pursuing extrinsic goals, but, following the positive psychology perspective (Seligman & Csikszentmihalyi, 2000), we also consider a positive alternative, that is, the pursuit of intrinsic goals. Furthermore, we move beyond the personal and social well-being correlates of people's goal pursuits (see Kasser, 2002, for an overview) by also focusing on the consequences of extrinsic versus intrinsic goals in the domains of ethical, ecological, and inter-group attitudes and performance and persistence.

This chapter consists of four different parts. In the first two parts, we discuss the implications of the personal pursuit of extrinsic relative to intrinsic goals and the exposure to the contextual promotion of extrinsic relative to intrinsic goals. After this, we review a number of theories that have challenged the distinction between extrinsic and intrinsic goals. Finally, we argue that the lack of satisfaction of the basic psychological needs for autonomy, competence, and relatedness (Ryan, 1995) that follows from endorsing or being exposed to the promotion of extrinsic goals at the expense of intrinsic goals might account for the differential effects of these goals on people's functioning (Kasser, 2002).

In addition to discussing the mechanism of basic need satisfaction, we also "zoom in" on the micro-mediational mechanisms that might play an intervening role between goal pursuits and basic need satisfaction. In doing so, we review research from the body image literature, from consumer psychology and from social psychology.

INTRINSIC- VERSUS EXTRINSIC-GOAL PURSUITS

Within SDT, it is argued that some goals are more likely to contribute to people's personal and social well-being than others (Ryan, Sheldon, Kasser, & Deci, 1996). Specifically, SDT-researchers (Kasser & Ryan, 1996; Vansteenkiste, Lens, & Deci, 2006) have distinguished two different types or contents of goals, that is, (a) extrinsic goals such as garnering social popularity or fame, being financially successful, attaining power and influence over others, and having a physical appealing image, and (b) intrinsic goals such as building meaningful relationships, developing one's talents, achieving a sense of physical fitness and good health, and meaningfully contributing to the community.

Extrinsic goals exemplify salient aspects of a consumer culture, in which fame, money, and good looks are portrayed as signs of success (Kasser, Cohn et al., 2007). The appeal of these goals lies in the anticipated power, admiration, and sense of worth that might result from realizing them (Kasser, Ryan, Couchman, & Sheldon, 2004). They are considered extrinsic because they would promote an "outward orientation" (Williams, Cox, Hedberg, & Deci, 2000) or a "having orientation" (Fromm, 1976), as they focus people on making a good impression on others. However, the pursuit of these goals is likely to be "exogenous" to basic need satisfaction, as their pursuit is unlikely to satisfy and might even thwart the need for autonomy, competence, and relatedness (Deci & Ryan, 2000).

In contrast, intrinsic goals are typically valued because their pursuit is inherently satisfying and health promoting. They reflect an inward oriented frame or a "being orientation" focused on the actualization of one's interests, values, and potential (Fromm, 1976; Van Boven & Gilovich, 2003). In agreement with humanist thinking, intrinsic goals are thought to reflect people's tendency to obtain meaning, to grow as a person, and to connect with others (Sheldon & Kasser, 2001). Thus, intrinsic goals can be considered manifestations of the organismic growth tendencies common to human beings; under sufficiently supportive circumstances, people would have the natural inclination to increasingly move away from extrinsic goals, toward intrinsic goals (Sheldon, Arndt, & Houser-Marko, 2003). The pursuit of intrinsic goals is more likely to lead the person to have experiences that can satisfy inherent psychological needs for autonomy, competence, and relatedness, so that intrinsic goal pursuit is said to be more "endogenous" or more inherently related to basic need satisfaction.

In contrast to researchers who aimed to chart the structure of all possible human values (e.g., Schwartz, 1992), the differentiation between intrinsic and extrinsic goals is not meant to be exhaustive: Not all possible goals can be classified as either intrinsic or extrinsic in nature, and goals that are neither means to impress others nor inherently growth-promoting (e.g., hedonism) might fit neither category. It should also be noted that the study of extrinsic goals is by no means unique to SDT. Although labeled differently, the concept of extrinsic goals has also received considerable attention in fields such as consumer psychology (e.g., Belk, 1985; Richins & Dawson, 1992), political sociology (e.g., Inglehart, 1990), and organizational psychology (e.g., Elizur, 1984), which have all primarily focused on the pursuit of one particular extrinsic goal, that is the pursuit of wealth. In the literature on body image and eating disorders (e.g., Stice & Shaw, 1994), researchers have focused on another single extrinsic goal, that is, the thin ideal. Although pursuing material success and physical appeal might be important for understanding different phenomena (e.g., ethical functioning versus the etiology of eating disorders), from a SDT perspective, they can both be studied under the extrinsic-goal concept, as they share an outward character.

Furthermore, rather than studying extrinsic goals in "isolation" from other goals, SDT argues that the pursuit of extrinsic goals needs to be contrasted with a positive alternative, that is, the pursuit of intrinsic goals. Accordingly, empirical studies in the SDT tradition often use a composite score reflecting the relative importance individuals attach to intrinsic compared to extrinsic goals. Thus, a higher score reflects a tendency to value more strongly intrinsic than extrinsic goals.

In the first studies on intrinsic and extrinsic goals, Kasser and Ryan (1993, 1996) developed the Aspiration Index, assessing the importance that individuals attribute to the pursuit of intrinsic and extrinsic aspirations. Initial factor-analytical work in U.S. samples indicated that these two types of goals fall apart in an intrinsic and extrinsic factor. More recently, using more sophisticated analytical techniques (i.e., multidimensional scaling), Grouzet, Kasser, et al. (2006) demonstrated the generalizability of the intrinsic–extrinsic goal distinction by showing that it holds up in 15 different nations varying in cultural foci and Bruto National Product, providing further evidence for the generalizability of the intrinsic–extrinsic dimension. Because intrinsic and extrinsic goals are said to result in qualitatively different modi of functioning, the critical issue at hand concerns whether living a life that is organized more strongly around the pursuit of intrinsic than extrinsic goals yields implications for individuals' adjustment. Note that it is not so much the absolute importance attributed to extrinsic goals that might be problematic rather than the relative weight these goals occupy in the person's total value-structure.

Personal Well-being and Health

A few dozen studies, conducted in countries as diverse as South-Korea, Russia, Belgium, Germany, and the UK, have now convincingly shown that the pursuit of extrinsic relative to intrinsic goals is associated with lower psychological well-being (e.g., self-actualization, vitality), lower subjective well-being (e.g., happiness, life satisfaction), and stronger signs of ill-being (e.g., depression, negative affect, proportion of time spent being unhappy, and anxiety; see Kasser, 2002, for an overview). Various studies in the consumer literature have confirmed these results by showing that the pursuit of materialism is negatively associated with self-esteem (e.g., Richins & Dawson, 1992) and quality of life (e.g., Roberts & Clement, 2007), while being positively associated with social anxiety, narcissism, and conduct disorders (Cohen & Cohen, 1996).

In a similar vein, Van Boven and Gilovich (2003) found that people who believe that money spent on experiential purchases (i.e., the "consumption" of a series of events, such as traveling) when compared to material purchases (i.e., the buying of a tangible object; e.g., jewelry) is "better spent" and that experiential relative to material purchases provoke more positive feelings. These findings were further corroborated by Kasser and Sheldon (2002), who reported that a happy and satisfying Christmas is positively associated with more frequent engagement in religious and family experiences and is negatively associated with engagement in materialist experiences (e.g., spending money). Furthermore, Kasser (2005) found materialist children of 10 to 11 years old to be more prone to depression and reduced well-being. In a related study, Dohnt and Tiggeman (2006a) showed that by 6 years old a large number of girls desired a thinner ideal figure; girls who looked at women's magazines were more likely to be dissatisfied with their appearance concurrently, whereas girls who watched more appearance-related television programs were more at risk for developing low appearance satisfaction prospectively (Dohnt & Tiggeman, 2006b). The finding that young children are already vulnerable for the adverse effects of extrinsic relative to intrinsic goal pursuits is alarming in light of the advertising industry's increasing attempts to seduce children to buy the message that achieving an ideal body and material goods guarantees happiness.

Finally, research in different domains, including exercise (Sebire, Standage, & Vansteenkiste, in press), sports (Vansteenkiste, 2007) and work (Vansteenkiste, Neyrinck, et al., 2007) starts to show that the valuation of intrinsic over extrinsic goals is associated with better domain-specific adjustment. In addition to studying adjustment and well-being, other studies have linked people's goals to self-reported (un)healthy behaviors. For instance, extrinsically oriented individuals were found to watch more TV and to smoke, drink, and use drugs more often (e.g., Williams, Cox, Hedberg, & Deci, 2000). Moreover, materialist individuals were more likely to be "shopaholics" (Dittmar, 2005). These behaviors can be considered self-medicating, because they may help extrinsically oriented individuals to compensate for their lack of daily need satisfaction. Such an interpretation of the findings suggests that extrinsic goal pursuits might not only result in poorer well-being but might also be undertaken to overcome and compensate for distress (Kasser, 2002).

Social and Ethical Functioning

The pursuit of extrinsic goals does not only yield personal well-being and health costs but also has a number of social implications, at both interpersonal and intergroup levels. For instance, extrinsically oriented individuals are more likely to engage in conflicting and less trustful love relationships (Kasser & Ryan, 2001), and materialists are found to be less satisfied with their family and friends (e.g., Richins & Dawson, 1992). In addition to affecting the quality of intimate and family relationships, the pursuit of intrinsic relative to extrinsic goals also seems to affect the interaction with opponents during sports games. For instance, on the ball field, extrinsic relative to intrinsic goal oriented soccer players have been found to be more likely to engage in aggressive behaviors, such as tackling (Vansteenkiste, 2007). Although such unfair behavior might be perceived by soccer players as necessary and instrumental for achieving their extrinsic goals (i.e., winning the game and making more money), they are unlikely to foster respectful relationships with one's opponents.

A similar lack of ethical functioning was observed in the organizational domain by Tang and Chiu (2003) who found materialist white collar employees to be more likely to overcharge customers, use their expense account inappropriately, and steal merchandise. The current findings thus suggest that the pursuit of extrinsic goals is associated with poorer ethical functioning (Kasser, Vansteenkiste, & Deckop, 2006).

Adopting an extrinsic relative to intrinsic goal orientation was not only found to be problematic for the quality of one's social relationships (i.e., the interpersonal level) but also for individuals' attitudes toward social groups (i.e., the intergroup level). For instance, Duriez, Vansteenkiste, Soenens, and De Witte (2007) found that an extrinsic- relative to intrinsic-goal orientation was associated with a less prejudiced attitude toward ethnic minorities (see also Roets, Van Hiel, & Cornelis, 2006).

This effect could be accounted for by the stronger social dominance orientation that is associated with an extrinsic relative to an intrinsic goal orientation. Specifically, extrinsic goal oriented individuals are more likely to adopt a social dominance orientation, that is, they want their group to maintain a superior position relative to other social groups (Pratto, Sidanius, Stallworth, & Malle, 1994). A social dominance orientation is likely to take root in extrinsically oriented individuals' belief that they live in a dog-eat-dog world that requires them to compete with others for scarce material goods. Hence, the adoption of a socially dominant attitude fits with these individuals' worldview and would be instrumental in achieving their extrinsic ambitions.

Conversely, the pursuit of material goods might also represent an instrument allowing socially dominant individuals to confirm their superior position in society. In line with this reasoning, Duriez, Vansteenkiste, et al. (2007) found that a social dominance attitude and an extrinsic relative to intrinsic goal orientation reciprocally predicted one another over time, suggesting that they form a mutually reinforcing constellation that is likely to contribute to the stability and even rise in prejudice over time.

Finally, the pursuit of intrinsic relative to extrinsic goals not only yields effects on the way one treats other people but also on the way one deals with our planet and the environment at large. For instance, Brown and Kasser (2005) demonstrated that an extrinsic- relative to intrinsic-goal orientation negatively predicted engagement in proecological behaviors and was associated with an enlarged ecological footprint. Similarly, Richins and Dawson (1992) found materialism to negatively predict voluntary simplicity, that is, a lifestyle that is characterized by low consumption and high ecological responsibility (see also Kilbourne & Pickett, in press). Finally, in an experimental role playing study, Sheldon and McGregor (2000) showed that extrinsic relative to intrinsic goal oriented individuals were more likely to keep a greater proportion of scarce natural resources to themselves.

CONTEXTUAL PROMOTION OF INTRINSIC VERSUS EXTRINSIC GOALS

The previous section detailed the differential consequences that are related to individuals' pursuit of intrinsic versus extrinsic goal contents. Hence, this line of SDT-research has investigated the impact of intrinsic versus extrinsic goals from an *individual difference* perspective, that is, the degree to which people focus upon the attainment of intrinsic versus extrinsic goals. However, authority figures, such as parents, teachers, managers, and doctors as well as the broader culture play an important role in spreading, promoting, and reinforcing these goals. From the SDT-perspective, analogous to the differential effects of holding intrinsic and extrinsic goals, the contextual promotion of these goal contents is likely to yield differential psychological dynamics as well. Several recent experimental and correlational studies have provided evidence for this notion.

In a set of experimental studies (Vansteenkiste, Simons, Lens, Sheldon, & Deci, 2004), the effects of framing a learning task in terms of intrinsic versus extrinsic goal attainment on quality of learning, performance, and persistence were examined. In a first study, students were invited to read a text on recycling and were either told that learning more about this could help them to attain the intrinsic goal of community contribution or the extrinsic goal of a monetary benefit. Then, they were tested on text knowledge and were given questionnaires assessing deep and rote learning. Finally, it was recorded which students visited the library to get additional information on recycling, and which students chose to visit a recycling plant on a weekday after school a few days after the experiment.

It was reasoned that intrinsic goals, because of their closer link with individuals' inherent growth tendencies, are more likely to promote a deep commitment toward the learning activity. In contrast, extrinsic goal framing would shift learners' attention from the learning toward external indicators of worth, thereby resulting in poorer commitment and reduced learning. Consistent with this, intrinsic relative to extrinsic goal framing promoted self-reported deep processing and resulted in superior performance and higher persistence. These results were replicated using different activities (i.e., exercising rather than reading), different intrinsic goals (i.e., self-development and health), different extrinsic goals (i.e., physical attractiveness), and different age groups (i.e., children instead of adolescents; Vansteenkiste, Simons, Lens, Soenens, & Matos, 2005).

In another series of experimental studies, Vansteenkiste, Simons, Braet, Bachman, and Deci (2007) explored the impact of intrinsic versus extrinsic goal framing among a group of severely obese children. They examined whether framing a learning text on the four-leafed clover (a simplified version of the food pyramid) in terms of the attainment of the intrinsic goal of physical fitness versus the extrinsic goal of physical attractiveness would affect (a) adoption and maintenance of healthy lifestyles, (b) continued engagement in a diet program, (c) longitudinal participation in physical exercise, and (d) weight loss assessed up to two years after participation in the experiment.

Although extrinsic goal framing might prompt some behavioral change, it was expected that initial changes were unlikely to be maintained over time, as the newly adopted behaviors were undertaken in a strategic and conditional fashion, that is, to attain the anticipated extrinsic goal of physical attractiveness. Consistent with this, it was found that both intrinsic and extrinsic goal framing promoted the adoption of a healthier lifestyle, but that these gains were only maintained among participants placed in the intrinsic goal condition. Furthermore, intrinsic relative to extrinsic goal framing resulted in a more continuous engagement in the diet program and greater weight loss at 6 weeks, 14 weeks, 1 year, and 2 year follow-up assessments.

Subsequent work (Duriez, Soenens, & Vansteenkiste, 2007) examined whether parents' promotion of intrinsic rather than extrinsic goals would affect children's social functioning, as indexed by their socially aggressive and domineering attitude towards other social groups. Thus, rather than studying the impact of intrinsic and extrinsic goal promotion at the situational level (i.e., with respect to a particular activity), intrinsic relative to extrinsic goal promotion was studied at the global level, as parenting is likely to affect children's general functioning. Complementing the experimental research, perceived parental intrinsic relative to extrinsic goal promotion was found to both concurrently and longitudinally predict adolescents' social dominance orientation which, as mentioned before, represents a strong predictor of ethnic prejudice (e.g., Pratto et al., 1994). Notably, the effects of parental goal promotion emerged above and beyond the effects of the quality of parents' rearing style (i.e., how parents interact with their children). These findings thus suggest that, in order to evaluate the impact of socializing agents (e.g., parents, coaches, managers, etc.), it is not only critical to consider the way people interact with others and the type of emotional climate they create but also to consider the type of goals they try to transmit.

Finally, Schwartz (2006) provided interesting evidence on how the extrinsic and capitalistic versus more intrinsic character of a country's economy is associated with and represented in the cultural orientation of that country as well as in the average importance individuals within these countries attribute to particular values. Using an index developed by Hall and Gingerich (2004) that reflects the extent to which a national economy is coordinated by competitive market principles rather than strategic principles, Schwartz (2006) showed that the strategic vs. competitive coordination index was strongly positively correlated with a cultural emphasis on intrinsic ideals including (a) harmony (i.e., a concern with nature and world peace), (b) egalitarianism (i.e., a focus on equality, social justice, and honesty), and (c) intellectual autonomy (i.e., a focus on broadmindedness, curiosity, and creativity), whereas it was negatively correlated with a cultural orientation toward more extrinsic oriented endeavors, including (a) mastery (i.e., an emphasis on ambition, and success), (b) hierarchy (i.e., an emphasis on authority, social power, and wealth), and (c) embeddedness (i.e., a focus on tradition, social order, and obedience). Along similar lines, individuals within more capitalistic societies were found to attribute, on average, a stronger importance to extrinsic values, such as achievement and power, whereas placing less importance on intrinsic values, such as universalism and self-direction.

ALTERNATIVE ACCOUNTS OF THE INTRINSIC VERSUS EXTRINSIC GOAL DISTINCTION

SDT's intrinsic versus extrinsic goal conceptualization has been criticized from different angles. One of the reasons why this distinction is critically received is the fact that the SDT perspective on goals is regarded as highly "value-laden." Indeed, the research reviewed previously suggests that intrinsic goals are to be preferred over extrinsic goals and, as such, should be encouraged at the expense of extrinsic goals. However, many scholars are hesitant to make such prescriptive suggestions. Skepticism vis-à-vis the desirability of intrinsic rather than extrinsic goals has even led some scholars to severely criticize the intrinsic-extrinsic goal distinction.

Specifically, three different types of criticisms have been forwarded. First, it has been argued that this distinction is a "false" one because it represents nothing but a different way of speaking about autonomous versus controlled regulations. Second, based on quantitative theories of motivation, it can be argued that intrinsic goal framing results in more adaptive learning than extrinsic goal framing because it induces a higher quantity or amount of motivation rather than a different quality of motivation. Third, it has been suggested that the negative impact of extrinsic relative to intrinsic goal pursuits would be limited (a) to individuals residing within intrinsic goal environments and (b) to individuals who do not attain their extrinsic ambitions (e.g., people with low income). Similarly, the detrimental impact of extrinsic goal framing would be limited to individuals with an intrinsic goal orientation. We will now discuss each of these critical claims in more detail.

Intrinsic versus Extrinsic Goals: A False Distinction

One of the problems that various theorists point out with a "self-actualization model" as provided by SDT is that it is difficult to specify a priori what anyone's true self consists of (e.g., Carver & Scheier, 2000). If an individual has a real interest in accumulating wealth, for example, why can this not be truly self-actualizing for that person? If an elderly individual wants to hide the signs of aging by buying new clothes, visiting a hair stylist, and purchasing the latest antiwrinkle cream, why would such an endeavor not represent a core goal for that person? Carver and colleagues thus doubt that some goals are more inherently need-satisfying and congruent with the self than others. In line with this, they suggested that the intrinsic–extrinsic goal distinction is a false one that can be conceptually reduced to the differentiation between an autonomous and controlled regulation (Carver & Baird, 1998; Srivastava, Locke, & Barthol, 2001). Carver and Baird (1998) argued that the effect of intrinsic versus extrinsic goals can be fully explained by the reasons or motives underlying people's goal pursuit. Specifically, these authors contend that extrinsically oriented individuals display more signs of ill-being because they feel more pressured and coerced (i.e., controlled) during their goal pursuits. In contrast, intrinsically oriented individuals are happier and more fulfilled because they pursue these goals in a more volitional (i.e., autonomous) manner. In other words, the impact of intrinsic versus extrinsic goal striving could be completely carried by the extent to which people pursue their goals for autonomous rather than for controlled reasons. If this were the case, the effect of goal pursuits on well-being would disappear after controlling for type of regulation, and the effect of the intrinsic versus extrinsic goal dimension would be fully accounted for by its underlying autonomous versus controlled regulation.

In spite of their criticism, Carver and Baird (1998) could not provide compelling evidence for their claim. Consistent with other work (e.g., Kasser & Ryan, 1996), the results of Carver and Baird's (1998) hierarchical regression analyses indicate that the intrinsic versus extrinsic goal dimension positively predicted well-being, even after controlling for the autonomous versus controlled reasons that underlie the goal pursuits. In another study, Srivastava et al. (2001) found the negative effect of pursuing financial success on well-being among business students and entrepreneurs to disappear after entering three types of motives for valuing financial success, that is, positive motives (e.g., helping one's family), freedom of action motives (e.g., charity), and negative motives (e.g., appearing worthy). Whereas positive motives were positively associated with well-being, negative motives yielded a negative relationship.

The findings of Srivastava et al. (2001) were criticized by Sheldon, Ryan, Deci, and Kasser (2004), who suggested that, among other things, some motive scales (e.g., charity) reflect higher order goals rather than reasons for pursuing a goal. Hence, because of this mixture of goals and motives in their motive measure, it should not be surprising that aspiring financial success could not explain additional variance.

However, although Sheldon, Ryan, et al. (2004) refuted Carver and Baird's (1998) criticism, they did recognize that intrinsic and extrinsic goals and autonomous and controlled regulations are correlated. Specifically, previous studies (e.g., Sheldon & Kasser, 1995) demonstrated that the pursuit of intrinsic goals is positively related to an autonomous regulation (correlation of about .30), whereas the pursuit of extrinsic goals is positively related to a controlled regulation (correlation of about .30). The strength of these correlations suggests that goals and regulations are indeed related, as suggested by Carver and Baird (1998). Yet, the size of these correlations also suggests that they are empirically distinguishable.

Indeed, it is quite possible to, for instance, follow a language course to develop one's talents (i.e., an intrinsic goal) because one is pressured by one's boss to improve one's language skills (i.e., controlled regulation) or because one is personally interested in learning languages (i.e., autonomous regulation). Conversely, a person can be focused on being attractive and good-looking (i.e., extrinsic goal) because he feels an inner obligation to do so (i.e., controlled regulation) or because he personally values beauty and attractiveness (i.e., autonomous regulation). In spite of these relationships between goals and motives, past research has shown that both predict independent variance in well-being and adjustment (Sheldon, Ryan, et al., 2004; Sheldon & Kasser, 1995), and similar results were reported in the exercise domain (Sebire et al., in press).

If intrinsic and extrinsic goal contents could be conceptually equated with an autonomous and controlled regulation, this would also imply that framing a learning activity in terms of the attainment of intrinsic versus extrinsic goals should be fully (instead of partially) accounted for by the autonomous versus controlled motives underlying one's activity engagement. The experimental work on goals thus opened new ways to test this criticism. Although autonomous motivation fully explained the goal framing effects on five out of 11 outcomes, it only partially reduced the relation in the remaining six outcomes (Vansteenkiste, Simons, et al., 2004), providing reasonable evidence for the assertion that the intrinsic- versus extrinsic-goal framing effect cannot be reduced to the underlying regulation it induces.

Although research to date suggests that goals seem to matter above and beyond their underlying motives, more research is needed to further test this alternative explanation of the effects of intrinsic versus extrinsic goals. We suggest that, if the criticism by Carver and Baird were true, *any* observed effect of intrinsic versus extrinsic goals on any outcome (e.g., well-being, ethical functioning, performance) should disappear when controlling for individuals' motives. In this respect, it should also be noted that, maybe, goals only have an independent effect in some domains or for some outcomes. Given that goals are more cognitive in nature than regulations or motives (which are more affective in nature), it is possible that goals yield unique effects on cognitive and attitudinal outcomes (e.g., prejudice, fair play attitudes) whereas motives would be more strongly related to affective and well-being outcomes. To the best of our knowledge, no study to date has explicitly tested this hypothesis of specialized effects of individuals' goals and motives.

Quantity rather than Quality of Motivation

Experimental goal-framing research has indicated that extrinsic goal framing hinders conceptual learning, presumably because it shifts attention away from the activity at hand toward external indicators of worth (Vansteenkiste, Lens, & Deci, 2006). In contrast, intrinsic goal framing promotes learning and achievement presumably because it leads to a qualitatively different approach of and engagement in the learning activity. However, based on quantitative conceptualizations of motivation, as articulated within expectancy-value theories (Eccles & Wigfield, 2002) and instrumentality models (Husman & Lens, 1999), the effects of goal framing on learning can also be explained in a different way. Given that intrinsic goals are, on average, more highly valued than extrinsic goals (Kasser, 2002), presenting a particular learning activity as serving a more highly valued intrinsic goal should increase the perceived utility value (Eccles & Wigfield, 2002) of the learning activity compared with framing that activity in terms of the attainment of a less valued extrinsic goal. This enhanced utility would increase learners' quantity or amount of motivation, resulting in higher performance and persistence.

This alternative account was tested in several studies. In a first study (Vansteenkiste, Simons, Soenens, Lens, Matos, & Lacante, 2004), a learning activity was portrayed as serving either an intrinsic goal, an extrinsic goal, or both an intrinsic and an extrinsic goal. This allowed investigating the effects of double versus single goal framing upon learning and achievement. From a quantitative motivational perspective, the perceived utility value in a double goal condition is higher than in the single goal conditions. Hence, providing two goals should always result in better learning than providing only a single goal. However, according to a qualitative view on goals, as defended within SDT, not only the number of goals but also their quality needs to be considered (Vansteenkiste, Lens, & Deci, 2006). Providing an extrinsic goal in addition to an already present intrinsic goal is likely to shift attention from the learning activity to external signs of worth, thereby hindering the learning process. In contrast, providing an intrinsic goal in addition to an extrinsic goal is likely to increase a thoughtful and task-focused commitment toward the activity, so that individuals in the double goal framing condition get more fully engaged in the activity. The predictions derived from SDT were supported such that intrinsic goal framing enhanced performance and persistence compared with both extrinsic goal framing and double goal framing; yet, the perceived utility of the activity was greater in the double goal condition.

Comparing the effects of intrinsic versus extrinsic goal framing does not allow the derivation of strict conclusions regarding the impact of extrinsic goal framing per se: It is quite possible that indicating how a learning task relates to an extrinsic goal leads to better learning outcomes compared to a control-group where no goal references are made. In fact, on the basis of quantitative theories on motivation, it can be hypothesized that extrinsic goal framing enhances the perceived utility of the activity, so that better outcomes should follow in the extrinsic goal condition compared with when the relevance of the activity is not stressed at all. However, in contrast to this view, SDT holds that extrinsic goal framing will result in poorer quality learning compared with a no-goal control group. The findings of an experimental study by Vansteenkiste, Simons, Soenens, and Lens (2004) were in line with SDT-based hypotheses: Whereas intrinsic goal framing resulted in better performance and greater persistence than no goal framing, extrinsic goal framing undermined performance and persistence.

Limited Negative Effects of Extrinsic Goal Pursuit and Extrinsic Goal Framing

Match Perspective

The match perspective, which maintains that optimal functioning and well-being will occur when individuals' own goals fit with the goals that are promoted within the environment, has received considerable attention in a broad array of fields, including social psychology (e.g., Sagiv & Schwartz, 2000), educational psychology (e.g., Harackiewicz & Elliot, 1998), organizational psychology (e.g., Edwards, 1991), developmental psychology (e.g., Eccles, Lord, & Midgley, 1991), and sports psychology (e.g., Amiot, Vallerand, & Blanchard, 2006).

One example of the match perspective is an employee who experiences lower well-being and job satisfaction when his own values are discrepant from those promoted in the organization. Hence, the impact of goals for well-being and functioning would not depend on the content of the goals as such but on the extent to which individuals' own goals correspond to or match with the goals promoted in the immediate social environment. In other words, the negative impact of extrinsic goals would be limited to people residing in an environment that promotes intrinsic goals. Also, the negative effects of pursuing extrinsic relative to intrinsic goals, as observed in a number of previous studies (e.g., Kasser & Ryan, 1996), would be primarily carried by individuals involved in intrinsic goal oriented climates. The negative effects of extrinsic relative to intrinsic goal pursuits would be offset or even reversed among people who find themselves in an extrinsic goal promoting environment.

Overall, the match perspective assumption posits, at least implicitly, that any kind of goal can be incorporated within one's sense of self. In this respect, the match perspective fits a social-constructivist viewpoint

(Berzonsky, 1990; Markus & Kitayama, 2003), which rejects the idea that individuals are inherently oriented toward particular goals (i.e., intrinsic goals). Instead, one's goals and the identity that is based on them are considered constructions, obtained in part through socialization processes.

The extent to which internalized goals are successful in regulating behavior and the extent to which they are associated with optimal functioning merely depends on the degree to which goals are also adopted in the social context. Thus, the same goals may be negatively associated to well-being in one environment but not in another. For instance, the pursuit of the extrinsic goal of financial success might be positively related to well-being in a business organization or in a culture that highlights such goals but may negatively predict adjustment in an organization that emphasizes intrinsic goal attainment or in a society that promotes generativity and solidarity between its members.

Yet, if one assumes that a fundamental, psychological make-up underlies the human psyche, as in an organismic theory such as SDT, it becomes important to consider whether individuals' goals or the goals promoted by the social environment are consistent with basic elements of human nature. SDT assumes that the basic psychological needs for autonomy, competence, and relatedness form an inherent part of the human organism. Thus, to derive predictions about the adaptive value of goals, SDT considers the extent to which people's goals are congruent with these universal propensities (i.e., people's basic psychological needs) rather than with the goals prevailing in the social environment. Therefore, SDT maintains that the pursuit of intrinsic relative to extrinsic goals should predict well-being because it is more likely to be associated with basic need satisfaction. In sum, within SDT the most important criterion to evaluate whether goals promote or detract from well-being is whether these goals contribute to the satisfaction of human basic needs and not whether goals match the requirements of particular environments (Vansteenkiste, Lens, & Deci, 2006).

In line with the match perspective, in a sample of psychology and business students, Sagiv and Schwartz (2000) showed that the effect of valuing extrinsic over intrinsic goals on well-being interacted with participants' study environment. Business students who valued extrinsic over intrinsic goals reported higher psychological well-being, whereas psychology students reported more optimal functioning when they valued intrinsic over extrinsic goals. In contrast to this, in two subsequent studies (Kasser & Ahuvia, 2002; Vansteenkiste, Duriez, Simons, & Soenens, 2006), extrinsic relative to intrinsic goal pursuits were associated with lower well-being and more internal distress among business students, even though extrinsic goals tend to be emphasized in their environment (see also Srivastava et al., 2001). Furthermore, Sheldon and Krieger (2004) reported that law students shifted away from intrinsic toward extrinsic goal pursuits during the first year of law school. Given that law schools typically foster status-seeking, competition, and image-building (Krieger, 1998), a match perspective would suggest that such changes should be adaptive. In spite of this, these changes were found to be positively related to a decline in psychological well-being.

The experimental induction of intrinsic and extrinsic goals provided a new avenue to further test these two conflicting perspectives, as it could examine whether extrinsic goal oriented individuals would benefit from being placed in an extrinsic goal framing condition. Based on the match perspective, it is suggested that the negative effects of extrinsic goal framing are limited to learners who value intrinsic over extrinsic goals and that the overall enhancement of learning and persistence in the intrinsic goal conditions of the studies reviewed earlier were primarily carried by learners whose goal orientation was more intrinsic than extrinsic. A study among business students provided preliminary counterevidence for this viewpoint by showing that extrinsic goal framing undermined business' students learning and performance (Vansteenkiste, Simons, Lens, et al., 2004, Study 2). Unfortunately, in this study, participants' personal goal orientations were not measured prior to the goal exposure. This was the case in a study among 5th- and 6th-grade children (Vansteenkiste, Timmermans, Lens, Soenens, & Van den Broeck, 2008). Results confirmed SDT as the performance and persistence of children preferring either intrinsic or extrinsic goals was enhanced when placed in an intrinsic instead of an extrinsic goal framing condition. Although more research is needed on this issue, the existing empirical evidence suggests that the negative effects of extrinsic relative to intrinsic goal pursuits are unlikely to be altered depending upon the goals that are promoted in the environment.

Aspiration Theory

Although a stronger valuation of extrinsic relative to intrinsic goals might be associated with lower well-being, the aspiration theory (e.g., Campbell, Converse, & Rodgers, 1967; McGill, 1967) would predict that the attainment of extrinsic goals should produce well-being as it provides people with rewards and a sense of self-efficacy. Thus, according to this theory, because well-being is a function of the discrepancy between people's aspirations or goals and their attaining these aspirations and goals, attaining one's materialist goals should be associated with enhanced well-being. For instance, the negative effects associated with aspiring financial success are limited to the pursuit of such success but should disappear or even be inversed once people are capable of attaining these aspirations.

In contrast to such predictions, Kasser and Ryan (2001) showed that, whereas intrinsic goal attainment was conducive to psychological well-being, extrinsic goal attainment was not. Similar results were reported by Ryan et al. (1999) in a sample of Russian adults. Furthermore, in a longitudinal study, Sheldon and Kasser (1998) showed that making progress at extrinsic goals over a semester did not result in an increase in well-being, whereas intrinsic goal progress positively predicted enhanced well-being. Most recently, in a sample of older adults (>65 years), Van Hiel and Vansteenkiste (2007) showed that reported attainment of intrinsic goals over the life course was positively predictive of feelings of ego integrity and death acceptance, whereas extrinsic goal attainment was not. These results fit the idea that, if people are able to attain goals that are consistent with their natural growth-trajectory, they experience more harmony and seem more ready to face the "final curtain."

The question whether the negative effects of aspiring financial success disappear when one is able to actually attain financial success has been examined in a second line of research as well. In a number of studies, it was examined whether the well-being effect of pursuing materialist goals would be different for individuals with low compared with high income. LaBarbera and Gürhan (1997) argued that pursuing materialist goals should positively predict well-being for individuals with a high income, because these individuals reached their materialist goals. LaBarbera and Gürhan (1997) provided partial support for the hypothesis derived from the aspiration theory: Two of their materialism subscales, nongenerosity and possessiveness (Belk, 1985), interacted with income in the prediction of general affect, and materialism did not negatively predict general affect for people with a high income. Similarly, in a longitudinal study, Nickerson, Schwartz, Diener, and Kahneman (2003) found that the negative impact of aspiring financial success on life and job satisfaction diminished for people earning a high income. Such moderation effects were not found for satisfaction with family life.

In contrast to these studies, Kasser and Ryan (1996) found that the negative effects of extrinsic relative to intrinsic goals on a broad range of self-reported and rated well-being outcomes (i.e., self-actualization, vitality, depression, anxiety, and physical symptoms) were not offset for people with a high level of income. Similarly, Vansteenkiste, Neyrinck, et al. (2007) found that the negative effect of holding an extrinsic relative to an intrinsic work value orientation on life and job satisfaction was not moderated by income, suggesting that the negative well-being effect of pursuing material goals equally applies to individuals with a low and a high income.

Instead, they reported that objectively earning a higher income had a small but positive effect on job and life satisfaction (Diener, Suh, Lucas, & Smith, 1999), whereas the personal valuation of a higher income over more intrinsic work aspirations was negatively related to well-being. This was referred to as the "income-paradox": Whereas objectively making more money increases happiness, subjectively valuing money seems to have the opposite effect.

This brief overview suggests that more research is needed in this area of inquiry. In particular, it would be interesting to explore whether the attributed meaning (e.g., autonomous versus controlled, Deci & Ryan, 2000) would be different for people with different income levels. This might help to achieve further insight in which circumstances (i.e., income level) and for which reason the pursuit of materialist aspirations yield negative well-being implications. We turn to the latter issue in more detail in the following section, when a number of macro- and micro-mediational mechanisms are proposed that might help clarify the link between intrinsic relative to extrinsic goals and optimal functioning.

MACRO- AND MICRO-MEDIATIONAL MECHANISMS UNDERLYING GOAL EFFECTS

Macro-Mediational Mechanisms: Basic Psychological Need Satisfaction

A variety of processes explain the relation between an intrinsic relative to an extrinsic goal pursuit and optimal functioning. For instance, because time is a limited resource requiring people to make choices that will determine the content and quality of their lives, it has been suggested that investing too much time pursuing extrinsic goals is likely to occur at the expense of devoting time to intrinsic goals (e.g., Ryan et al., 1996; Sheldon, Ryan, et al., 2004). As stated by Csikzsentmihalyi (1999, p. 823), for materialist individuals, "the opportunity costs of playing with one's child, reading poetry, or attending a family reunion might become too high, and so one stops doing these irrational things." Put differently, intrinsic activities are likely to be crowded out by an overly strong investment in extrinsic goals.

Furthermore, within SDT, it is suggested that the pursuit of intrinsic, relative to extrinsic, goals is likely to be differentially linked to psychological well-being because of their differential effect on basic psychological need satisfaction. SDT maintains that people are endowed with three basic innate psychological needs (Ryan, 1995): (a) the need for *autonomy* or the desire to feel volitional with respect to one's behavior, (b) the need for *belonginess* or relatedness or the desire to care for and feel cared for by others, and (c) the need for *competence* or the desire to feel effective in the actions one undertakes.

These basic needs—which can best be remembered through the acronym "ABC", because of the first letter of the three basic terms—propel and instigate a wide variety of human behaviors across different contexts, and their satisfaction is said to promote the realization of one's basic growth tendencies. Indeed, the satisfaction of these psychological needs is considered equally fundamental for people's psychological thriving, integrity, and well-being, as satisfaction of physical needs (e.g., hunger and thirst) is for their physical survival and growth (Ryan, 1995).

Basic need satisfaction is thus considered to be the energizing and driving force behind individuals' growth, so that basic need satisfaction would foster the pursuit of intrinsic rather than extrinsic goals. The relationship between people's growth tendencies and basic need satisfaction is, however, likely to be bidirectional, as the pursuit of intrinsic relative to extrinsic goals is likely to yield more optimal functioning because it allows for a greater satisfaction of the basic needs for autonomy, competence, and relatedness (Deci & Ryan, 2000; Kasser, 2002).

Although various studies provide indirect evidence for these claims (see Kasser, 2002, for an overview), the mediational role of basic need satisfaction has only recently been investigated. For instance, fashion models—who are likely to personally value the body ideal and definitely work in a social environment that places high emphasis on physical attractiveness and body image—were recently found to experience lower daily need satisfaction relative to a control-group (Meyer, Enström, Harstveit, Bowles, & Beevers, 2007). This lower need satisfaction could in turn, account for the mean-level differences in psychological well-being between models and nonmodels. Further, Rijavec, Brdar, and Miljikovic (2006) found intrinsic relative to extrinsic goal pursuits to relate positively to need satisfaction.

Similarly, in the organizational domain, Vansteenkiste, Neyrinck, et al. (2007) found that intrinsic relative to extrinsic work value orientations positively predicted need satisfaction at work, which, in turn, predicted job well-being. Finally, Sebire et al. (2008) reported intrinsic relative to extrinsic goal pursuits during exercising to be more strongly linked to basic need satisfaction, which, in turn, predicted a variety of well-being outcomes.

What kind of mechanisms can account for the link between intrinsic relative to extrinsic goal pursuit and basic need satisfaction? We believe that people will approach activities and other people differently depending on their dominant goal orientation, resulting in different need satisfaction opportunities. In the following section, three different micro-mediational mechanisms are discussed that might explain how and why pursuing extrinsic versus intrinsic goals or being exposed to extrinsic versus intrinsic goal promotion is differentially linked to need satisfaction: (a) attention shift, (b) interpersonal comparison, and (c) conditional approach (see also Vansteenkiste, Soenens, & Lens, 2007). We suggest that these attentional and cognitive mechanisms help break down the marco-mediational mechanism of basic need satisfaction into lower-level processes.

Micro-Mediational Mechanisms: Cognitive-Attentional Processes

Attention Shift

Let us assume that an absorbed and committed activity engagement represents the best way to get one's basic needs for autonomy, competence, and relatedness met. When people are fully immersed in an activity, they are more likely to express their own interests and values (autonomy) and are more likely to effectively deal with the challenges of the activity (competence). Similarly, when people are fully absorbed in a conversation, they are more likely to derive a sense of satisfaction from it and to experience a sense of connectedness with the other person (relatedness). If an absorbed activity engagement is a necessary condition for basic need satisfaction, it can be concluded that any goal that precludes such an engagement will yield less optimal effects. We suggest that extrinsic goals are likely to shift individuals' attention away from the activity at hand and, as such, forestall need satisfaction (see Figure 4.1).

Consider an extrinsic goal oriented female exerciser who is exercising as a way to improve her sex appeal and attractiveness. Instead of being immersed in the exercise activity at hand, she is likely to be "number-checking" during a work-out session (e.g., "how many calories did I already burn?") because such information helps her to monitor her progress toward the extrinsic goal ambitions. Or consider an academic who is

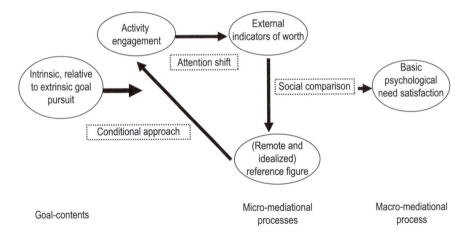

Figure 4.1. Graphical Representation of Different Micro-Mediational Processes involved in the Pursuit of Intrinsic versus Extrinsic Goals.

focused on building up a prestigious academic career. When giving a talk at a conference, instead of being focused on the content of the talk, he is likely to feel stressed and anxious because his perceived academic status and worth is contingent upon the quality of the presentation.

These anecdotes suggest that extrinsic goal oriented people's attention is more likely to shift away from the content of the activity. In line with this, experimental studies have shown that extrinsic relative to intrinsic goal framing resulted in poorer conceptual integration of the learning material and lower subsequent achievement because it hindered committed and task-oriented learning (e.g., Vansteenkiste, Simons, Lens, et al., 2005; Vansteenkiste, Simons, Lens, Soenens, et al., 2004). A number of other empirical studies, although not based on the SDT-perspective, also provided evidence for the distracting role of extrinsic goals. Quin, Kallen, Twenge, and Frederickson (2006) reported that when women's attention was oriented toward their physical looks, they displayed decreased performance on a Stroop task, presumably because their attention focus was disrupted. Furthermore, Kashdan and Breen (2007) showed that the pursuit of materialism is associated with greater experiential avoidance, representing a lack of willingness to be in contact with negatively evaluated thoughts, feelings, and bodily sensations. Thus, materialist individuals do not seem as receptive to their momentary unfolding emotions, presumably because their attention is focused on attaining external indicators of worth (Kasser, 2002).

As a consequence of shifting their attention away from the activity at hand, people are less likely to fulfill their needs. First, a lack of thorough engagement in an activity typically results in poorer performance and achievement, thus undermining individuals' need for competence. Second, a focus on external indicators of worth is stressful and autonomy inhibiting because it induces a preoccupation with self-worth concerns. Third, such a focus is also likely to elicit ego-involvement and egoism, such that extrinsic goal oriented individuals may fail to be attuned to the needs and concerns of others.

Interpersonal Comparison

After becoming concerned with her bodily attractiveness during a work-out session, the female exerciser is likely to gaze in the mirror to check her own figure and to check the difference with other exercisers' figures or with role models. Similarly, being concerned with academic status, a researcher is likely to compare the own publication record with the record of his colleagues or with an admired researcher. Indeed, several researchers in different fields of psychology, including consumer psychology (Sirgy, 1998; Van Boven, 2005) and health psychology (Dittmar, 2007), have suggested that a focus on extrinsic goal pursuits is likely to increase people's tendency to engage in interpersonal comparisons. That is, after turning to the external indicators of worth, individuals are likely to start comparing their own extrinsic goal realizations with those of others (see Figure 4.1).

Several studies have now provided evidence for this claim. For instance, studies in the body image literature have shown that women engage in social comparison processes after being exposed to attractive comparison targets (e.g., Patrick, Neighbors, & Knee, 2004; Tiggeman & McGill, 2004). Furthermore, in the domain of education, extrinsic relative to intrinsic goal framing was found to provoke a stronger performance-approach orientation (Elliot, 1999), that is, a desire to outperform others (e.g., Vansteenkiste, Matos, Lens, & Soenens, 2007). By definition, a performance orientation involves making comparisons of one's own achievements with the achievements of others. Extrinsic goals are not only associated with interpersonal but also with intergroup comparisons, as indexed by a stronger adoption of a social dominance attitude (Duriez, Vansteenkiste, et al., 2007).

A first likely result of such comparisons is that the pursuit of extrinsic goals or the exposure to extrinsic goal messages will be experienced as stressful and controlling, as people experience an inner urge to achieve the high standards exemplified by reference figures. Consistent with this, extrinsic goal framing was found to result in a more stressful learning experience and to prompt more controlled engagement in learning activities, signaling lack of autonomy satisfaction (Vansteenkiste, Simons, Lens, Sheldon, et al. 2004; Vansteenkiste, Simons, Soenens, et al., 2004).

Second, in addition to failing to provide autonomy satisfaction, engagement in interpersonal comparisons is likely to make people feel inferior to others because there are always people that outperform a person in attaining an extrinsic goal. Moreover, extrinsic goal oriented individuals tend to overidealize wealth and physical appeal and are more likely to monitor their success against the success of romanticized and rather remote reference figures (e.g., models, successful managers; Kasser, 2002). As a result, extrinsic goal oriented individuals are more likely to make upward comparisons (Sirgy, 1998), which provoke a sense of frustration and unhappiness and fuel their feelings of incompetence and insecurity. Even if people are momentarily able to meet their extrinsic ambitions, the benefits associated with extrinsic goal attainment are said to be quite short-lived. This is because, although extrinsic goal attainment might yield some hedonic satisfaction, its attainment is unlikely to engender a sense of eudaimonia and self-realization (Ryan, Huta, & Deci, 2008). As a result, new extrinsic ambitions are likely to set quickly in place, leading extrinsic goal oriented people to get trapped in a "hedonic treadmill" (Brickman & Campbell, 1977). This treadmill would be further fed by the ongoing gap extrinsic oriented individuals experience between their current realized and desired extrinsic ambitions (Solberg, Diener, & Robinson, 2004).

The notion that extrinsic aspirations would result in reduced competence satisfaction through processes of social comparison has recently received some evidence. In a meta-analytical review, Groesz, Levine, and Murnen (2002) showed that the experimental exposure to the thin ideal resulted in decreased body satisfaction ($d = -.31$), an effect that was more pronounced among women with an eating disorder or body dissatisfaction history.

Similarly, in a sample of male participants, Gulas and McKeage (2000) reported that self-esteem dropped when presented with ads referring to physical appeal or financial success, especially if participants were sensitive to idealized images. Notably, not only the exposure to attractive professional models but also to thinner peers was found to result in decreased body satisfaction (e.g., Krones, Stice, Batres, & Orjada, 2005). Research even suggests that expose to attractive peers might be more harmful than exposure to attractive models (Cash, Cash, & Butters, 1983), presumably because one might perceive attaining an attractive body of a peer as easier, such that a failure to do so might engender a stronger sense of incompetence, body dissatisfaction, and related psychological insecurity compared with being exposed to a professional attractive model.

Several studies have begun to explicitly elucidate the explanatory role of social comparison. Strahan, Wilson, Cressman, and Buote (2006) showed that, when being asked to freely describe their weight and body shape, women (but not men) appear more likely to make upward rather than downward comparisons, and, more important, that the number of spontaneously generated upward comparisons was positively correlated with the number of negative self-statements with regard to their physical appearance.

Using an experimental design, Tiggeman and McGill (2004) reported that the frequency of engaging in social comparisons mediated the negative effect of exposure to media images on negative mood and body dissatisfaction. Thus, after being exposed to ads depicting highly attractive models with (presumably) unattainable appearances, women tended to feel less competent and worthy of their own bodies because they compared their own appearance and figure with an unattainable ideal in a critical and self-evaluative fashion (Martin & Gentry, 1997). Similar mediational findings were reported by Bessendorf (2006), who showed that women who experienced a large discrepancy between their current and ideal body images were especially vulnerable to social comparison processes and, as a result, were also more at risk for increased body dissatisfaction and depressive feelings after being exposed to thin-ideal advertisements.

Third, upward interpersonal comparisons are also likely to be experienced as socially alienating and to interfere with the possibility of deeply relating to others. By devoting attention and energy to interpersonal comparisons, the woman in the fitness room would fail to share exercise enjoyment with her friends and would be less likely to feel connected to them. By comparing the own publication record with the record of others, the extrinsic goal oriented academic might become envious of other people's successes and less inclined to collaborate with them. Thus, the competitive and performance-oriented focus that is activated through engaging in interpersonal comparisons is unlikely to contribute to the development of trustful relationships.

Conditional Approach

The lack of need satisfaction that is associated with an attention shift and with engagement in interpersonal comparison might lead people to feel insecure about their competencies, relationships, and personal values. Such insecurity might provoke two different reactions.

First, insecurity and anxiety are likely to prompt various defensive behaviors that are intended to reduce anxiety and threat. For instance, an individual could try to minimize the extrinsic goal attainments of others when observing that he or she was less successful in attaining these goals, or such an individual might be more likely to provide external, and hence more self-protective, explanations (i.e., attributions) for failure to attain extrinsic goals. Second, the heightened insecurity might also prompt people to acquire more external indicators of worth to improve their standing relative to others, as a way to prove their worth (see Figure 4.1).

To illustrate, after having observed that she was a bit fatter than her friends, the woman in the fitness room might put extra effort into the exercises to show her friends that she is able to live up to the extrinsic ideals. Alternatively, she might put her friends down or provide a self-protective excuse for her failure to attain a slim body in an attempt to ameliorate her insecurity and feel better about herself. Similarly, after finding out that his colleagues are more successful, the extrinsically oriented academic might decide to work harder to get another project finished, increasing the chances of work–family interference (Vansteenkiste, Neyrinck, et al., 2007). Alternatively, this person might defensively minimize the publication record of colleagues or provide rather external attributions for his lack of academic success.

Previous research has provided evidence for these hypotheses. For instance, Schimel, Arndt, Pyszczynski, and Greenberg (2001) demonstrated that defensive behavior in a new situation is more likely to occur when people's extrinsic goals rather than their intrinsic goals are activated. Duriez, Vansteenkiste, et al. (2007) found that extrinsically oriented individuals were more right-wing authoritarian, presumably because adopting such attitudes helped them to alleviate the intraindividual insecurity that extrinsic goal pursuits engender. Similarly, Duriez, Soenens, et al. (2007) showed that parents who emphasized the attainment of extrinsic relative to intrinsic goals in their child rearing had children who displayed stronger right-wing authoritarian attitudes.

In addition to these defensive reactions, more extrinsically oriented individuals might display more interest in other people or put extra effort in activities that help them attain the desired external indicators of worth. Unfortunately, they are likely to approach other people and activities in a nonoptimal, that is, a conditional way. Specifically, extrinsic goal oriented individuals would only select activities and would only interact with individuals as far as other people are perceived as being useful or instrumental for the achievement of their own extrinsic ambitions. Kasser (2002) used the term "objectifying stance" to refer to the conditional interest that extrinsically oriented individuals show in other people. Extrinsically oriented individuals would perceive others as objects that need to be used (and even abused) in the most efficient way to get ahead in their extrinsic strivings.

Such a self-centered approach stands in opposition with the more empathic stance that characterizes an intrinsic goal orientation. In line with this, an intrinsic relative to an extrinsic goal orientation has been found to be inversely related to Machiavellian attitudes (McHoskey, 1999) while being positively associated with empathy (Sheldon & Kasser, 1995). As a result of these different relational attitudes, individuals will be more or less likely to get their basic need for relatedness satisfied. It is interesting to note that extrinsic goal oriented individuals not only consider others as objects but also tend to adopt a self-objectifying stance toward themselves as well (Frederickson & Roberts, 1997). Specifically, when people are self-objectifying, they perceive their bodies from a third-person perspective, thereby focusing on body attributes ("How does my bum look?") rather than from a first-person perspective, thereby focusing on nonobservable body attributes ("How do I feel?"). Such a self-objectifying stance would increase the vulnerability for low competence satisfaction, as illustrated by the finding that self-objectification predicts body shame, which, in turn, predicts low body satisfaction (Noll & Frederickson, 1998).

In addition to observing oneself and others in a conditional fashion, more extrinsically oriented individuals tend to approach activities in a conditional way, which is equally unlikely to contribute to one's need satisfaction because activities are more likely to be carried out in a rigid and narrowly focused way. In line with this, it has been shown that, although participants in an extrinsic goal condition are engaged in the learning activity, the learning material is processed in a relatively superficial fashion (Vansteenkiste, Simons, Lens, Sheldon, et al., 2004; Vansteenkiste, Simons, Lens, et al., 2005).

This suggests that extrinsically oriented students only focus on those elements that are perceived as instrumental in performing on the test, which is likely to preclude feeling a sense of competence. Further, although such a rigid approach promoted initial persistence, these gains were not maintained in the longer run (e.g., Vansteenkiste, Simons, Soenens, et al.,

2004), leaving individuals with a sense of ineffectiveness and incompetence for failing to persist at the requested behaviors.

In sum, extrinsic versus intrinsic goal pursuits and the exposure to extrinsic versus intrinsic goal promotion seem to affect a set of related attention and cognitive processes that might explain why these different goals are differentially related to basic need satisfaction. Drawing upon the existing data on extrinsic and intrinsic goals, we propose that extrinsic relative to intrinsic goals promote an attention shift away from the activity at hand toward external indicators of worth. When people become concerned with living up to these external indicators, they are more likely to compare their own realizations with those of others, which can involve both romanticized and remote reference figures as social partners in one's direct environment. These upward comparisons will, on average, hinder basic need satisfaction and will leave people with a sense of insecurity and intraindividual threat. Such insecurity and threat can evoke defensive behavior or a more proactive tendency to garner external indicators of worth. As a result, and rather paradoxically, such individuals' attention shifts back to the activity at hand, as the instigated insecurity might lead them to become more strongly focused on attaining their extrinsic ideals (Kasser et al., 2004). However, more extrinsically goal oriented people approach the activity at hand and other people around them in a conditional, and hence, more rigid and self-centered fashion, which, is—rather unfortunately—likely to further interfere with basic need satisfaction, thereby fuelling a sense of insecurity and thus further activating the negative vicious cycle.

CONCLUSION

The question whether materialist strivings buy happiness has received increasing attention by psychologists over the past 15 years. Self-determination theory discerns materialist strivings and other extrinsic aspirations such as social status and physical appeal from more organismic and intrinsic strivings such as self-acceptance and emotional intimacy. The articulation of a positive alternative for the pursuit of extrinsic strivings is very much needed, as researchers within the fields of consumer psychology and the body image literature have tended to study extrinsic goals in relative isolation from a more rewarding and growth-promoting alternative. Moreover, the study of such a positive alternative seems to fit very well within the current zeitgeist in the psychological literature to focus on those social conditions and personal attributes that facilitate the deployment of one's potential and contribute to growth.

The work reviewed in this chapter suggests the pursuit and promotion of intrinsic, relative to extrinsic, goals yields a host of differential effects, including people's personal well-being and health, the quality of their social relationships, their ethical functioning, their concern with ecological welfare, and their performance. Moreover, several lines of research begin to show that these conclusions are not only valid for people's general life aspirations but also hold when looking at different life domains as diverse as sports and exercising, work, education, and health care. Future research might shed further insight in why these effects occur. The proposed macro-mediatonal process of basic need satisfaction as well as the three intervening micro-mediational mechanisms might provide some inspiration in this regard.

PERSONAL MINI-EXPERIMENT

**Discovering the Intrinsic and Extrinsic Goal Importance
of your Daily Strivings**

Personal Strivings: Try to think for a while about your personal strivings. These are midlevel goals you have set for yourself. They represent what you typically try to do in your daily behavior, such as learning to play guitar, trying to exercise more, trying to put extra effort in your job, spending more time with your children, or cleaning your house. Please write down three different personal strivings you have set for yourself for the next 3 months.

Intrinsic and Extrinsic Goal Importance of Your Strivings: Now, ask yourself why these strivings are so important for you? To what extent is the pursuit of each of these strivings helpful in achieving different life goals? To help you brainstorm, you can write down how helpful each striving is in terms of achieving the following:

1) financial success in your life
2) helping other people in need
3) increasing your physical appeal to others
4) developing your talents
5) being more socially admired by others
6) being in better physical shape
7) having a stronger influence over others
8) developing stronger relational bonds with others

For each of these goals, indicate whether your current strivings help you in achieving them by scoring them from 1 (*not helpful at all*) to 5 (*very helpful*). Then, sum your scores across the three strivings for goals 1, 3, 5, and 7, and your scores for goals 2, 4, 6, and 8. The first set of goals assesses the importance of extrinsic goal strivings, and the second set of goals measures the importance of intrinsic goal strivings.

Look at your results. If your intrinsic goal score is much higher than your extrinsic goal score, your daily strivings are centered around goals that promote growth. If your extrinsic goals score is higher than your intrinsic goal score, your daily strivings are focused on material gain. Take a moment to reflect on your goals. What is it that makes extrinsic goals so important for you? What are the benefits to pursuing them? What are the costs? How do you pursue other people around you when you have an extrinsic goal on your mind when engaging in an activity? If you manage to attain an extrinsic goal, how long does the satisfaction of goal attainment last?

These kinds of questions might help you to gain further insight in the dynamic effects that are associated with the pursuit of intrinsic and extrinsic goals and might perhaps ultimately lead you to alter your perspective on your goals, to abandon some of them, and to select new ones.

REFERENCES

Amiot, C. E., Vallerand, R. J., & Blanchard, C. M. (2006). Passion and psycholog-ical adjustment: A test of the person-environment fit hypothesis. *Personality and Social Psychology Bulletin, 32,* 220–229.

Belk, R. W. (1985). Materialism: Trait aspects of living in the material world. *Journal of Consumer Research, 12,* 265–280.

Berzonsky, M. D. (1990). Self-construction over the life-span: A process perspec-tive on identity formation. *Advances in Personal Construct Psychology, 1,* 155–186.

Bessendorf, G. R. (2006). Can the media affect us? Social comparison, self-discrep-ancy, and the thin ideal. *Psychology of Women Quarterly, 30,* 239–251.

Brickman, P., & Campbell, D. (1977). Hedonic relativism and planning the good society. In M. H. Appley (Ed.), *Social comparison processes: Theoretical and empirical perspectives.* New York: Wiley/Halsted.

Brown, K. W., & Kasser, T. (2005). Are psychological and ecological well-being compatible? The role of values, mindfulness, and lifestyle. *Social Indicators Research, 74,* 349–368.

Campbell, A., Converse, P. E., & Rodgers, W. L. (1967). *The quality of American life: Perceptions, evaluations, and satisfactions.* New York: Russell Sage.

Carver, C. S., & Baird, E. (1998). The American dream revisited: Is it what you want or why you want it that matters? *Psychological Science, 9,* 289–292.

Carver, C. S., & Scheier, M. F. (2000). Autonomy and self-regulation. *Psychologi-cal Inquiry, 11,* 284–290.

Cash, T. F., Cash, D. W., & Butters, J. W. (1983). "Mirror, mirror, on the wall?": Contrast effects and self-evaluations of physical attractiveness. *Personality and Social Psychology Bulletin, 9,* 351–358.

Csikszentmihalyi, M. (1999). If we are so rich, why aren't we happy? *American Psychologist, 54,* 821–827.

Cohen, P., & Cohen, J. (1996). *Life values and adolescent mental health.* NJ: Erlbaum.

Deci, E. L., & Ryan, R. M. (2000). The "what" and the "why" of goal pursuits: Human needs and the self-determination of behavior. *Psychological Inquiry, 11,* 227–268.

Diener, E., Suh, E. M., Luca, R. E., & Smith, H. L. (1999). Subjective well-being: Three decades of progress. *Psychological Bulletin, 125,* 276–302.

Dittmar, H. (2005). Compulsive buying—a growing concern? An examination of gender, age, and endorsement of materialistic values as predictors. *British Journal of Psychology, 96,* 467–491.

Dittmar, H. (2007). The costs of consumer culture and the "cage within": The impact of the material "good life" and "body perfect" ideals on individuals' identity and well-being. *Psychological Inquiry, 18,* 23–59.

Dohnt, H. K., & Tiggeman, M. (2006a). Body image concerns in young girls: The role of peers and media prior to adolescence. *Journal of Youth and Adolescence, 35,* 141–151.

Dohnt, H. K., & Tiggeman, M. (2006b). The contribution of peer and media influences on the development of body satisfaction and self-esteem in young girls: A prospective study. *Developmental Psychology, 42,* 929–936.

Duriez, B., Soenens, B., & Vansteenkiste, M. (2007). In search of the antecedents of adolescent authoritarianism: The relative contribution of parental goal promotion and parenting style dimensions. *European Journal of Personality, 21,* 507–527.

Duriez, B., Vansteenkiste, M., Soenens, B., & De Witte, H. (2007). The social costs of extrinsic relative to intrinsic goal pursuits: Their relation with social dominance and racial and ethnic prejudice. *Journal of Personality, 75,* 757–782.

Eccles, J. S., Lord, S., & Midgley, C. (1991). What are we doing to early adolescents? The impact of educational contexts on early adolescents. *American Journal of Education, 99,* 521–541.

Eccles, J. S., & Wigfield, A. (2002). Motivational beliefs, values, and goals. *Annual Review of Psychology, 53,* 109–132.

Edwards, J. R. (1991). Person-job fit: A conceptual integration, literature review, and methodological critique. In C. L. Cooper, & I.T. Robertson (Eds.). *International review of industrial and organizational psychology* (pp. 283–357). Oxford: Wiley.

Elizur, D. (1984). Facets of work values: A structural analysis of work outcomes. *Journal of Applied Psychology, 69,* 379–389.

Elliot, A. J. (1999). Approach and avoidance motivation and achievement goals. *Educational Psychologist, 34,* 169–189.

Frederickson, B. L., & Roberts, T. A. (1997). Objectification theory: Toward understanding women's lived experiences and mental health risks. *Psychology of Women Quarterly, 21,* 173–206.

Fromm, E. (1976). *To have or to be?* New York: Continuum.

Groesz, L. M., Levine, M. P., & Murnen, S. K. (2002). The effect of experimental presentation of thin media images on body satisfaction: A meta-analytical review. *International Journal of Eating Disorders, 31,* 1–16.

Grouzet, F. M. E., Kasser, T., Ahuvia, A., Dols, J. M. F., Kim, Y., Lau, S., et al. (2006). The structure of goal contents across 15 cultures. *Journal of Personality and Social Psychology, 89,* 800–816.

Gulas, C. S., & McKeage, K. (2000). Extending social comparison: An examination of the unintended consequences of idealized advertising imagery. *Journal of Advertising, 2,* 17–28.

Hall, P. A., & Gingerich, D. W. (2004). Varietiess of capitalism and institutional complementarities in the macroeconomy: An empirical analysis. *Berliner Journal fur Soziologie, 14,* 5.

Harackiewicz, J. M., & Elliot, A. J. (1998). The joint effects of target and purpose goals on intrinsic motivation: A mediational analysis. *Personality and Social Psychology Bulletin, 24,* 675–689.

Husman, J., & Lens, W. (1999). The role of the future in student motivation. *Educational Psychologist, 34,* 113–125.

Inglehart, R. (1990). *Culture shift in advanced industrial society.* Princeton, NJ: Princeton University Press.

Kashdan, T. B., & Breen, W. E. (2007). Materialism and diminished well-being: Experiential avoidance as a mediating mechanisms. *Journal of Social and Clinical Psychology, 26,* 521–539.

Kasser, T. (2002). *The high price of materialism.* London: MIT Press.

Kasser, T. (2005). Frugality, generosity, and materialism in children and adolescents. In K. A. Moore, & L. H. Lippman (Eds.), *What do children need to flourish?: Conceptualizing and measuring indicators of positive development* (pp. 357–373). New York: Springer Science.

Kasser, T., & Ahuvia, A. (2002). Materialistic values and well-being in business students. *European Journal of Social Psychology, 32,* 137–146.

Kasser, T., Cohn, S., Kanner, A. D., & Ryan, R. M. (2007). Some costs of American corporate capitalism: A psychological exploration of value and goal conflicts. *Psychological Inquiry, 18,* 1–22.

Kasser, T., & Ryan, R. M. (1993). A dark side of the American dream: Correlates of financial success as central life aspiration. *Journal of Personality and Social Psychology, 65,* 410–422.

Kasser, T., & Ryan, R. M. (1996). Further examining the American dream: Differential correlates of intrinsic and extrinsic goals. *Personality and Social Psychology Bulletin, 22,* 280–287.

Kasser, T., & Ryan, R. M. (2001). Be careful for what you wish: Optimal functioning and the relative attainment of intrinsic and extrinsic goals. In P. Schmuck, & K. M. Sheldon (Eds.), *Life goals and well-being: Toward a positive psychology of human striving* (pp. 116–131). Goettingen, Germany: Hogrefe & Huber.

Kasser, T., Ryan, R. M., Couchman, C. E., & Sheldon, K. M. (2004). Materialistic values: Their causes and consequences. In T. Kasser, & A. D. Kanfer (Eds.), *Psychology and consumer cultures: The struggle for a good life in a materialistic world* (pp. 11–28). Washington, DC: American Psychological Association.

Kasser, T., & Sheldon, K. M. (2002). What makes for a merry Christmas? *Journal of Happiness Studies, 3,* 313–329.

Kasser, T., Vansteenkiste, M., & Deckop, J. R. (2006). The ethical problems of a materialist value orientation for business. In J. R. Deckop (Ed.), *Human resource management ethics.* Greenwich, CT: Information Age Publishers.

Kilbourne, W., & Pickette, G. (in press). How materialism affects environmental beliefs, concern, and environmentally responsible behavior. *Journal of Business Research.*

Krieger, L. S. (1998). What we're not telling law students—and lawyers—that they really need to know: Some thoughts-in-acting toward revitalizing the profession from its roots. *Journal of Law and Health, 13,* 1–48.

Krones, P., Stice, E., Batres, C., & Orjada, K. (2005). In vivo social comparison to a thin-deal peer promotes body dissatisfaction: A randomized experiment. *International Journal of Eating Disorders, 38,* 134–142.

LaBarbera, P., & Gürhan, Z. (1997). The role of materialism, religiosity, and demographics in subjective well-being. *Psychology and Marketing, 14,* 71–97.

Markus, H. R., & Kitayama, S. K. (2003). Models of agency: Socio-cultural diversity in the construction of action. In V. Murphy-Berman, & J. J. Berman (Eds.), *Nebraska symposium on motivation: Vol. 49. Cross-cultural differences in perspectives on the self* (pp. 1–57). Lincoln, NE: University of Nebraska Press.

Martin, M. C., & Gentry, J. W. (1997). Stuck in the model trap: The effects of beautiful models in ads on female pre-adolescents and adolescents. *The Journal of Advertising, 2,* 19–33.

McGill, V. J. (1967). *The idea of happiness.* New York: Praeger.

McHoskey, J. W. (1999). Machiavellianism, intrinsic versus extrinsic goals, and social interest: A self-determination theory analysis. *Motivation and Emotion, 23,* 267–283.

Meyer, B., Enström, M. K., Harstveit, M., Bowles, D. P., & Beevers, C. G. (2007). Happiness and despair on the catwalk: Need satisfaction, well-being, and personality adjustment among fashion models. *Journal of Positive Psychology, 2007,* 2–17.

Nickerson, C., Schartz, N., Diener, E., & Kahneman, D. (2003). Zeroing in on the dark side of the American dream: A closer look at the negative consequences of the goal for financial success. *Psychological Science, 14,* 531–536.

Noll, S. M., & Frederickson, B. L. (1998). A mediational model linking self-objectification, body shame and disorder eating. *Psychology of Women Quarterly, 22,* 623–636.

Patrick, H., Neighbors, C., & Knee, C. R. (2004). Appearance-related social comparisons: The role of contingent self-esteem and self-perceptions of attractiveness. *Personality and Social Psychology Bulletin, 30*, 501–514.

Pratto, F., Sidanius, J., Stallworth, L. M., & Malle, B. F. (1994). Social dominance orientation: A personality variable predicting social and political attitudes. *Journal of Personality and Social Psychology, 67*, 741–763.

Quin, D. M., Kallen, R. W., Twenge, J. M., & Frederickson, B. L. (2006). The disruptive effect of self-objectification on performance. *Psychology of Women Quarterly, 30*, 59–64.

Richins, M. L., & Dawson, S. (1992). A consumer value orientation for materialism and its measurement: Scale development and validation. *Journal of Consumer Research, 19*, 303–316.

Rijavec, M., Brdar, I., & Miljikovic, D. (2006). Extrinsic vs. intrinsic life goals, psychological needs and life satisfaction. In A. Delle Fave (Ed.), *Dimensions of well-being. Research and Intervention* (pp. 91–104). Milan: Franco Angeli.

Roberts, J. A., & Clement, A. (2007). Materialism and satisfaction with overall quality of life and eight life domains. *Social Indicators Research, 82*, 79–92.

Roets, A., Van Hiel, A., & Cornelis, I. (2006). Does materialism predict racism? Materialism as a distinctive social attitude and a predictor of prejudice. *European Journal of Personality, 20*, 155–168.

Ryan, R. M. (1995). Psychological needs and the facilitation of integrative processes. *Journal of Personality, 63*, 397–427.

Ryan, R. M., Chirkov, V. I., Little, T. D., Sheldon, K. M., Timoshina, E., & Deci, E. L. (1999). The American dream in Russia: Extrinsic aspirations and well-being in two cultures. *Personality and Social Psychology Bulletin, 25*, 1509–1524.

Ryan, R. M., & Deci, E. L. (2000). Self-determination theory and the facilitation of intrinsic motivation, social development, and well-being. *American Psychologist, 55*, 68–78.

Ryan, R. M., Huta, V., & Deci, E. L. (2008). Living well: A self-determination theory perspective on eudaimonia. *Journal of Happiness Studies, 9*, 139–170.

Ryan, R. M., Sheldon, K. M., Kasser, T., & Deci, E. L. (1996). All goals were not created equal: An organismic perspective on the nature of goals and their regulation. In P. M. Gollwitzer, & J. A. Bargh (Eds.), *The psychology of action: Linking motivation and cognition to behavior* (pp. 7–26). New York: Guilford.

Sagiv, L., & Schwartz, S. H. (2000). Value priorities and subjective well-being: Direct relations and congruity effects. *European Journal of Social Psychology, 30*, 177–198.

Schimel, J., Arndt, J., Pyszczyinski, T., & Greenberg, J. (2001). Being accepted for who we are: Evidence that social validation of the intrinsic self reduces general defensiveness. *Journal of Personality and Social Psychology, 80*, 35–52.

Schwartz, S. H. (1992). Universals in the content and structure of values: Theoretical advances and empirical tests in 20 countries. In M. P. Zanna (Ed.), *Advances in experimental social psychology* (Vol. 25, pp. 1–65). San Diego, CA, and London: Academic Press.

Schwartz, S. H. (2006). Cultural and individual value correlates of capitalism: A comparative analysis. *Psychological Inquiry, 18*, 52–57.

Sebire, S., Standage, M., & Vansteenkiste, M. (2008). *Exploring exercise goal content: Intrinsic vs. extrinsic exercise goals, exercise outcomes, and psychological need satisfaction.* Manuscript submitted for publication.

Sebire, S., Standage, M., & Vansteenkiste, M. (in press). Development and validation of the Goal Content for Exercise Questionnaire. *Journal of Sport and Exercise Psychology.*

Seligman, M. E. P., & Csikszentminhalyi, M. (2000). Positive psychology: An introduction. *American Psychologist, 55,* 5–14.

Sheldon, K. M., Arndt, J., & Houser-Marko, L. (2003). In search of the organismic valuing process: The human tendency to move toward beneficial goal choices. *Journal of Personality, 71,* 835–886.

Sheldon, K. M., & Kasser, T. (1995). Coherence and congruence: Two aspects of personality integration. *Journal of Personality and Social Psychology, 68,* 531–543.

Sheldon, K. M., & Kasser, T. (1998). Pursuing personal goals: Skills enable progress, but not all progress is beneficial. *Personality and Social Psychology Bulletin, 24,* 1319–1331.

Sheldon, K. M., & Kasser, T. (2001). Goals, congruence, and positive well-being: New empirical support for humanistic theories. *Journal of Humanistic Psychology, 41,* 30–50.

Sheldon, K. M., & Krieger, L. S. (2004). Does legal education have undermining effects on law students? Evaluating changes in motivation, values, and well-being. *Behavioral Sciences and the Law, 22,* 261–286.

Sheldon, K. M., & McGregor, H. (2000). Extrinsic value orientation and the tragedy of the commons. *Journal of Personality, 68,* 383–411.

Sheldon, K. M., Ryan, R. M., Deci, E. L., & Kasser, T. (2004). The independent effects of goal contents and motives on well-being: It's both what you pursue and why you pursue it. *Personality and Social Psychology Bulletin, 30,* 475–486.

Sirgy, M. J. (1998). Materialism and quality of life. *Social Indicators Research, 43,* 227–260.

Solberg, E. G., Diener, E., & Robinson, M. D. (2004). Why are materialists less satisfied? In T. Kasser & A. D. Kanner (Eds.), *Psychology and consumer culture: The struggle for a good life in a materialistic world* (pp. 29–48). Washington, DC: American Psychological Association.

Srivastava, A., Locke, E. A., & Bartol, K. M. (2001). Money and subjective well-being: It's not the money, it's the motives. *Journal of Personality and Social Psychology, 80,* 959–971.

Stice, E., & Shaw, H. E. (1994). Adverse effects of the media portrayed thin-ideal on women and linkages to bulimic symptomatology. *Journal of Social and Clinical Psychology, 13,* 288–308.

Strahan, E. J., Wilson, A. E., Cressman, K. E., & Buote, V. M. (2006). Comparing to perfection: How cultural norms for appearance affect social comparisons and self-image. *Body Image, 3,* 211–227.

Tang, T. L., & Chiu, R. K. (2003). Income, money ethic, pay satisfaction, and unethical behavior: Is the love of money the root of evil for Hong Kong employees? *Journal of Business Ethics, 46,* 13–30.

Tiggeman, M., & McGill, B. (2004). The role of social comparison in the effect of magazine advertisements on women's mood and body dissatisfaction. *Journal of Social and Clinical Psychology, 23,* 23–44.

Van Boven, L. (2005). Experientialism, materialism, and the hedonics of consumption. *Review of General Psychology, 9,* 132–142.

Van Boven, L., & Gilovich, T. (2003). To do or to have? That is the question. *Journal of Personality and Social Psychology, 85,* 1193–1202.

Van Hiel, A., & Vansteenkiste, M. (2007). *"Ambitions fulfilled?" The effects of intrinsic versus extrinsic goal attainment on psychological well-being and ego-integrity, and death attitudes among the elderly.* Manuscript submitted for publication.

Vansteenkiste, M. (2007, September). *The effects of intrinsic vs. extrinsic goal pursuit on ethical functioning.* Paper presented to the British Association of Sport and Exercise Sciences Annual Conference, Bath, United Kingdom.

Vansteenkiste, M., Duriez, B., Simons, J., & Soenens, B. (2006). Materialistic values and well-being among business students: Further evidence for their detrimental effect. *Journal of Applied Social Psychology, 36,* 2892–2908.

Vansteenkiste, M., Lens, W., & Deci, E. L. (2006). Intrinsic vs. extrinsic goal contents in self-determination theory: Another look at the quality of academic motivation. *Educational Psychologist, 41,* 19–31.

Vansteenkiste, M., Matos, L., Lens, W., & Soenens, B. (2007). Understanding the impact of intrinsic versus extrinsic goal framing on exercise performance: The conflicting role of task and ego involvement. *Psychology of Sport and Exercise, 8,* 771–794.

Vansteenkiste, M., Neyrinck, B., Niemiec, C. P., Soenens, B., De Witte, H., & Van den Broeck, A. (2007). On the relations among work value orientations, psychological need satisfaction, and job outcomes: A self-determination theory approach. *Journal of Occupational and Organizational Psychology, 80,* 251–277.

Vansteenkiste, M., Simons, J., Braet, C., Bachman, C., & Deci, E. L. (2007). *Promoting maintained weight loss through healthy lifestyle changes among severely obese children: An experimental test of self-determination theory.* Manuscript submitted for publication.

Vansteenkiste, M., Simons, J., Lens, W., Sheldon, K. M., & Deci, E. L. (2004). Motivation learning, performance and persistence: The synergistic effects of intrinsic goal contents and autonomy-supportive contexts. *Journal of Personality and Social Psychology, 87,* 246–260.

Vansteenkiste, M., Simons, J., Lens, W., Soenens, B., Matos, L., & Lacante, M. (2004). "Less is sometimes more": Goal-content matters. *Journal of Educational Psychology, 96,* 755–764.

Vansteenkiste, M., Simons, J., Lens, W., Soenens, B., & Matos, L. (2005). Examining the impact of extrinsic vs. intrinsic goal framing and internally controlling vs. autonomy-supportive communication style upon early adolescents' academic achievement. *Child Development, 76,* 483–501.

Vansteenkiste, M., Simons, J., Soenens, B., & Lens, W. (2004). How to become a persevering exerciser? Providing a clear, future intrinsic goal in an autonomy supportive way. *Journal of Sport and Exercise Psychology, 26,* 232–249.

Vansteenkiste, M., Soenens, B., & Lens, W. (2007). Intrinsic versus extrinsic goal promotion in sport and exercise: Understanding their differential impact on performance and persistence. In M. S. Hagger and N. Chatzisarantis (Eds.) *Self-Determination Theory in exercise and sport* (pp 167–180). Champaign, IL: Human Kinetics.

Vansteenkiste, M., Timmermans, T., Lens, W., Soenens, B., & Van den Broeck, A. (2008). Does extrinsic goal framing enhance extrinsic goal oriented individuals' learning and performance? An experimental test of the match-perspective vs. self-determination theory. *Journal of Educational Psychology, 100,* 387–397.

Williams, G. C., Cox, E. M., Hedberg, V. A. & Deci, E. L. (2000). Extrinsic life goals and health-risk behaviours among adolescents. *Journal of Applied Social Psychology, 30,* 1756–1771.

CHAPTER 5

Positive Schooling

Richard Gilman, E. Scott Huebner, and Matthew Buckman

There is much agreement that youth development takes place in three major contexts: families, peer groups, and out-of-home contexts, such as schools (Cox & Harter, 2003). Nevertheless, research investigating the relationship between school experiences and positive youth development has lagged behind scholarship examining the other two contexts. The purpose of this chapter is to summarize studies that have focused on factors contributing to positive school experiences, or school satisfaction. In this chapter, the definition and measures of school satisfaction will be provided, followed by a review of the linkages between individual difference and environmental factors and school satisfaction. Finally, we provide a discussion of the implications of the research for the design of healthy school environments.

DEFINITION AND THEORETICAL OVERVIEW

Simply stated, positive or "good" schools are those that are experienced as positive by students. Although the primary goal of schools is to prepare students for life beyond graduation, the quality of experiences *during* the formal school years dictates in some part the choices one makes post-high school. Indeed, students who report positive school experiences also report more favorable life experiences (e.g. Mahoney, Cairns, & Farmer, 2003), and they are less likely to report unfavorable experiences such as chronic alcohol use and heightened mental distress years after graduating (Locke & Newcomb, 2004). These findings emphasize that when students report positive school experiences, good things tend to happen for them both as current students and in the future as adults. Understanding factors that contribute to positive schooling should thus be an important consideration in the evaluation of school effectiveness (Hegarty, 1994).

In this regard, life satisfaction provides a useful conceptual framework to assess school effectiveness. Life satisfaction is an individual's cognitive appraisal of his or her current life circumstances, with these appraisals taking into account both internal (e.g., self-beliefs) and external factors (see Diener, 2000, for a review). Among youth, life satisfaction has been primarily studied from a global perspective, that is, asking youth to evaluate the positivity of their life as a whole (e.g., "overall, my life is going well"). The importance of global evaluations in adults and children and youth has been well established (Gilman & Huebner, 2003; Huebner, 2004). However, studies of domain-specific perceptions, such as satisfaction with family and peer relationships have emerged and have proven successful as well. Students as young as 8 years old are able to provide meaningful assessments of major life domains, and they are also able to differentiate life satisfaction judgments from positive and negative emotions, showing that life satisfaction reports are related to, but not limited to, their experiences of different emotions (Huebner, 1991, 2004). In other words, students who are satisfied with their lives do not have to be happy all the time.

School is considered an important life domain for most youth, and to this end research efforts have been made to assess youth's school satisfaction. School satisfaction has been defined as a student's judgment of the positivity of her or his school experience *as a whole* (Huebner, 1994). Nevertheless, although there may be some consensus on important criteria that are necessary for positive school experiences (e.g., "fair" teachers, small class sizes), students are likely to assign different weights to these criteria or, in some cases, develop their own criteria (see Pavot & Diener, 1993). As a result, items on measures of school satisfaction reflect global (e.g., I like my school) rather than specific (e.g., I like my school building; I like my school curriculum) characteristics. These measures allow students to weight or incorporate domains of unique criteria for positive schooling.

Such measures are thus differentiable from school climate measures, which include researcher-generated domains that are predetermined to be important for the respondents. The usefulness of each measure is, of course, dependent upon the aims of the researcher.

Although research remains in its beginning stage, it is evident that the levels of students' school satisfaction judgments are related to a number of favorable psychological, psychosocial, and psychoeducational outcomes. For example, Huebner and Gilman (2006) found that "very high" levels of school satisfaction are associated with school-related benefits above and beyond "average" and "below average" levels, such as higher grade point averages, a greater sense of motivation and personal control, and fewer psychological symptoms. Also, higher school satisfaction has been shown to be associated with fewer adolescent problem behaviors concurrently (DeSantis-King, Huebner, Suldo, & Valois, 2006) and prospectively (Elmore, 2006). Most important, school satisfaction appears to be a precursor of student engagement behaviors and academic progress even in students as young as kindergartners (Ladd, Buhs, & Seid, 2000). Thus, school satisfaction appears to serve as one clinically useful and important indicator of positive school adaptation and its accompanying benefits.

MEASUREMENT OF SCHOOL SATISFACTION

School satisfaction measures are often designed to be used for a particular research study or for a single grade level, which often limits their generalizeability to other groups and ages of interest. Nevertheless, there are some measures that have been used across multiple studies, and they will be the focus of this section. The earliest measure was the Quality of School Life Scale (QSL; Epstein & McPartland, 1976), which consists of 27 items that assess three domains believed to be most relevant to positive school experiences: satisfaction with school in general, commitment to school work, and attitudes towards teachers. Item response formats range from dichotomous true–false options to multiple response options. The QSL was originally administered to over 4,000 elementary, middle, and high school students in one U.S. state. Results supported the psychometric properties of the scale, with adequate internal consistency for each of the three domains (generally ranging from .70 to .85), and moderate consistency across a 1-year time span. Evidence for the convergent and discriminant validity of the scale was obtained via significant and expected positive correlations with school performance and negative and significant correlations with school anxiety and poor school behaviors such as cutting class or school. Finally, the QSL yielded evidence of construct validity via exploratory factor analytic methods. Subsequent studies have generally supported these original findings (e.g., Johnson & Johnson, 1993). Other measures have largely adapted the QSL but have expanded the number of domains and applied them to students from different nationalities (e.g. Karatzias, Power, & Swanson, 2001; Mok & Flynn, 2002).

Other school satisfaction measures are embedded within larger multidimensional scales to provide a comprehensive understanding of factors that contribute to students' overall well-being. For example, the Multidimensional Students' Life Satisfaction Scale (MSLSS; Huebner, 1994) assesses global life satisfaction as well as satisfaction with school, family, friends, living environment, and self. The School Satisfaction subscale consists of seven items that reflect the degree of positivity surrounding students' relationships with teachers and classmates, as well as their overall impression of their school environment (e.g., "school is great"). All items are responded to on a 6-point rating scale. Extant findings reveal that the scale yields strong psychometric properties, including internal consistency estimates of .80 or greater, adequate internal consistency across multiple time frames, and evidence of convergent and discriminant validity across youth representing different age and grade ranges (see Gilman & Huebner, 2003). The School Satisfaction subscale also demonstrates solid evidence of construct validity for students across many nationalities (Gilman et al., in press).

Other scales are incorporated into standardized instruments, to be used as part of a comprehensive assessment to establish clinical diagnoses. The Behavioral Assessment System for Children, Second Edition (BASC–2;

Reynolds & Kamphaus, 2004) is one example of such an instrument, which includes the Attitude to Teachers and Attitude to School subscales. Both subscales evidence strong psychometric properties and have been used in recent studies (e.g. Gilman & Anderman, 2006b).

In summary, evidence from available school satisfaction instruments indicates that positive school perceptions can be reliably and validly assessed among youth. It should be noted like most satisfaction measures, school satisfaction is primarily assessed via self-report, using written responses on measures that are administered in group settings. Considering that such perceptions are based on internalized beliefs that may not be shared with others, self-reports will continue to prevail as the primary assessment method. Nevertheless, such measures cannot completely address potential limitations such as social desirability, positive impression management, and faking responses. For this reason, other methods have been recently utilized to limit these response artifacts.

For example, the use of momentary time sampling, where students are given a pager and then randomly "beeped" throughout the day to assess their in-the-moment perceptions have been recently applied and have garnered reliable results (e.g. Shernoff, Csikszentmihalyi, Schneider, & Shernoff, 2003). Other methods also have included having students keep an ongoing diary or having the students respond to questions via computer survey at home. Finally, reports of others who know the student well (such as peer, teacher, and parent reports) have been used to address limitations inherent in self-reports.

FINDINGS ON SCHOOL SATISFACTION

Until recently, studies have largely focused on the presumed consequences related to school dissatisfaction, including disengagement from the academic curriculum, increased behavior problems, and other difficulties. Nevertheless, research has now turned to understanding antecedent conditions that presumably contribute to elevated levels of school satisfaction such as demographic variables—as well as temperament variables (e.g., outgoing personality and emotional regulation styles). Other antecedents include environmental factors ranging from proximal variables (e.g., student–teacher relationships, academic expectations of the school) to more indirect, distal ones (parent–school relationships, cultural expectations).

Most research has been largely atheoretical, although recent models adapted from motivational and school engagement research (Marchand & Skinner, 2007), sociological research (Locke & Newcomb, 2004), developmental psychology (Baker, Dilly, Aupperlee, & Patil, 2003), and population studies (Evans, 1994) have all been used as conceptual frameworks to examine the influence of antecedent conditions on perceived school quality. Common beliefs held by many of these frameworks are that (a) subjective appraisals (such as school satisfaction reports) are thought to mediate the relationship between personal and environmental antecedents and behavioral consequences, and (b) the relationship between subjective appraisals and behavioral outcomes can move in both directions. Thus, school satisfaction can both influence and be influenced by changes in environmental conditions as well in student behaviors. It should be noted that although some efforts have been undertaken to test unique aspects of these models with respect to students' school satisfaction (see DeSantis-King et al., 2006; Elmore, 2006), much work remains to be done. For one example, among kindergarten students, Ladd et al. (2000) found support for a longitudinal path model in which school satisfaction predicted classroom participation and achievement, rather than the converse. Considering the young age of the participants however, elements of this model (and others) may require revision when applied to students of different ages, backgrounds, and so forth.

Proximal Factors

Research suggests the importance of key proximal factors in the promotion of school satisfaction. It should first be noted that demographic variables such as age, gender, and race have relatively little influence on school satisfaction reports. Indeed, regardless of composition studied, whatever differences are found are quite small, with effect sizes typically ranging between 2% and 7% (see Huebner, Gilman, Reschly, & Hall, in press).

What appears more influential to school satisfaction reports are qualities and characteristics within students. For example, among the highest relationships shared with school satisfaction are self-esteem and self-efficacy, and more specifically academic self-efficacy (Verkuyten & Thijs, 2002). That is, students who believe that they can competently complete their academic work report higher school satisfaction.

Other personal characteristics include external locus of control, with students reporting that their academic successes are due to effort and ability (rather than through chance or luck) often reporting higher school satisfaction (Gilman & Anderman, 2006b). Related to locus of control is hope, a multidimensional construct consisting of motivational tendencies and goal strategies. In general, students who can formulate alternative academic strategies when their primary strategy becomes impeded, and who are motivated to pursue these alternative strategies tend to report higher satisfaction (Valle, Huebner, & Suldo, 2006).

Other proximal factors related to school satisfaction extend beyond internal characteristics to the choices students make while in school. For example, the type of activities that youth spend their time on outside of their school work has been a topic of increasing interest. It has been estimated that 40–50% of youths' waking hours are spent in unsupervised and nonstructured leisure pursuits, such as watching television or playing videogames (Larson & Verma, 1999). Although these activities are largely innocuous and enjoyable, research finds that an over-reliance on them can lead to chronic boredom, lack of initiative, and maladaptive behaviors. Participation in structured extracurricular activities (SEAs) is one class of leisure pursuits that has drawn increasing attention from researchers given their unique characteristics. For example, SEAs differ from more relaxed leisure pursuits in that one or more adult leaders who are judged as competent within the interest area lead them. Further, SEAs contain some established standards of performance or work effort and require voluntary and ongoing participation, rather than activities that are required or held at only one point in time (or only occasionally). SEAs also emphasize skill development and growth, with the skill set continually increasing in both challenge and complexity. Finally, the activities require sustained attention, and clear and consistent feedback from the adult is provided regarding the participant's level of performance (Mahoney et al., 2003). With respect to school satisfaction, research finds that students who report higher involvement in SEAs also tend to report higher levels of school satisfaction than do students reporting little or no SEA involvement (Gilman, 2001). Further, more recent findings suggest that the relationship between school satisfaction and SEA participation may be mediated by motivational factors. For example, borrowing from Deci and Ryan's (1985) self-determination theory of motivation, Gilman and Stacy (2007) found that the effect of moderate-to-high SEA participation on school satisfaction was significant only if such activities promoted feelings of individual autonomy, competency, and social relatedness. Activities that were selected to fulfill a course requirement, to satisfy a request from a parent, or participated in for reasons other than personal preference (e.g., because the student's peer group was engaged in the activity) were less influential on school satisfaction reports.

In addition to internal characteristics and individual choices, there are other proximal factors that contribute to school satisfaction. Most notably, peer support and social acceptance by teachers are also significantly related to school satisfaction (Baker, 1998). In general, students who are connected to their peers and report positive relationships with teachers also report higher school satisfaction than students who report moderate-to-high levels of social stress and problems with their teachers (Huebner & Gilman, 2006).

Clearly, these positive relationships can be explained in part by attitudes and behaviors demonstrated by the student, including possessing adequate social skills and having an outgoing personality; both of which increase the probability of initiating and maintaining positive interactions with peers and teachers and thus increasing school satisfaction.

Nevertheless, other proximal factors outside of the student's control also can also facilitate or discourage positive interactions. For example, students whose teachers promote positive peer interactions via shared learning tasks and other social activities also report higher school satisfaction (Verkuyten & Thijs, 2002). Further, teachers who have clearly developed and enforced classroom rules, and who create predictable classroom structures also promote positive peer relations and school satisfaction (see Baker et al., 2003). Conversely, teachers who establish class structures characterized as authoritarian or who avoid praising appropriate behaviors can diminish students' positive interactions and reduce school satisfaction (Baker, 1998; Carey & Bourbon, 2005).

The relevance of classroom instruction methods also has been shown to be correlated with positive school experiences. For example, classrooms that incorporate intrinsically interesting activities that challenge students to use their developing skills (such as those found in group work activities or individual activities that involved active learning) were far more satisfying to students than passive activities (such as lectures; Shernoff et al., 2003). Finally, the larger goals of the school may influence school satisfaction as well. For example, research indicates that more positive psychological outcomes (including perceived positive school experiences) are obtained from schools that incorporate mastery learning strategies. These strategies focus on having students master new skills and material, where the level of self-growth reported by the student largely determines success. Conversely, less satisfying school experiences have been found in schools that embrace performance learning strategies, in which success is determined by comparing a student's performance against that of his or her peers, or against a standardized criterion (Meece, Anderman, & Anderman, 2006).

Distal Factors

In comparison to proximal factors, few studies have investigated how more remote factors influence school satisfaction reports. Cultural expectations about academic performance may be one factor to consider when assessing school satisfaction. One recent study of adolescents from America, Ireland, China, and South Korea found that while there were differences in school satisfaction scores between students from America and Ireland versus China and South Korea, these differences were quite small, suggesting that students hold comparable views of the quality of their school experiences regardless of cultural nuances (Gilman et al., in press).

Another distal factor to consider when assessing school satisfaction is the amount of stress experienced by students as they transition between school levels (i.e., from elementary school to middle school, and from middle school to high school). As noted by Akos and Galassi (2004), transitions between school levels are quite difficult for many students and mark a time of heightened ambivalence. Meeting new peers, having specific teachers for specific classes, having greater opportunities to participate in activities of interest, and even having a locker are frequently cited as positive aspects, while increasing academic demands, less flexible school rules, and the fear of being bullied are commonly noted as negative aspects.

Although research continues to explore factors that increase school satisfaction as the student transitions between levels, two of the more prominent factors are positive relationships with adult figures and the types of goal strategies adopted by teachers. For example, regardless of the student's age, parents (and to a great extent, teachers) serve as an important base from which students appraise their school satisfaction (Rosenfeld & Richman, 1999), and these relationships appear to be most critical during the time preceding and after school transitions. Further, positive school experiences are most noted by teachers who report a greater mastery learning focus and a reduced performance focus (Kumar, 2006).

Finally, the size of the school may partially influence school satisfaction reports. For example, in a study of schools with differing enrollment sizes, Bowen, Bowen, and Richman (2000) found that school satisfaction was lower among schools with populations of 1,000 students or more. Nevertheless, other studies reported no differences across enrollment sizes (Verkuyten & Thijs, 2002). These conflicting findings are likely due to sample differences and the manner in which school satisfaction was assessed, underscoring the need for further research in this area.

PUTTING IT ALL TOGETHER: THE IMPORTANCE OF SCHOOL SATISFACTION TOWARD THE PROMOTION OF POSITIVE SCHOOLING

As noted elsewhere (Gilman & Anderman, 2006a), if examined through the lens of objective indicators, much can be positively written about the American education system. In the past 2 decades, school enrollment has steadily increased, the high school dropout rate has steadily decreased, and there has been a significant increase in basic math, reading, and writing skills scores. Yet in spite of these improvements there has been a marked decrease in the number of youth who report that their school curriculum is meaningful or relevant to their future and an increase in those who report that they are passive participants in the learning process and who report high levels of anger, boredom, and stress. Indeed, large scale studies find that a significant number of students report hating school or liking it very little (Huebner, Drane, & Valois, 2000). Thus, for all the academic gains that have been made, the school experiences of many children are often pessimistic at best and miserable at worst.

Noddings (2003) cogently argued that the seeming overemphasis on academic outcomes by school systems has largely come at the expense of understanding important affective and experiential factors. Such factors, which include school satisfaction, are believed necessary for the formation of positive school environments that would facilitate enjoyment in learning. To create such environments, several key attributes of positive schools assembled from the school satisfaction literature can be delineated and will be described for future recommendations.

First, there is a significant relationship between students who report elevated levels of school satisfaction and academic outcomes (e.g., Huebner & Gilman, 2006), underscoring the notion that positive school perceptions and achievement variables are interrelated rather than distinct. An evaluation of school satisfaction reports by individuals and across groups would provide useful information for school personnel to evaluate the overall psychological "health" of their schools. Such reports can easily be integrated into existing evaluation strategies that often rely on standardized scores to determine how well schools are meeting their academic goals. Yet standardized scores do little to address the ultimate goal of schools, which is to produce graduates who are productive, self-actualizing individuals throughout their life span. Assessing school satisfaction provides essential information in this regard, which can be used in both promotion and intervention strategies.

Second, the review of antecedents contributing to school satisfaction emphasizes the importance of supportive parent, teacher, and peer relationships. Indeed, the highest levels are reported by students who also report positive relationships with each group, indicating that parents, peers, and teachers add unique and significant variance to school satisfaction reports (DeSantis-King et al., 2006; Rosenfeld & Richman, 1999). That is, school satisfaction is lower if relationships with members of one of these three groups are unfavorable. Unfortunately, the relationship between parents and schools is less than optimal. These poor relationships may directly and indirectly influence a student's perception of his or her school experiences.

Third, although research remains in the beginning stages, the type of instructional method and tasks that are provided to students may influence levels of school satisfaction. It appears that school and classroom settings that emphasize instructional tasks that are appropriately challenging, interesting, and taught in group format (versus lecture) facilitate positive school perceptions. Csikszentmihalyi and Schneider (2000) provide useful recommendations pertinent to educational policy for secondary schools. These recommendations include the development of curricula that emphasize creativity and emotional intelligence and increased provision of instructional activities that are intellectually engaging (vs. passive), social in nature (e.g., activities with peers) and intrinsically motivating; underscoring the importance of lifelong learning for students, clarifying the links between time management and vocational preparation, and greater parental involvement in teenagers' lives.

Finally, schools that promote mastery learning goals and capitalize upon individual differences in personality, abilities, and interests also facilitate positive school experiences. In contrast to traditional efforts to "repair" what is either missing or broken in children, schools that promote elevated levels of school satisfaction focus their attention to students' unique personal strengths and environmental assets, in addition to their deficits. This situation applies not only to "normal" students but also to students with special needs and at-risk students. In the latter cases, the articulation of personal strengths and environmental supports can balance the identification of "pathology" so that such students can be perceived and educated in a more holistic manner. In this regard, students are treated as persons with unique strengths and characteristics, rather than being viewed simply as students with a "disability."

PERSONAL MINI-EXPERIMENTS

Increasing School Satisfaction in Students

In this chapter, we have shown how positive school satisfaction relates to a variety of academic and behavioral performance measures. Use a combination of your personal observations, input from significant others (e.g., parents, other school professionals), and self-report measures (e.g., measures of school satisfaction, school climate, positive and negative emotions) to monitor your students' sense of well-being in school. These assessments should be conducted at least once per academic semester for the entire academic year. Once the data are collected and examined, hold classroom discussions with the students to discuss the results and develop plans to improve the classroom climate. As appropriate, utilize individual student data to promote healthy individual student functioning and prevent the development of problems.

Recognize and Utilize Students' Unique Personal Strengths in the Classroom and at Home: Hold occasional parent conferences in which the purpose of the conference is to work with children and their parents to identify and recognize the child's individual differences, focusing on his or her areas of strength and interest. Develop individual action plans to facilitate the child's use of her or his strengths in school and at home. Develop specific strategies that reward (e.g., praise, privileges) students' efforts. For example, adopt a 5:1 ratio between providing rewards and providing negative evaluation. That is, five instances of praising a student when he or she displays a personal strength for every instance where the student needs to be corrected for a behavior. Anecdotal evidence indicates that the most positive classrooms adopt this 5:1 ratio, while the least positive classrooms provide far less positive feedback in relation to providing negative evaluations.

Provide Daily Acts of Kindness Toward Others: To foster positive peer relationships in the classroom and school, start each day with a morning group meeting in which the children are asked to think about one kind thing they can do for a peer during the day. Near the end of the day, hold another group meeting. Have the children describe briefly one act of kindness they performed during the day and reward appropriately.

Provide Frequent "Flow" Activities: Teach students to understand the concept of flow experiences. Set aside time each week for students experience a "flow activity" in the classroom. Facilitate student participation in personal flow experiences in other school setting as well (e.g., extracurricular activities, recess time). Discuss the importance of flow activities and their impact on student engagement, well-being, and academic functioning, encouraging students to thoughtfully plan, manage, and evaluate the extent of their flow experiences in a manner appropriate to their developmental level.

REFERENCES

Akos, P., & Galassi, J. P. (2004). Middle and high school transitions as viewed by students, parents, and teachers. *Professional School Counseling, 7,* 212–221.

Baker, J. A. (1998). The social context of school satisfaction among urban, low-income, African-American students. *School Psychology Quarterly, 13,* 25–44.

Baker, J. A., Dilly, L. J., Aupperlee, J. L., & Patil, S. A. (2003). The developmental context of school satisfaction: Schools as psychologically healthy environments. *School Psychology Quarterly, 18,* 206–221.

Bowen, G. L., Bowen, N. K., & Richman, J. M. (2000). School size and middle school students' perceptions of the school environment. *Social Work in Education, 22,* 69–82.

Carey, T. A., & Bourbon, W. T. (2005). Countercontrol: What do the children say? *School Psychology International, 26,* 595–615.

Cox, M. J., & Harter, K. S. M. (2003). Parent-child relationship. In M. H. Bornstein, L. Davidson, C. L. M. Keyes, & K. A. Moore (Eds.), *Well-being: Positive development across the life course* (pp. 191–204). Mahwah, NJ: Erlbaum.

Csikszentmihalyi, M., & Schneider, B. (2000). *Becoming adult: How teenagers prepare for the world of work.* New York: Basic Books.

Deci, E. L., & Ryan, R. M. (1985). *Intrinsic motivation and self-determination in human behavior.* New York: Plenum Press.

DeSantis-King, A., Huebner, E. S., Suldo, S. M., & Valois, R. F. (2006). An ecological view of school satisfaction in adolescence: Linkages between social support and behavior problems. *Applied Research in Quality of Life, 1,* 279–295.

Diener, E., (2000). Subjective well-being: The science of happiness and a proposal for a national index. *American Psychologist, 55,* 34–43.

Elmore, G. (2006). *The role of school satisfaction in moderating and mediating the relationship between attachment relationships and negative school behavior in adolescents.* Unpublished doctoral dissertation, University of South Carolina.

Epstein, J. L., & McPartland, J. M. (1976). The concept and measurement of the quality of school life. *American Education Research Journal, 13,* 15–30.

Evans, D. R. (1994). Enhancing the quality of life of the population at large. *Social Indicators Research, 33,* 47–88.

Gilman, R. (2001). The relationship between life satisfaction, social interest, and frequency of extracurricular activities among adolescent student. *Journal of Youth and Adolescence, 30,* 749–767.

Gilman, R., & Anderman, E. M. (2006a). Motivation and its relevance to school psychology: An introduction to the special issue. *Journal of School Psychology, 44,* 325–329.

Gilman, R., & Anderman, E. M. (2006b). The relationship between relative levels of motivation and intrapersonal, interpersonal, and academic functioning among older adolescents. *Journal of School Psychology, 44,* 375–391.

Gilman, R., & Huebner, E. S. (2003). A review of life satisfaction research with children and adolescents. *School Psychology Quarterly, 18,* 192–205.

Gilman, R., & Stacy, C. (2007). *Are all structured extracurricular activities meaningful?* Unpublished manuscript. University of Kentucky.

Gilman, R., Huebner, E. S., Tian, L., Park, N., O'Byrne, J., Schiff, M., et al. (in press). Cross-national adolescent multidimensional life satisfaction reports: Analyses of mean scores and response style differences. *Journal of Youth and Adolescence.*

Hegarty, S. (1994). Quality of school life. In D. Goode (Ed.), *Quality of life for persons with diabilities: International perspectives and issues* (pp. 241–250). Cambridge, MA: Brookline Books.

Huebner, E. S. (1991). Further validation of the Students' Life Satisfaction Scale: The independence of satisfaction and affect ratings. *Journal of Psychoeducational Assessment, 9,* 363–368.

Huebner, E. S. (1994). Preliminary development and validation of a multidimensional life satisfaction scale for children. *Psychological Assessment, 6,* 149–158.

Huebner, E. S. (2004). Research on assessment of life satisfaction of children and adolescents. *Social Indicators Research, 66,* 3–33.

Huebner, E. S., Drane, W., & Valois, R. F. (2000). Levels and demographic correlates of adolescent life satisfaction reports. *School Psychology International, 21,* 281–292.

Huebner, E. S., & Gilman, R. (2006). Students who like and dislike school. *Applied Research in Quality of Life, 1,* 139–150.

Huebner, E. S., Gilman, R., Reschly, A., & Hall, R. (in press). Positive schools. In S. Lopez (Ed.), *Handbook of positive psychology II.* Oxford: Oxford University Press.

Johnson, W. L., & Johnson, A. M. (1993). Validity of the Quality of School Life Scale: A primary and second-order factor analysis. *Educational and Psychological Measurement, 53*, 145–153.

Karatzias, A., Power, K. G., & Swanson, V. (2001). Quality of school life: Development and preliminary standardisation of an instrument based on performance indicators in Scottish secondary schools. *School Effectiveness and School Improvement, 12*, 265–284.

Kumar, R. (2006). Students' experiences of home-school dissonance: The role of school academic culture and perceptions of classroom goal structures. *Contemporary Educational Psychology, 31*, 253–279.

Ladd, G. W., Buhs, E. S., & Seid, M. (2000). Children's initial sentiments about kindergarten: Is school liking an antecedent of early classroom participation and achievement? *Merrill-Palmer Quarterly, 46*, 255–279.

Larson, R. W., & Verma, S. (1999). How children and adolescents spend their time across the world: Work, play, and developmental opportunities. *Psychological Bulletin, 125*, 701–736.

Locke, T. F., & Newcomb, M. D. (2004). Adolescent predictors or young adult and adult alcohol involvement and dysphoria in a prospective community sample of women. *Prevention Science, 5*, 151–168.

Mahoney, J. L., Cairns, B. D., & Farmer, T. W. (2003). Promoting interpersonal competence and educational success through extracurricular activity participation. *Journal of Educational Psychology, 95*, 409–418.

Marchand, G., & Skinner, E. A. (2007). Motivational dynamics of children's academic help-seeking and concealment. *Journal of Educational Psychology, 99*, 65–82.

Meece, J. L., Anderman, E. M., & Anderman, L. H. (2006). Classroom goal structure, student motivation, and academic achievement. *Annual Review of Psychology, 57*, 487–503.

Mok, M., & Flynn, M. (2002). Establishing longitudinal factorial construct validity of the Quality of School Life Scale for secondary students. *Journal of Applied Measurement, 3*, 400–420.

Noddings, N. (2003). *Happiness and education.* Cambridge: Cambridge University Press.

Pavot, W., & Diener, E. (1993). Review of the Satisfaction with Life Scale. *Psychological Assessment, 5*, 164–172.

Reynolds, C. R., & Kamphaus, R. W. (2004). *Manual for the Behavior Assessment System for Children* (2nd ed.). Circle Pines, MN: American Guidance Service.

Rosenfeld, L. B., & Richman, J. M. (1999). Supportive communication and school outcomes. Part II: Academically "at-risk" low income high school students. *Communication Education, 48*, 294–307.

Shernoff, D. J., Csikszentmihalyi, M., Schneider, B., & Shernoff, E. S. (2003). Student engagement in high school classrooms from the perspective of flow theory. *School Psychology Quarterly, 18*, 158–176.

Valle, M. F., Huebner, E. S., & Suldo, S. (2006). An analysis of hope as a psychological strength. Journal of School Psychology, 44, 393–406.

Verkuyten, M., & Thijs, J. (2002). School satisfaction of elementary school children: The role of performance, peer relations, ethnicity and gender. *Social Indicators Research, 59*, 203–228.

CHAPTER 6

Employee Engagement: How Great Managing Drives Performance

James K. Harter

THE ENGAGEMENT STORY OF BOB

The menu was pretty simple in 1958 when Bob was a short-order cook and waiter at McDonalds in Battle Creek, Michigan. For minimum wage, he and his coworkers sold 15-cent hamburgers, 19-cent cheeseburgers, fries, shakes, and cokes. The organization and its menu have expanded considerably in nearly 5 decades. But like young adults just out of high school today, a first job back then was mainly an economic transaction. This 18-year-old wasn't married and just wanted to make some money and spend time with his friends. This job was hardly a career. Bob enjoyed meeting and serving the guests at McDonalds, getting his job done right, and making some of his own money for the first time. Bob's first exposure to the world of management was positive. His manager made work expectations clear, kept the employees continually busy, cooking, serving, and cleaning. He even sat down with Bob and talked about opportunities in the future. As much as Bob could tell, the manager had a genuine concern for the employees he managed. But since this was Bob's first real job, he didn't really think much about the important qualities of great managing, and what impact that might have on his life. He wanted a job, and he wanted to improve his pay. And to day, he can't remember the name of that first manager. About 5 decades, three companies, three children, six grandchildren, and 45 years of marriage later, Bob found himself working in the electronics department of a home improvement store in Lincoln, Nebraska. He had retired from an auto manufacturer about 5 years earlier and had gone to work as a consultant for another auto manufacturer, and had then retired for good. Well, almost. About 6 months into retirement he became a little uneasy. His wife Sandy was still working, and he needed something to do. He didn't watch much TV and "you can only clean the same closet so many times," he said. Like many who enter into retirement, Bob found himself missing the sense of purpose and importance that work once provided, no matter the unnecessary struggles and hassles wrapped up within it.

The home improvement store was a good fit; it was close to his home and Bob was an avid do-it-yourselfer.... With the right retirement job, he could give other people advice on how to get their projects done. He applied for a job and was quickly hired, and then went through an extensive training regimen that lasted about 3 weeks, teaching him nearly everything about every department in the store (from lawn mowers to plants to TVs). He loved his work. He enjoyed the customers and got to know many of them quite well. From the little kids to the older folks, Bob loved to greet them, ask them about their day, tease them, hug them, and of course, help them find products. This reminded him of how much he enjoyed serving guests, even in his very first job, 50 years earlier. He liked helping out his coworkers at the checkout counter, when they needed a break. He had good relationships with many of the store managers. Bob felt he was doing something important, enjoyed doing it, and could see his impact on the success of the store.

Customer service was, of course, the store's mantra. Not unlike other businesses around the world, this organization said the right things. The corporate communication made it clear that the "customer comes first." Executives know their bread and butter, and their well-intended messages were effectively spread to the stores throughout the country, including the one Bob worked at in Lincoln.

And Bob believed in the importance of the message, because he had seen it firsthand throughout his career, including his last "pre-retirement" consulting job. After a long career at an automobile parts manufacturer, he had taken a consulting job with his brother-in-law, Johnny, who managed another automobile parts manufacturing organization. Bob's job had been to travel around the country to assist suppliers in processing, meeting timelines, financial obligations, and ultimately in meeting customer requirements.

Over the course of 5 years, he had met with a lot of suppliers and vendors. He could see the impact of each conversation on the end customer, either in meeting timelines or producing quality products. If the suppliers weren't getting the information or finances they needed from the company, they couldn't do what they needed to do, and the customers would eventually suffer. Bob also had seen the impact of each problem, however large or small it seemed from a distance, on the suppliers themselves. Many of the suppliers employed the majority of workers in small communities. And so they were dependent on the parts company for their own well-being.

As a consultant, Bob would sit down with each person and discuss problems that were causing inefficiencies. He quickly recognized that each supplier had their own unique issue, and that if he could help make each supplier more successful, it would ultimately make the business more successful. "Every issue is an individual issue—you just have to sit down and listen—each has a different solution," Bob had said. "These are good companies; we just need to help them out. Every day that I went to each facility, I tried to make their day. These companies' whole existence was based on supplying our company." By sitting down and listening to each supplier, and then responding, Bob had helped save them, and the company, millions of dollars. Bob had been amazed by how much could be discovered and resolved by simply listening to the needs of each supplier. And Johnny let him do what he needed to do to ultimately serve the customer, and their company.

These lessons weren't lost on Bob when he entered his "retirement job" at the "customer service focused" home improvement store. One afternoon Bob responded to a call from a customer from his usual station in the electronics department. Like many customers, this one did business in many departments throughout the store. The customer inquired about a product in the "lawn & garden" department. Bob listened to the customer, and, then rather than transferring the call to someone in lawn and garden, walked over, himself, to get the customer what she needed. But the next thing that happened stunned Bob. The store manager saw Bob walking outside his department and jumped to the conclusion that he must be slacking on his duties in electronics. As Bob walked by, rather than asking him what he was doing, or thanking him for his exemplary customer service, the store manager proceeded to page Bob's direct supervisor on the intercom to inquire as to why he was not doing his job. When confronted by his supervisor, Bob, of course, explained that he was helping a customer. He was doing what he thought was right for that customer. But such behavior didn't fit into the structure and accountability that had been built into the store by the store manager. The whole situation did not seem sensible to Bob and the part that irritated him the most was that, rather than stopping and asking *him*, the store manager paged his supervisor, subordinating his role and value to the organization.

As you can tell, Bob's store manager was strong on setting structure, and accountability, but weak on the human elements that often make the difference between serving customers effectively, or not. He put process ahead of service.

With the company vice president coming to the home improvement store in a few days, Bob noticed the increased attention to detail around the store. An unkempt area in one department was specifically targeted for cleanup prior to the VP's arrival, only left to return to clutter after his departure. Given his strong sense of ownership for the store's success and desire to serve customers, Bob asked his manager, "What did the vice president buy today?" His manager responded, "Nothing, but he *is* the vice president." Bob countered, "Now he leaves and we let it look sloppy again? Shouldn't everything we do be about the customer? Aren't they the ones that make this store successful?"

The store manager was soon promoted.

For Bob, the final straw came a few months later when a new store manager proved ineffective in managing his four supervisors, each operating with separate agendas, not in sync toward the common purpose of the store. This resulted in confusion for many employees who served multiple departments. Employees were directed to do things that might benefit one department but jeopardize the success of other departments. Merchandise often found itself in the wrong places. And something as simple as getting the shelves stocked on time each morning was compromised. The management solution was to have each employee sign a form that says "I will get the shelves stocked by 10 a.m. each morning," to insure each employee's commitment to this most basic task.

Bob's manager asked him to sign the form; it was a requirement. "When I tell you I am going to do something, I will do it … and I don't need to sign a form that says I'm going to do my job," Bob told his manager. It was degrading, dehumanizing, to want to come to work and help customers every day and have management get in the way. And to sign a form that says he will do something he already intended to do reminded Bob of the lack of trust he had witnessed in the battle between his union and supervisor in former work at an automobile manufacturing plant. Bob had a long history of quality work and customer service.

Many employees, maybe most, would have gone ahead and signed the form and went about their day. After repeatedly attempting to voice his opinion to management about how they were jeopardizing customer service, and company sales, Bob had enough. He resigned. He, of course, had a choice. He was retired and didn't have to work for financial reasons. But he also resigned because he knew there was a different side to management, and that he didn't have to tolerate the form of management he was experiencing. This was particularly unfortunate for the home improvement store, not to mention its customers. With unnecessarily high turnover rates and a lot of opportunity for work in most industries, many other employees make the same choice Bob made.

The good news for Bob was that he had many good management experiences in those 5 decades between McDonalds and the home improvement store. In fact, his best lessons about himself, and management, came in a 35-year career at an auto manufacturer, his third job. Having 20 different managers during his tenure, he learned a lot about different styles of managing, and eventually became a manager himself.

MANAGING ENGAGED EMPLOYEES

Bob moved from being "engaged" to "actively disengaged," in months, based on the quality of his encounters with management. I will continue with Bob's story a little later. But first, I want to describe how we, as scientists, can know which elements of great managing best describe high performing, engaged, cultures.

Each week contains 168 hours. For most people, more than half of our awake time is spent working. For most of us, several of the nonwork hours are spent either preparing for or commuting to work. And with e-mail, cell phones, and handheld computers, we are often reminded by our families that we are working when we are not at work. And so it should not be a surprise that the quality of our work experience contributes significantly to our overall well-being. But what makes a good work experience? What do most people expect from work? Over the past several decades, in more than 120 countries, Gallup has had a chance to study the quality of workplaces all over the world.

George Gallup studied human needs and satisfactions all over the world, starting in the 1930s. In the 1970s Gallup reported that less than half the people in North America were highly satisfied with their work lives (Gallup & Kettering, 1977). The percentages were even lower in other countries.

In addition to the polling work, Gallup researchers have spent decades studying what happens within organizations and the factors that drive their performance. During this time, they have conducted thousands of in-depth interviews with high performing managers and employees, in a wide range of occupations, industries, and countries. This research was originally led by Dr. Donald O. Clifton, a former professor and chairman of Gallup, and the "Father of Strengths-Based Psychology." The interviews by Gallup researchers led to the identification of factors that described the top performing teams and then questions were written to measure the factors. For the most part, surveys were written under the assumption that every organization is unique and needs its own survey questions. The surveys were very long and attempted to measure just about everything you might imagine, from pay and benefits to the organizational structure to perceptions of senior management.

In the early and mid-1990s researchers accumulated data from many long surveys across hundreds of organizations, literally thousands of questions. One of the findings was that the answer to what defines a productive work environment was much simpler than we originally thought was the case. We found there are some basic elements that consistently define high performing environments in any setting we had studied. The following are the 12 statements (called the Q12) that describe an engaging and productive culture:

Q01. I know what is expected of me at work.
Q02. I have the materials and equipment I need to do my work right.
Q03. At work, I have the opportunity to do what I do best every day.
Q04. In the last 7 days, I have received recognition or praise for doing good work.
Q05. My supervisor, or someone at work, seems to care about me as a person.
Q06. There is someone at work who encourages my development.
Q07. At work, my opinions seem to count.
Q08. The mission or purpose of my company makes me feel my job is important.
Q09. My associates or fellow employees are committed to doing quality work.
Q10. I have a best friend at work.
Q11. In the last 6 months, someone at work has talked to me about my progress.
Q12. This last year, I have had opportunities at work to learn and grow.[1]

The statements start with very basic employee perceptions that are often overlooked. Knowing what's expected, for instance, is the most basic employee perception you can ask about, and act on. Yet only a little over half of employees in Gallup's large international database clearly know what is expected of them at work. This most basic perception is often overlooked. The 12 statements measure basic needs (Q01, Q02), individual contribution (Q03–Q06), belonging (Q07–Q10), and growth (Q11, Q12). Wagner and Harter (2006) present research and practical application of each the 12 elements.

Employee engagement is defined as the *involvement with* and *enthusiasm for* work (Harter, in press; Harter, Schmidt, & Hayes, 2002). As William

Kahn (1990) described, engagement is best understood through the day-to-day experiences employees have within their work situation. Employees can become engaged when they find meaning in their work, feel safe to do good work, and can then transfer their energy into performance. Engaged employees are both cognitively and emotionally connected to their work and workplace. Employees become involved in their work when their basic needs are met consistently, and when they have a chance to make an individual contribution.

In addition to the fulfillment that comes from being in the right job and getting recognized for good work, employees that feel connected to their coworkers and the larger organization, and those that can clearly see their future in their work, have high levels of enthusiasm, or positive emotional energy. Engaged employees use their discretionary effort to help their organization improve through higher productivity, greater efficiency and innovation, and more meaningful customer impact, leading to higher profitability. Disengaged employees withhold effort or withdraw from the organization, thus jeopardizing the organization's future through higher absenteeism, higher turnover rates, more theft or merchandise shrinkage, and more accidents on the job. The Q12 have now been responded to by more than 10 million employees in 124 countries around the globe.

As we were studying the data across companies, we found something quite interesting. Companies were certainly different in how satisfied and committed their employees were, in aggregate. But when we sliced the data across teams within companies, we found some of the best run companies had some poorly committed teams, at the bottom of our overall database. We also found some of the worst run companies had some highly committed teams, at the top of our database. There was wide variation within every company we studied, across manager-led teams. Mapping the data to the team level took some work, but it was well worth it, because it revealed variation in its most critical place ... the local level, where managers have great influence. Rather than finding a common company culture, we found there were almost as many cultures as there were managers ... tremendous variation in employee opinions across manager-led teams.

The Gallup database has employee engagement data mapped for work units (such as teams or departments) or business units (such as stores, restaurants, or bank branches). Many of these business units also have performance data (such as profitability, productivity, customer ratings, employee turnover, safety records, absenteeism, and theft or lost merchandise) that can be studied alongside the employee engagement data. This allows us to study the relationship between employee engagement and performance within companies and then to pool those data across companies using a statistical technique called meta-analysis (Hunter & Schmidt, 2004). And what we found was that business or work units that have a critical mass of engaged employees also tend to be in work units that perform better on all of the metrics listed above. We've had a chance to repeat this analysis six times, most recently across 125 companies, and 23,910 independent teams or business units (Harter, Schmidt, Killham, & Asplund, 2006). The results have led us to essentially the same conclusion each time—that employee engagement is related to work unit performance and has great practical value, if understood and applied correctly.

A separate meta-analysis, across thousands of employees, found a substantial correlation between individual job satisfaction and performance (Judge, Thoresen, Bono, & Patton, 2001). As you might expect, the 12 engagement items listed above correlate highly with job satisfaction (Harter et al., 2002) and other important work attitudes (Le, Schmidt, Lauver, & Harter, 2007) such as passion, dedication, commitment, and absorption in work (Schaufeli, Bakker, & Salanova, 2006).

Just because work attitudes *correlate* with performance doesn't mean they *cause* performance. By collecting data across time, we've also been able to statistically test two different causal scenarios. Scenario 1 tests whether employee engagement predicts future performance. Scenario 2 tests whether performance predicts future employee engagement. The research to this date suggests Scenario 1 is more valid than Scenario 2 (Harter, Schmidt, Asplund, & Killham, 2004).

Employee engagement predicts performance. But wide variation in engagement exists across manager-led teams in nearly any organization we study for the first time, with some teams at the very top of our database, some teams at the very bottom of our database, and a lot of teams in the middle (the typical bell shaped curve you may be familiar with from your statistics classes). This pattern is ideal for researchers (because we love to study variance), but it is terrible for organizations (because it means the culture is not constant, and thus less predictable). While organizations may have reduced the variation on operational elements, they have often overlooked the human elements. But why does so much variation exist within companies, across manager-led teams? The reason has something to do with how people have been put into management roles historically, and how people management has been valued within organizations. The problem also stems from how we have historically valued (or not valued) non-management positions. Historically, managers have earned their right to manage through promotion due primarily to two factors: tenure within the company, and success in a prior, nonmanagement job. Since management is viewed as a senior position hierarchically, and often compensated as such, most employees aspire to be a manager. And so there are many successful sales people, engineers, analysts, accountants (among many other nonmanagement roles) who end up with stewardship over the company's "greatest assets." Some become successful managers, but most don't.

You might notice, as you look through the 12 engagement items, that they all represent elements that can be influenced and improved on. In fact, organizations that focus on measuring the 12 elements, while providing good education for managers and holding them accountable, often double the number of top quartile work units, over time. Top quartile business units outperform their bottom quartile counterparts by 12% on profit, and 18% on productivity. Bottom quartile units have 30–50% higher turnover, 62% more accidents on the job, and 51% more theft on average (Harter et al., 2006).

Not all managers improve the engagement of their employees, and some aren't suited psychologically for managing people. But measurement and education can create awareness and change for many. The average organization has about two engaged employees for every actively disengaged employee. But due to the heavy downward tug of the disengaged employees, two to one is not enough. Publicly traded organizations, for instance, that double that ratio (four to one), have achieved 18% greater earnings per share than their competitors and a growth trajectory that is 2.6 times greater than below average engagement organizations, who have closer to one engaged employee for every actively disengaged employee (The Gallup Organization, 2006).

BACK TO BOB

Bob's varied experiences in the organizations parallel the general pattern seen in workplaces throughout the world. Most organizations have well-intended corporate messages about what they want to get done … their purpose or mission. But what impacts workers every day is what they experience locally, and this has a lot to do with their immediate manager.

About a year into his first job, at McDonald's, Bob took an entry level job with a local insurance company where his brother, Richard, worked. He was paid to be a clerk, distributing business forms and taking orders from customers. During this time, he and Sandy got married and focused on making a good living for their family. Like his first job, his first manager in the insurance company, Norm, took the time to get to know him, helped think about his future. Bob got to know Norm and his family quite well, and he enjoyed the closeness of the relationship. Bob didn't know it at the time, but he was leading a charmed life, as he was two for two in getting a good manager in his early career. Based on our research, Bob was defying the odds. But, like gambling in Vegas, the winning streak wouldn't continue.

Looking to advance within the insurance company, he put in for a promotion and was relocated to the home office where he had opportunities for better pay and career advancement. His job was to provide quotes on insurance accounts in addition to some odd jobs in other departments. While he was beginning to advance in his status at the insurance firm, he was also advancing in exposure to the wide variety of management styles he would come across in his career. Contrary to his previous supervisors, his new manager, Jack, was "stand-offish," and had the philosophy that "if you don't hear from me, you are doing your job" … basically, "no news is good news." Bob got the sense that Jack was filling time until retirement. The door was never open to have discussions with him, a stark contrast from his previous experiences. Bob recalls the relationship being "all about work … he didn't really show much confidence in us." He doesn't recall much, if any, recognition from Jack. Bob and his fellow employees would often "work the manager over a little" when he wasn't around.

And so it shouldn't be a surprise that Bob jumped at an opportunity to work for a local automobile manufacturer, a large international organization, employing more than 44,000 workers. It was an entry level job, but promised a 30% increase in pay and good benefits. This local unionized plant employed about 1,200 workers in the area. Bob worked on the "floor" for 16 years, rotating among various jobs and shifts. For about 5 years he helped manufacture engine valves. Bob recalls a time when he had difficulty forging the valves and they continued to crack, even after considerable effort on his part. He went to his supervisor, Lou, to explain the situation, because he wanted to do good work. Lou was a well-liked person but may not have been the right fit for management. In classic company-union speak Lou said "the only reason you are coming to me is that you don't want to work." And so Bob did his best work and reluctantly sent the parts through. The next day, Bob received a "work-back" tag with his name on it labeled "insufficient." One of his coworkers, Norm, a veteran of 25 years, was doing the same job. Norm was accustomed to the relationship between company representatives and union employees and had reached a point of "learned helplessness," and no longer cared about the quality of the products. He would send his parts through, even if deficient. Norm found it was easier not to raise a fuss about parts deficiencies, because Lou didn't seem to care one way or another, unless it inconvenienced Norm. They were both putting in their time. There came a point, down the road, when the company had to take deficient parts seriously, because the automobile company they were manufacturing the parts for eventually rejected all of them and told them they had to be corrected immediately. Bob, a regular guy on "the floor," had discovered the problem, but no one wanted to listen. Management didn't take the issue seriously until a crisis occurred. Fixing all these deficient parts led to a major financial burden on the company, which impacted various budget items, including pay and benefits. In the late 1970s the union went on strike. The company temporarily gave the union what it wanted and then eventually had major layoffs. Bob was one of the victims.

This was a turning point in Bob's career. He noticed the contrast between him and Norm, and as he described it, "if you take something to your boss and he doesn't listen or care, you begin to stop caring too." In this case, it affected the fate of hundreds of workers. It bothered Bob that they didn't care. And he started believing there had to be something better. Bob was only laid off for 5 days, but it was the first time in his life when panic started to set in. He had a wife and three kids by this time and it "scared the hell out of me," he said later. He wasn't going to let someone like Lou affect his job and the future of his company. He saw how much one poor manager could destroy things for so many people.

After the layoff, Bob's new boss was Mike. Whether by providence or pure chance, Bob was given a manager who was very different from Lou and many of the other managers he had worked with over the years. "Mike knew how to have fun at work. He was a happy person," Bob described, "we laughed at a lot of things, but we were also a team, where people had different roles, responsibilities, where each person was important." Bob's analogy, given his Michigan heritage, was a football team where some were blockers, a quarterback, a running back ... with each person knowing their role on the team. Mike organized everyone at the start of each day and "got us going," Bob said, "he got us in a group huddle and made us feel like a team, that what we were doing as a team was important and had a purpose." "Mike liked me," Bob explained, "he had talks with me along the way and asked me whether I had ever thought about being a supervisor, and then he came to me one day and said they're going to offer you a supervisory job ... and you'd better take it.'" Bob knew that Mike had been looking out for him and, behind his back, talking to upper management about his potential, getting him this opportunity. But Bob was a long-time union member, and he believed in the union. He didn't like how supervisors were disliked by union members. He had built close relationships with his fellow employees and was hesitant to take a supervisory job. Eventually, with Mike's coaxing, Bob got to the point where he knew he had to take the initiative himself. He had to be an active player in making a difference and couldn't sit back and watch another supervisor do what he had seen Lou do before. "I think Mike saw I had some leadership, that I could make things happen and make friends," said Bob.

And so Bob got his first taste of supervising for a year and a half until, after union negotiations, the plant closed and he was eventually repositioned to another plant in Nebraska where he would spend 18 years. But those 18 months were some of the most valuable Bob had experienced. "Mike would mentor me along the way. We had morning meetings where we shared thoughts and ideas, and he gave me direction," explained Bob, "Mike and I were on the same level, but he was still my mentor. Early on, I kept asking our boss, Tom, what I should do next, because I was new, and second guessing myself. Mike gave me some good advice. He told me they are paying you to be the supervisor, you need to do what's best for the company.'" That gave Bob the push to create his own style of managing, rather than try to follow a set of prescribed steps. The outcome he was working toward was clear. Do what is best for the company. The union people he managed were his best friends. He had fun with them, picked on them, teased them, and even hugged them. They did things for Bob because they liked him. But it was more than having fun. If one of his employees needed something, a machine repaired, some fine tuning of equipment, whatever was getting in their way, Bob would write the order and chase it down to be sure they got what they needed. In some situations, he had to work the internal politics to get his employees what they needed. He pushed until he could get them what they needed. "If you do something good for your people, they'll do something good for you," he explained.

He spent the first 4 years in Nebraska as a technician and engineer, given his knowledge of the manufacturing process and the organization's products. After a lot of success in that role, he was offered another supervisory job. This time there was no hesitation. Supervising gave Bob a lot of gratification. He took initiative to inspect the machines and expected his employees to do the same. He expected his employees to question the current process, to evaluate its efficiency. He held many discussions with them about improving the current processes, and over time, "they took charge and did it all themselves," Bob said. During his 9 years of supervision at the plant in Nebraska, his team saved about $500,000 in tooling and increased productivity from 182,000 to 350,000 valves per day, at the same cost. Bob attributes this to the ownership his employees had for their own performance and that of their organization. They took pride in their work, and knew their work was important. Needless to say, his employees were engaged. And their company was better *because* their lives were better. This had something to do with what Bob did for them, and years earlier, what Mike did for Bob.

PERSONAL MINI-EXPERIMENTS

Being and Becoming an Engaged Employee

In this chapter, you read about the role of managers in employee engagement. Take some time to learn about engagement and good managing by conducting informational interviews with a family member and a manager at your favorite business.

Interview an Engaged Employee: What do you really know about the work lives of your loved ones? Take some time to learn more about the work of a family member and about employee engagement by sitting down and asking the following questions.

- Of all the work you have done, what gave you the most positive energy?
- When you have good days at work, what are the contributing factors?
- What makes you feel successful at work?
- How can you use your strengths to positively impact the performance of your coworkers?
- How do you continually clarify what you are expected to do in your work?
- What do your best friends at work do well, and how do they like to be recognized?
- Who do you want to recognize you when you do good work?

Interview an Engaging Manager: Emerging research suggests that a high quality workplace is associated with health and overall well-being. It is clear that engagement at work is important to organizations, but it is also important to the overall quality of life for individuals. Identify a manager at one of your favorite businesses who you believe is good to his or her employees. Ask the manager three or four good questions about how they foster the well-being and health of their employees.

Future Work Fantasy: Just take a few minutes and imagine you spending a day at your dream job. Begin by shutting off all media and becoming as relaxed as possible. Then, just let your mind wander through a full day at work. How are you being your best at work? Who is supporting you at work? How are you being acknowledged for a job well done?

NOTE

1. Each of the Q12(R) statements are proprietary. They cannot be reprinted or reproduced in any manner without the written consent of Gallup. Copyright © 1993–1998 Gallup, Inc., Washington, DC. All rights reserved.

REFERENCES

Gallup G., & Kettering, C. F. (1979). *Human needs and satisfactions: A global survey.* Omaha, NE: Charles F. Kettering Foundation & Gallup International Research Institutes.

The Gallup Organization (2006). *Engagement predicts earnings per share.* Omaha, NE: Author.

Harter, J. K. (in press). Employee Engagement. In S. J. Lopez (Ed.) *The Encyclopedia of Positive Psychology.*

Harter, J. K., Schmidt, F. L., Asplund, J. W., & Killham, E. A. (2005). *Employee engagement and performance: A meta-analytic study of causal direction.* Omaha, NE: The Gallup Organization.

Harter, J. K., Schmidt, F. L., & Hayes, T. L. (2002). Business-unit-level relationship between employee satisfaction, employee engagement, and business outcomes: A meta-analysis. *Journal of Applied Psychology, 87,* 2.

Harter, J. K., Schmidt, F. L., Killham, E. A., & Asplund, J. W. (2006). *Q12 meta-analysis.* Omaha, NE: The Gallup Organization.

Hunter, J. E., & Schmidt, F. L. (2004). *Methods of meta-analysis: Correcting error and bias in research findings* (2nd ed.). Newbury Park, CA: Sage.

Judge, T. A., Thoresen, C. J., Bono, J. E., & Patton, G. K. (2001). The job satisfaction–job performance relationship: A qualitative and quantitative review. *Psychological Bulletin, 127,* 376–407.

Kahn, W. A. (1990). Psychological conditions of personal engagement and disengagement at work. *Academy of Management Journal, 33,* 692–724.

Le, H., Schmidt, F. L., Lauver, K., & Harter, J. K. (2007). *Empirical re-examinations of the relationships between the constructs underlying measures of job attitudes.* Omaha, NE: The Gallup Organization.

Schaufeli, W. B., Bakker, A. B., & Salanova, M. (2006). The measurement of work engagement with a short questionnaire—A cross national study. *Educational and Psychological Measurement, 66,* 701–716.

Wagner, R., & Harter, J. K. (2006). *12: The elements of great managing.* Washington, DC: Gallup Press.

CHAPTER 7

Families That Work

John Eagle

T here is not one formula for developing and maintaining families that work. First of all, all families have strengths. Healthy functioning families exist in many different compositions, cultures, and interaction styles. Just looking around at your neighbors' or friends' families is an indication of this; no two families are the same. However, there are common characteristics of families that function well. In general, families that have found a balance between structure and flexibility tend to be families that support family members' emotional, physical, social, and educational development. These families also tend to be more resilient during challenging times.

In the past families were typically viewed with respect to the "traditional" family, complete with two biological parents and consisting of one parent in the workforce and the other in a caregiver role. However, during the past few decades, the landscape of the family structure has changed dramatically. The United States has seen a decrease in the "traditional" family. It is now being replaced with an ever-increasing diverse family structure. The population of children living with two parents has decreased significantly since 1980. There has been an increase in single-parent and step-parent families, which, in turn, may place children from these families at a greater risk for lower academic achievement, dropping out of school, teenage pregnancy, and mental health concerns such as anxiety, depression, and aggression (Fields, Smith, Bass, & Lugaila, 2001; McLanahan & Sandefur, 1994). The proportion of single-parent families headed by women more than doubled between the years of 1960 and 1988 (Carlson, 1996), and grandparents are playing a larger role as caregivers, even when a parent is present (Fields, 2003).

The cultural climate of the American family has also changed over the years. In 2004, 59 percent of children were identified as White, non-Hispanic; 30 percent lived in households that did not include two biological/adoptive parents; 17 percent lived in a blended family; 12 percent had at least one half-sibling; and 17 percent lived in poverty (Kreider, 2007). Given the challenges associated with discrimination, differing family structures, language barriers, and poverty, it is critical that resilience and well-being in children and families be promoted consistently.

To appropriately present the qualities of families that work, it is first best to depict how family functioning is viewed by clinicians and researchers. Family functioning is typically conceptualized within both a systems and developmental framework. Family systems theory conceptualizes the family as a complex composition made up of interdependent groups of individuals who (a) have a mutual sense of history, (b) experience a degree of emotional bonding, and (c) develop strategies for meeting the needs of individual family members and the family as a whole (Anderson & Sabatelli, 1995). Although the family is considered a single unit, the unit is comprised of individual family members. Additionally, the family unit is affected by the interactions between individual family members. Within the family system, positive or negative interactions between individual members have significant effects upon all other member of the family, both young and old.

There is only one hard and fast rule about families; they change over time. Throughout the years, families change with respect to family composition, age of family members, family characteristics (e.g., economic or social status), and environmental factors (e.g., location). Due to this, family functioning is often looked at according to a developmental, or life-cycle, orientation. Characteristics of healthy functioning families differ based on where the family exists along the developmental continuum. For example, a family with two toddlers operates and interacts in a different manner than a family with two children heading off to college. In a similar vein, there are different expectations for healthy functioning in families that are facing crises, loss, or grief and those who are not. A developmental perspective views healthy family functioning based on the developmental context, or the current situation. In this way a family's ability to function effectively is a multifaceted process occurring over time and developed in response to complex and changing conditions (Walsh, 2003).

MODELS OF FAMILY FUNCTIONING

Although there are several different theories or models of family functioning, three of the more prevalent are discussed below. All of these models are based on a systems approach to family functioning.

One of the most renowned theories is the McMaster Model of Family Functioning, developed by Epstein and colleagues (2003). The McMaster Model has been evolving and evaluated over the past 30 years. According to this model, the primary function of the family is to provide an environment that supports the physical, social, and emotional development of family members. Within the McMaster Model are six dimensions of family functioning that determine the family structure, organization, and transactional patterns. These dimensions include problem solving, communication, roles, affective responsiveness, affective involvement, and behavior control. Healthy family functioning is not represented by one sole dimension; rather, many dimensions are needed to represent the complexity of functioning families.

Similarly, the Circumplex Model of Marital and Family Systems (Olson & Gorall, 2003) has been developed and researched over the past 25 years. Three dimensions of family functioning are represented in the Circumplex Model: family cohesion, flexibility, and communication. The level of cohesion, flexibility, and communication describes both the nature of interactions within the family system and between family members and the larger community. Not only do these dimensions provide insight into family dynamics, but they also have implications for how community members can support and strengthen the family unit. Within cohesion and flexibility dimensions of the model, balanced or moderate levels (versus extreme levels) are associated with more optimal functioning. Positive communication skills allow families to modify their levels of cohesion and flexibility based on the demands of the situation or developmental context.

The Beavers Systems Model of Family Functioning, as described by Beavers and Hampson (2000), provides a cross-sectional approach to family functioning. In this model family functioning falls along two dimensions: family competence and family style. Family competence refers to the structure, available information, and adaptive flexibility of the family system. High levels of family competence require both structure and the ability to adapt the structure to meet the needs of family members. Family style relates to a stylistic quality of interactions within the family unit. Healthier functioning is associated with families that place importance on their relationships both within and outside the family.

RESILIENCE IN FAMILIES

It is almost impossible to talk about families that work without discussing the notion of resilience within families. Resilience refers to how well families adapt to situations or address crises. Patterson (2002b) defined resilience as the process of successfully overcoming adversity. Historically, the notion of resilience solely focused upon individuals and individual factors associated with adaptive adjustment, such as personality traits and coping strategies (Walsh, 1996). Gradually, the concept of resilience was expanded to include larger social constructs, such as families and communities (Patterson, 2002a).

A resilient family is one that values itself as a collective unit, has a common set of values, communicates effectively, responds successfully to changing conditions or crises, and solves problems collaboratively. For example, families demonstrate resilience by effectively functioning in the face of family crises, including parental job loss, relocation to a different region of the country, parental divorce, chronic medical conditions of a family member, or death of a family member. The idea that families bond together after facing a crisis is connected with the concept of family resilience.

The concept of family resilience recognizes not only key processes that help families address persistent challenges but also those that strengthen the family unit. In this way, family resilience enables the family to foster resilience in all individual members (Walsh, 1996). Family resilience is exemplified by (a) rising in the face of hardship, (b) returning to previous levels of functioning, and (c) being viewed in terms of wellness versus pathology (Hawley & DeHaan, 1996).

In many circles resilience is almost synonymous with, or at least very closely tied to, family functioning. That is, the more resilient a family is, the better it functions. Every family faces adversity at one point or another, thus resilience is a characteristic of every family. In fact this is a core aspect of positive psychology with respect to families; how do families utilize their strengths to function effectively and adapt to adverse situations?

The concept of family resilience is made up of several different family characteristics that are described below.

Family Cohesion

Family cohesion is defined as "family members' close emotional bonding with each other as well as the level of independence they feel within the family system" (Turnbull & Turnbull, 1997, p. 108). The degree of emotional connectedness varies significantly between and within families and is influenced by the culture, age, and stage of life of the family members.

Olson and Gorall (2003) presented a continuum for family cohesion, ranging from *enmeshed/overly connected* (very high), to *very connected* (moderate to high), to *connected* (moderate), to *somewhat connected* (moderate to low) to *disengaged/disconnected* (very low). An enmeshed style of interaction is characterized by overidentification with the family, resulting in extreme levels of consensus and limited individual autonomy and independence. At this level of cohesion loyalty is demanded and individuals are very dependent upon each other. Disengaged families are marked by high autonomy and low bonding, in which there is little attachment to the family system. Along with this independence comes an inability to receive support from other family members.

Within Olson's model of cohesion there are three "balanced" levels of cohesion and two "unbalanced" levels. Family functioning in enhanced when there is a balance between enmeshment and disengagement. Thus, the three central levels (somewhat connected, connected, and very connected) are considered to provide optimal family functioning across the life-cycle. Balanced levels of cohesion indicate a family in which individuals experience both separateness and togetherness. There is no one "best" level of cohesion, but families that exist at the extremes (e.g., enmeshed, disengaged) tend to have more difficulties over time.

Family Involvement

Affective involvement, as defined by Epstein and colleagues (2003), refers to the extent to which family members value and display interest in the activities of other family members. An emphasis is placed on the amount of interest as well as the manner in which family members demonstrate their interest and investment in each other. Family involvement exists on a continuum, ranging from lack of involvement to overinvolvement. The lowest level, *lack of involvement*, indicates a complete absence of interest in other members of the family. The second level, *involvement devoid of feelings*, represents some involvement among family members, but it is typically intellectual in nature. The third level, *narcissistic involvement*, refers to a degree of interest among family members, but only to the degree that it reflects on oneself. The fourth, and optimal level, *empathetic involvement*, depicts a genuine interest; family members are invested for the sake of others in the family unit. The development of healthy functioning in families is enhanced through empathetic family involvement practices. Level five, *overinvolvement*, represents an excessive degree of interest among family members. A *symbiotic involvement*, the most extreme level of involvement, indicates an interest that is so extreme that there is a marked difficulty distinguishing one family member from another (Epstein et al., 2003).

Family Adaptability and Flexibility

Every family faces situations throughout the course of life that present challenges to the manner in which family members relate to one another or how the family unit functions within the community. Although related to resilience, family adaptability differs from resilience in that it does not encompass the characteristics and qualities of families necessary to strengthen the family unit. In other words, a family may be adaptive and flexible, but that does not ensure effective communication, collaborative problem solving, and strong family unity, all of which are also components of family resilience.

Olson and Gorall (2003) indicated that families have differing degrees of adaptability falling along a continuum from *rigid/inflexible* (extremely low) to *somewhat flexible* (low to moderate) to *flexible* (moderate) to *very flexible* (moderate to high) to *chaotic/overly flexible* (extremely high). Similar to the construct of family cohesion, moderate, or "balanced" degrees of adaptability (e.g., somewhat flexible, flexible, very flexible) may allow for healthier degrees of family functioning than those on the extremes (e.g., rigid or chaotic).

A *somewhat flexible* relationship between family members tends to follow a democratic leadership with stable roles, some role sharing, enforced rules, and few rule changes. A *flexible* relationship provides a leadership that believes in the equality of all members and with decision making that is democratic. Thus, children also have a say in family decision making. Family roles are fluid and shared, and rules can be changed based on the developmental needs of the family. A relationship that is *very flexible* is characterized by frequent changing in leadership and family roles. Rules are often changed and are very flexible based on the needs of the family.

In contrast, "unbalanced" levels of flexibility depict families that are too stable or too fluid. *Rigid* families consist of one dominant leader who is always in charge. Leadership roles do not change, and there is very limited negotiation within family decision making. Family rules are explicit and do not change. Chaotic families have inconsistent or limited leadership and provide impulsive decision making. Family roles are not well defined, and rules differ from family member to family member.

To function as a healthy system, families must be both adaptive and stable. The ability to determine when it is appropriate to maintain stability or address change is a characteristic of healthy, functional families. Such families are both proactive in the development of individual family members and also understand the importance of maintaining the family unit.

Parenting Styles and Problem-Solving Processes

Family functioning is related to the family's parenting styles and problem-solving skills. The interactions between parents and children often serve as a model for the family's overall style and ability to communicate and problem-solve. Walsh (2003) reported that family functioning benefits from collaborative problem-solving that includes shared decision making among family members, is goal-oriented, follows concrete steps, and builds on successes.

Parenting style refers to "a constellation of attitudes toward the child that are communicated to the child and that, taken together, create an emotional climate in which the parents' behaviors are expressed" (Darling & Steinberg, 1993, p. 493). Diana Baumrind (1991) identified four main types of parenting styles: authoritarian, authoritative, neglectful, and indulgent.

The *authoritarian* parenting style is restrictive and punitive. It is characterized by high levels of authority and control, with limited negotiation regarding standards of behavior. This is often exemplified by a parent indicating "Do it my way, or it's the highway." Strict limits are placed on children, and there is very limited discussion between parents and children regarding the fairness of rules. Authoritarian parenting is associated with children who have decreased social and communication skills, have difficulty initiating activity, and are more anxious about social comparisons (Santrock, 2007).

Parents using an *uninvolved* parenting style are neglectful with their children's activities and lives. Neglectful parents allow children to regulate their own activities, standards, and rules, with few decisions imposed by caregivers. Children of uninvolved parents are more likely to have poor self-control, are less motivated by achievements, and have difficulty handling independence well (Santrock, 2007).

Indulgent parenting depicts style of parenting in which parents are extremely involved in the lives of their children. These parents provide support but do not place a great deal of restrictions or limits on their children's activities or behaviors. Often, parents utilizing this parenting style believe that this environment will foster creativity and independence in their children. However, children of indulgent parents are not placed in an environment in which they learn to control their own behavior (Santrock, 2007).

Authoritative parenting, considered the optimal parenting style for healthy family functioning, is marked by a balance between freedom and responsibility. Parents adopting this style engage family members in problem-solving processes to negotiate compromise and manage conflict. These parents are nurturing and limiting at the same time. There is often a verbal give-and-take and learning process associated with this style of parenting. This type of parenting fosters social competence, higher levels of self-esteem, and more appropriate decision making in children (Santrock, 2007).

Shared Beliefs and Values

Another critical component for the development of healthy family functioning is the establishment of a shared belief system within the family. Shared values and beliefs are essential for family resilience and reinforce specific patterns regarding how a family reacts to new situations, life events, and crises (Walsh, 1996). A common belief system assists families in making meaning of crisis events and facilitates hope and a positive outlook. The concept of shared beliefs appears in the literature under similar constructs, including family schema, family worldview, and family coherence.

A strong family schema represents a belief in the family unit that views its interactions with the world from a collective "we" versus "I" orientation. Families with a strong schema, as discussed by McCubbin and colleagues (1993), are likely to perceive life in a realistic manner and not expect perfect solutions to the difficulties that life presents. Families with higher levels of resilience have a shared set of values regarding the critical components of life, such as time management and financial issues. Additionally, resilient families have a shared worldview of confidence that the outcomes of situations will be positive (McCubbin, Thompson, Thompson, Elver, & McCubbin, 1994).

Family Communication

Effective communication among family members is another critical characteristic of families that work. How family members communicate with each other either verbally or nonverbally impacts the functioning of the family. Family communication not only refers to how family members present information but also how they attend, listen, and receive information from other members. There are two categories of family communication: instrumental and affective (Epstein et al., 2003). Instrumental communication represents an exchange of factual information between one another.

Affective communication refers to how family members express their emotions to each other. Both are critical for effective family communication.

Within instrumental and affective communication there are four styles of communication have been described by Epstein and colleagues (2003): clear and direct, clear and indirect, masked and direct, and masked and indirect. These styles of communication differ based on their position on two continuums: clear versus masked and direct versus indirect. Clear communication is straightforward and easily understood by family members. Content provided through masked communication is difficulty to comprehend and confusing. Direct communication is presented specifically to the intended recipient; whereas, indirect communication is not clearly directed to the person intended. These communication styles are associated with both instrumental and affective communication,

Clear and Direct Communication

This is the most effective manner for families to communicate with each other. In this communication style, the content of the message is plainly stated and directed at the person it was intended for. An example of this is when a father says to his son "I am upset that you missed curfew, but let's get you to bed." As communication styles become more masked and indirect, family communication becomes less effective.

Clear and Indirect Communication

In this case the message remains plainly stated but the intended person is not the recipient. Following the example, this would occur when a father says to his wife while their son is present, "I am upset with our son because he missed curfew."

Masked and Direct Communication

This communication style presents a muddled and confusing message directly to the intended recipient. Using our example, this would occur when a father says to his son "Are you okay? It seems like you had some difficulty getting home."

Masked and Indirect Communication

This represents the least effective family communication style. In this case not only is the message muddled and confusing but it is also not directed towards the intended family member. To conclude with our example, this would occur when a father says to his wife while his son is present, "People who miss curfews are obnoxious."

Communication styles associated with healthy family functioning include clear, direct, and honest communication, active listening, and positiveness.

Peterson & Green (1999) identified key strategies for families to use that will increase the effectiveness of their communication. These include: (a) communicate frequently, (b) communicate clearly and directly, (c) be an active listener, (d) think about the person with whom you are communicating, (e) pay attention to nonverbal messages, and (f) be positive.

Characteristics of Television Families

Although not always the best representation of American families, television has provided us with a wide variety of examples of functioning families. The Wilder family from the television show *Little House on the Prairie* and the Salingers from the 1990s television show *Party of Five* are examples of families that demonstrate the characteristics of resilience and adaptability. Set in the Midwest prairie during the late 1800s, the Wilders faced many hardships, including medical, environmental, and economic crises. However, though these crises the family was able to maintain its ability to function as an effective family unit; thus demonstrating great resilience.

Similarly, the Salinger family, comprised of five children orphaned when their parents died in a car crash, provided a profile of a family that showed adaptability. In this case, the older siblings took up the familial roles previously held by the children's parents after their parents' death. This adaptability of familial roles was clearly depicted as the five siblings functioned as a family unit without any other external support. The family operated in a democratic fashion with specific roles and leadership shared among the siblings in a flexible fashion that was neither rigid nor constantly changing.

Cliff and Clair Huxtable from *The Cosby Show* are examples of an authoritative parenting style that uses clear and direct communication. These parents provided their children with clear boundaries and effectively set limits. However, they also allowed their children to have some say in the family rules as was developmentally appropriate. The Huxtables' communication style consisted of explicit expectations and clear meanings and included a process for checking with their children for understanding.

The Walkers from the recent show *Brothers and Sisters* characterize a family that has a strong family schema. This family approaches all aspects of life with a "we" versus "I" approach. The family unit is what is most important to them. This family schema is so strong that in-laws, or outsiders, have difficulty feeling as though they are part of the family unit.

The Barones from *Everybody Loves Raymond* depict a family that is enmeshed and overinvolved. Partially contributed to by the proximity of living conditions, this family does not have clear established boundaries between family members. For example, it is commonplace to watch Marie, the grandmother, clean her son's house without any invitation and against the wishes of his wife. In addition, the members of the Barone family exhibit a high degree of dependence upon each in their daily lives.

In contrast, the Bundy family from the television series *Married ... with Children* portrays a family that demonstrates a lack of involvement. Often, the father, Al Bundy, is seen watching television with his favorite beverage and ignoring other members of the family. The family members are not involved in the lives of each other, and there is little genuine interest from the parents in their children's lives. However, although there is a lack of involvement, the Bundys still show a somewhat connected level of cohesion as a family. The family members do bond over the fact of being Bundys and demonstrate pride in family name.

FAMILIES AND SCHOOLS

Parents in healthy functioning families are engaged in the academic, socio-emotional, and behavioral development of their children in settings other than home, particularly schools. These parents strive to develop partnerships with their children's teachers and other school personnel. A key component of building effective home–school relationships is the understanding of parents and teachers as *partners* in the educational, social, and behavioral development of children. This includes the concept of shared meaning and shared responsibility between families and schools. Thus, home–school relationships consist of families and schools working, as partners, towards a common goal: the establishment and maintenance of a supportive environment for a child's educational, social, and behavioral development.

Types of Family Involvement

Families that are looking to become more involved in their children's lives at schools should be aware of different opportunities available to connect with schools and school personnel. Schools use a variety of models to make connections between a child's school and home environments. These different models fall along a continuum based on differing degrees of interaction, collaboration, and focus. However, the goals of all family involvement models are "to enhance success for students and to improve learning opportunities and outcomes for children and youth, including those that are academic, social, and behavioral in nature" (Christenson & Godber, 2001, p. 455).

Epstein (1996) describes six types of family involvement that fall along a continuum (low to high). These include parenting, communicating, volunteering, learning at home, decision making, and collaborating with the community. These types of family involvement have been adopted by the National Parent and Teachers Association. However, not all families need to become involved in their children's schooling at the highest levels. It is best for families to recognize and utilize their strengths and resources in ways that are appropriate.

Parenting

The first type of family involvement their children's educational development is to provide and environment that is supportive to their children's schooling. This includes providing the necessities, such as food, shelter, love, safety, and health supports that enable a child to enter school ready to learn. This also involves developing parental literacy.

Communicating

This level of involvement consists of communication between the home and school. Ideally, this communication is bidirectional and reciprocal, coming from both home and school. Parent–teacher conferences and home–school notes are a few ways parents become involved at this level.

Volunteering

Parental involvement through volunteering includes activities through which parents can offer support for the school environment. Such activities include becoming playground monitors, assisting with classroom management, conducting bake sales or money raising initiatives, or running the snack bar at athletic events. Most often, these are ways that bring parents onto the school grounds and make their presence available.

Learning at Home

Family involvement at this level of support includes assisting their children with academic tasks in the home setting. This goes beyond providing a supportive environment and consists of assisting with homework, helping establish appropriate educational goals, and providing assistance with other curriculum-related activities.

Decision Making

Parents active in the school's PTA/PTO or other parent organizations are demonstrating their involvement at this level. This also includes becoming involved in schoolwide decision making, serving as a representative for parents on committees, and being active in curriculum considerations or school reform.

Collaborating with Community

Involvement at this level consists of identifying and connecting community supports and resources with the school. This includes helping develop community partnerships for after-school programs, mentoring, or transition services. At this level, community resources are used to support and enhance student learning, family functioning, and school operations.

Socialization and Development of Children

Establishing effective home–school connections is extremely important because both environments are essential to the socialization and development of a child. Scott-Jones (1988) reported, "There is no doubt that children's development is enhanced by connections between the major contexts in which children grow and develop—family and school" (p. 66). Pianta and Walsh (1996) referred to the family, child, and school as the "invidious triangle." They contend that problems cannot be isolated as existing solely in the child, home, or school; rather, problems are located in a reciprocal relationship between all three. Therefore, efforts to support a child must include both home and school environments. Problems in the socialization and education of children can occur if there is a disconnect between the home and school environments or a lack of shared meaning across these two contexts.

Families grant a child an informal education that is considered a prerequisite for successful experiences in the classroom. Although the school environment sets up developmental tasks for students, the family serves as an important resource for the acquisition of these developmental tasks. Parents provide opportunities and learning experiences from the beginning of childhood through adult years. Such experiences consist of (a) exposing a child to ideas and activities that promote the acquisition of knowledge, (b) assisting in the socialization of gender, cultural, and peer roles, and (c) parental standards, expectations, rules, rewards, and praise (Clark, 1988).

Conoley (1987) stated that not only are schools and families more similar than previously thought but they also share similar ways of socializing a child, through support, teaching, nurturing, punishment, rewards, and evaluation. Parents are also responsible for the "curriculum of the home" that is an essential component to a child's educational development in school (Walberg, 1984). The "curriculum of the home" refers to activities families can participate in that enhance a child's learning and educational success. Thus, parents can impact educational development by providing academic guidance and support, modeling effective work habits and educational activities (e.g., reading), and demonstrating interest and expectations for academic growth.

Benefits of Family Involvement in Education Settings

Parental involvement in their children's schooling is beneficial in many ways to many different people and different environments. Henderson (1989) conducted a highly cited review of the literature, consisting of 48 studies, on the effect of parental involvement in education. Christenson and colleagues (1992) concluded that all empirical reviews of this literature, including Henderson's, could be summarized in to five major findings.

1. Parental involvement is related to student achievement—students' tests scores and grades are higher when there is parental involvement.
2. Other aspects of student success at school are also positively impacted. (e.g., higher attendance rates, better attitudes toward school, and more appropriate behaviors).
3. Not only do parental involvement strategies benefit students but they also have a positive impact on teachers, parents, and schools.

4. While all different forms of parental involvement appear to be helpful, programs that are more comprehensive and meaningful seem to be more effective.
5. Gains in student achievement seem to be higher when parental involvement is incorporated at an earlier age.

It is important to note that although positive benefits have been ascertained for parents, not all forms of parental involvement are appropriate for each family. Kerbow and Bernhardt (1993) conducted a study evaluating cultural differences in parental involvement. They found that Asian American parents preferred to be involved in out-of-school activities, whereas African American parents were more actively involved in at-school activities. They also concluded that minority parents in the study already demonstrated a high level of involvement that equaled or surpassed nonminority parents of the same socioeconomic status level.

FAMILY-CENTERED POSITIVE PSYCHOLOGY

One model for providing positive psychological services to children and families was developed by Susan Sheridan and her colleagues at the University of Nebraska–Lincoln. Building upon two fundamental philosophies for providing services for families, these researchers and clinicians promoted a means of enhancing family functioning by incorporating aspects of both family-centered service delivery and positive psychology. Family-centered positive psychology (FCPP; Sheridan et al., 2004) is defined as a framework for working with families that promotes strengths and capacity building, instead of focusing on resolving problems or focusing on deficiencies. Within the family-centered positive psychology model, there are five key principles.

First, FCPP is *concerned with the process as well as the outcomes.* Not only are positive outcomes important in delivering services through a FCPP framework, but the process in which services are delivered is also emphasized. Family-centered positive psychology, as a process, encourages engagement, self-efficacy, skill acquisition, and self-determination (Sheridan et al., 2004). Thus, families are involved through identifying their own needs and selecting appropriate resources that match their needs and strengths as a family.

Second, FCPP focuses on *family-identified rather than professional determined needs.* The family determines what their needs are. Although professionals can collaboratively assist the family identify these needs, the family is responsible for determining what type of assistance will ultimately be helpful.

Third, FCPP *uses existing family strengths and capabilities to access and mobilize family resources.* A major premise of FCPP is that all families have strengths and resources. The professional is there to assist the family in identifying, getting in touch with, and assembling these resources. Helping the family utilize their own strengths provides an environment in which the family's feeling of self efficacy and ability to function can be enhanced.

Fourth, FCPP *promotes the acquisition of new skills and competencies through specific types of helping behavior and professional roles.* Family-centered positive psychology seeks to support the attainment of skills within the family unit. The goal is to establish a level of empowerment within the family, so that the family feels that they are able to address further needs as they arise. The focus is on developing skills, assets, and strengths and not only on the remediation of deficiencies (Sheridan et al., 2004).

Finally, FCPP *emphasizes strengthening social supports and networks.* A purpose of this model is to develop and maintain relationships between the family and community supports. These relationships are best conceptualized as "partnerships" in which the family has shared ownership and responsibilities for identifying needs, accessing resources, acquiring new skills, and evaluating the effectiveness of supports.

CONJOINT BEHAVIORAL CONSULTATION

One technique for providing services to families that follows the family-centered positive psychology model is conjoint behavioral consultation (CBC; Sheridan, Kratochwill, & Bergan, 1996). CBC is a model of service delivery for families and children that brings together family members, educators, and other key community stakeholders within a partnership framework. Within this framework, members of the consultation team work collaboratively to address the developmental, academic, social, and behavioral needs of a child and the family. CBC is an extension of the traditional behavioral consultation model (BC; Bergan & Kratochwill, 1990) that has been used as the basis for school-based, problem-solving teams.

CBC follows a structured but flexible, evidence-based problem-solving model and is based on (a) a family-centered service delivery model, (b) the principles of positive psychology, and (c) an ecological-systems perspective (Bronfenbrenner, 1979). Through the process of CBC, parents and educators share in the identification of the strengths and needs of children and families and the development, implementation, and evaluation of supports to address those needs in home and school environments.

The problem-solving model of CBC follows four stages (i.e., needs identification, needs analysis, treatment implementation, treatment evaluation) and allows for each phase to be recycled as needed.

CBC recognizes the importance of bidirectional, reciprocal influences between systems (i.e., children, families, schools, and other systems) and that securing the connections between these systems is critical in establishing positive support and outcomes for children and families. Based on elements of family-centered services, CBC (a) provides an opportunity for families to be equal partners in the process of addressing the needs of their children, (b) focuses on both family-identified and professional-identified needs, (c) uses identified family and educator strengths and capabilities to access and mobilize services, (d) promotes family and educator empowerment through the acquisition of new skills and competencies, and (e) emphasizes strengthening social supports and networks (Sheridan,

Warnes, Cowan, Schemm, & Clarke, 2004). CBC fosters an environment that promotes home–school partnerships by providing a structured environment in which trust, collaboration, effective communication, shared responsibility, and mutual support between families and educators can be developed.

This method of service delivery is a process that fosters a healthy attitude towards the home environment. The process adheres to a no-fault philosophy that neither the school nor home is responsible for the targeted concerns. In accordance with Christenson and Sheridan (2001), CBC focuses on the "contextual circumstances that can be altered, not the individuals" (p. 75) and instead places an emphasis on solutions. Inherent in the CBC model is a focus upon the strengths, not deficits, of the family and child. All participants in CBC are considered to have distinct areas of expertise and knowledge related to the identified concerns or needs. Thus, families are not only highly encouraged to provide their own knowledge and experiences to the problem-solving process; it is built within the collaborative, partnership model.

CBC is a solution-focused model, based upon the strengths and needs of the participants. The CBC process follows a four-stage, staggered process; however, the model is fluid and cyclical in practice. Thus, the model allows itself to be responsive to the present and immediate strengths and needs of the family. Another goal of CBC is to facilitate collaboration between home, school, and community supports. To achieve this goal, CBC implores the use of two-way collaborative communication between parents, teachers, and community agency representatives. Supports developed in CBC are often structured in a fashion that encourages an increase in collaboration and communication between the home and school environments.

Goals in CBC

Inherent in the implementation of CBC is the understanding that the process is just as important as the outcomes. In addition to the goals listed previously that parallel family-centered services, there are several other process goals that have been identified for CBC. These are to (a) increase communication and knowledge about the family, (b) improve the relationship among the child, family, and school personnel, (c) promote shared ownership for the identified need and solution, (d) recognize the need to address problems as occurring across, rather than within, settings, (e) promote greater conceptualization of the problem, (f) increase the diversity of expertise and resources available, and (g) establish and strengthen the home–school relationship and home–school partnership (Sheridan et al., 1996).

CBC Research

There is extensive body of research demonstrating the effectiveness of CBC in addressing a variety of needs for families and children. These studies have evaluated CBC both on direct observational outcomes as well as the acceptability and perceived effectiveness of services. Case studies have demonstrated that CBC is effective in supporting students with emotional and behavioral difficulties in mainstream classrooms, increasing positive social interactions of children with attention-deficit/hyperactivity disorder, increasing social initiation behaviors of socially withdrawn children, and improving academic performance. A large-scale study also found CBC to be effective in addressing behavioral, social, and academic difficulties in home and school settings, resulting in high levels of reported satisfaction from parents and teachers (Sheridan, Eagle, Cowan, & Mickelson, 2001). In addition, CBC has been reported to be effective in supporting families from diverse backgrounds (Sheridan, Eagle, & Doll, 2006).

Additional social validity research has indicated that parents, teachers, and practitioners (e.g., school psychologists) rate CBC as a highly acceptable model for addressing behavioral, social-emotional, and academic concerns. Process research also suggests that CBC is effective in establishing a collaborative environment, characterized by reciprocal and cooperative verbal interchanges between participants (Sheridan, Meegan, & Eagle, 2002).

Case Example

The following case example depicts the use of CBC within an FCPP framework. George Stevenson was a 14-year-old Caucasian male diagnosed with obsessive-compulsive disorder. George lived at home with his mother in a Midwest urban setting. Resulting from his obsessions and compulsions, George found it difficult to complete schoolwork and had failing grades that were due to incomplete assignments. He was referred to the CBC process because of academic difficulties. Following are four ways in which the CBC process was able to help George and his family.

CBC Focuses on Family-identified Rather than Professionally Determined Need

The consultation team, consisting of his mother, school personnel, and a CBC consultant, met together to discuss and prioritize the needs of the family. Ms. Stevenson reported that although the school was interested in focusing on work completion, she preferred to focus on school attendance. She indicated that George commonly stayed home from school or did not attend school until the afternoon. This was due to his obsessions and compulsions that made it difficult for him to be present at school. Her interest in initially focusing on this behavior was because of her own employment. She reported that she was unable to go to work when George remained home from school. Working from a family-focused perspective, the team agreed to target school attendance.

CBC Uses Existing Family Strengths and Resources

Based on information attained from the family, a plan was developed that took into account the strengths and resources available. Throughout this process, Ms. Stevenson demonstrated her own strengths and expertise. She was the expert regarding George's medical, social, educational, and psychological history and provided invaluable information. Ms. Stevenson reported that she was familiar and comfortable with positive reinforcement techniques and that she preferred them to punishment strategies. Resulting from her strength in this area, a strength-based intervention was developed using positive reinforcement to encourage school attendance.

Ms. Stevenson's skill in assisting George to resist performing compulsions was also utilized. A second component of the plan was for her to help George relax when his anxiety was elevated and help him get to school. Further, the consultation team evaluated additional family resources. Ms. Stevenson reported that she would begin to ask Georges's grandmother to watch over him when he remained at home during the school day. This strategy would allow Ms. Stevenson to go to work on those days.

CBC Strengthens Social Supports to Promote Partnership and Collaboration Among Systems

A major goal of the consultation was to establish partnerships between the family, school, and community systems. Through collaboration with George's individual therapist, Ms. Stevenson and school personnel were able to acquire additional skills in learning how to respond effectively when George experienced elevated anxiety. This provided a support system that crossed over settings; both home and school environments consistently responded to George's obsessions and compulsions in the same manner. Further, Ms. Stevenson's support system now extended to the school setting as school personnel learned more about George's difficulties and the subsequent stress placed upon the family unit. Moreover, the two environments began to work towards a common goal.

CBC Promotes Acquisition of Family and Child Competencies

Throughout the CBC process, the procedures and steps used during consultation were made overt to all parties. This was done to increase the family's understanding of how to proceed in future situations. For example, through this process the steps of (a) prioritization of need, (b) identification and use of existing resources, and (c) collaboration and partnership development were modeled and described for Ms. Stevenson. The plan was also designed to enhance George's ability to resist his compulsions, because of the support received at home and school. Foremost, the CBC process is designed to promote the use of existing and new resources to establish hope within the family.

CONCLUSION

In sum, all families work in some way or fashion. Families are more diverse in structure than ever before, but all families have strengths. The key is that some families work more efficiently or with less conflict. These families typically have some common characteristics. First, families that work have found a nice balance between structure and flexibility. Second, these families are positively involved in the developmental aspects of their children's lives in school and community settings. Third, families that work are also utilize effective communication techniques, appropriate parenting strategies, and valuable problem-solving skills.

There are effective ways to help families function better and to become empowered in their ability to demonstrate resilience. One such model for assisting families to function better is through family-centered positive psychology. This framework allows families to develop skills based upon their own strengths and available resources. Effective families also develop strategies that are goal and solution oriented. They look at how to mobilize resources and supports instead of focusing on problems or deficiencies.

PERSONAL MINI-EXPERIMENTS

Discovering and Capitalizing on Your Family's Strengths

In this chapter, we have discussed the characteristics of families that work. We encourage you to learn more about your family's strengths both as a unit and as individual family members.

Discovering Your Family's Weaknesses and Strengths: Conduct a family meeting and have family members write down a list of family strengths and weakness. Have each member read the list out loud and ask the remaining family members to provide feedback regarding their opinion of the comments. Ask family members to identify at least one strength that other individual family members bring to the family. Have each family member read the list of individual strengths aloud.

Capitalizing on Your Family's Strengths: We would like each member of the family to capitalize on one strength. Each member should pick one individual strength and try to use that strength five times a day for 5 days. Your 25 attempts to capitalize on that strength have the potential to bolster it and create a habit of using that strength more each day.

Keep track of how many positive comments family members give each other. One way to do so is to keep a bunch of pennies in your left pocket. When you make a positive comment to another family member then switch a penny to your right pocket. At the end of the day count how many pennies are in your right pocket. Try to make 40 to 50 positive comments to family members each day.

REFERENCES

Anderson, S. A., & Sabatelli, R. M. (1995). *Family interaction: A multigenerational developmental perspective.* Boston, MA: Allyn & Bacon.

Baumrind, D. (1991). The influence of parenting style on adolescent competence and substance use. *Journal of Early Adolescence, 11*(1), 56–95.

Beavers, R., & Hampson, R. B. (2000). The Beavers Systems Model of family functioning. *Journal of Family Therapy, 22,* 128–143.

Bergan, J. R., & Kratochwill, T. R. (1990). *Behavioral consultation and therapy.* New York: Plenum.

Bronfenbrenner, U. (1979). *The ecology of human development.* Cambridge, MA: Harvard University Press.

Carlson, C. (1996). Best practices in working with single-parent and step-family systems. In A. Thomas and J. Grimes (Eds.), *Best practices in school psychology III* (pp. 1097–1110). Washington, DC: National Association of School Psychologists.

Christenson, S. L., & Godber, Y. (2001). Enhancing constructive family-school connections. In J. Hughes, A. M. La Greca, & J. C. Conoley (Eds.), *Handbook of psychological services for children and adolescents* (pp. 455–476). New York and Oxford: Oxford University Press.

Christenson, S. L., Rounds, T., & Franklin, M. J. (1992). Home-school collaboration: Effects, issues, and opportunities. In S. L. Christenson and J. C. Conoley (Eds.) *Home-school collaboration: Enhancing children's academic and social competence* (pp. 19–51). Silver Spring, MD: National Association of School Psychologists.

Christenson, S. L., & Sheridan, S. M. (2001). *Schools and families: Creating essential connections for learning.* New York: Guilford Press.

Clark, R. M. (1988). Parents as providers of linguistic and social capital. *Educational Horizons, 66,* 93–95.

Conoley, J. C. (1987). Schools and families: Theoretical and practical bridges. *Professional School Psychology, 2,* 191–203.

Darling, N., & Steinberg, L. (1993). Parenting style as context: An integrative model. *Psychological Bulletin, 113,* 487–496.

Epstein, J. L., (1996). Perspectives and previews on research and policy for school, family, and community relationships. In A. Booth & J. F. Dunn (Eds.), *Family-school links: How do they affect educational outcomes* (pp. 209–246). Mahwah, NJ: Erlbaum.

Epstein, N., Ryan, C., Bishop, D., Miller, I., & Keitner G. (2003). The McMaster model: A view of healthy functioning. In F. Walsh (Ed.), *Normal family processes* (3rd ed., pp. 581–607). New York: Guilford Press.

Fields, J. (2003). *Children's living arrangements and characteristics: March 2002.* Current Population Reports, P20-547. Washington, DC: U.S. Census Bureau.

Fields, J., Smith, K., Bass, L., & Lugaila, T. (2001). *A child's day: Home, school, and play (Selected indicators of child well-being).* Current Population Reports, P70-68. Washington, DC: U.S. Census Bureau.

Hawley, D. R., & DeHaan, L. (1996). Toward a definition of family resilience: Integrating life-span and family perspectives. *Family Process, 35,* 283–298.

Henderson, A. T. (1988). Good news: An ecologically balanced approach to academic improvement. *Educational Horizons, 66,* 60–62.

Kerbow, D., & Bernhardt, A. (1993). Parental intervention in the school: The context of minority involvement. In B. Schneider & J. Coleman (Eds.), *Parents, their children, and school* (pp. 115–146). San Francisco: Westview Press.

Kreider, R. M. (2007). *Living arrangements of children: 2004.* Current Population Reports, P70–114. Washington, DC: U.S. Census Bureau.

McCubbin, H. I., & McCubbin, M. A., & Thompson, A. I. (1993). Resiliency in families: The role of family schema and appraisal in family adaptation to crises. In T. H. Brubaker (Ed.), *Family relations: Challenges for the future* (pp. 153–177). Newbury Park, CA: Sage.

McCubbin, H. I., Thompson, A. I., Thompson, E. A., Elver, K. M., & McCubbin, M. A. (1994). Ethnicity, schema, and coherence: Appraisal processes for families in crisis. In H. I. McCubbin, E. A. Thompson, & J. E. Fromer (Eds.), *Sense of coherence and resiliency: Stress, coping and health* (pp. 41–67). Madison: University of Wisconsin Press.

McLanahan, S., & Sandefur, G. (1994). *Growing up with a single parent: What hurts, what helps.* Cambridge, MA: Harvard University Press.

Olson, D. H., & Gorall, D. M. (2003). Circumplex model of marital and family systems. In F. Walsh (Ed.) *Normal family processes* (3rd ed.; pp. 514–547). New York: Guilford Press.

Patterson, J. M. (2002a). Integrating family resilience and family stress theory. *Journal of Marriage & Family, 64,* 349–360.

Patterson, J. M. (2002b). Understanding family resilience. *Journal of Clinical Psychology, 58,* 233–246.

Peterson, R. & Green, S. (1999). Communication. In *Families First: Keys to Successful Family Functioning.* Blacksburg, VA: Virginia Cooperative Extension.

Pianta, R., & Walsh, D. B. (1996). *High risk children in schools: Constructing sustaining relationships.* New York: Routledge.

Santrock, J. W. (2007). *Educational psychology.* Boston, MA: McGraw Hill.

Scott-Jones, D. (1988). Families as educators: The transition from informal to formal school learning. *Educational Horizons, 66,* 66–69.

Sheridan, S. M., Eagle, J. W., Cowan, R. J., & Mickelson, W. (2001). The effects of conjoint behavioral consultation: Results of a 4-year investigation. *Journal of School Psychology, 39,* 361–385.

Sheridan, S. M., Eagle, J. W., & Doll, B. J. (2006). An examination of the efficacy of conjoint behavioral consultation with diverse clients. *School Psychology Quarterly, 21,* 396–417.

Sheridan, S. M., Kratochwill, T. R., & Bergan, J. R. (1996). *Conjoint behavioral consultation: A procedural manual.* New York: Plenum Press.

Sheridan, S. M., Meegan, S., & Eagle, J. W. (2002). Exploring the social context in conjoint behavioral consultation: Linking processes to outcomes. *School Psychology Quarterly, 17,* 299–324.

Sheridan, S. M., Warnes, E. D., Cowan, R. J., Schemm, A. V., & Clarke, B. L. (2004). Family-centered positive psychology: Focusing on strengths to build student success. *Psychology in the Schools, 4,* 7–17.

Turnbull, A. P., & Turnbull, H. R. (1997). *Families, professionals, and exceptionality: A special partnership.* Upper Saddle River, NJ: Prentice-Hall.

Walberg, H. J. (1984). Families as partners in educational productivity. *Phi Delta Kappan, 65,* 397–400.

Walsh, F. (1996). The concept of family resilience: Crisis and challenge. *Family Process, 35,* 261–281.

Walsh, F. (2003). Family resilience: A framework for clinical practice. *Family Process, 42,* 1–18.

CHAPTER 8

How Smart Girls Become Talented Women

Barbara A. Kerr and Amber Lynn Larson

Much of the literature on gifted girls has lamented that fact that so many bright young females lose sight of their dreams and goals. Early works such as *Smart Girls, Gifted Women* (Kerr, 1985) and *Meeting at the Crossroads* (Brown & Gilligan, 1993) detailed the ways in which internal and external barriers prevent gifted girls from finding their own voices and fulfilling their true potential. National Science Foundation gender equity studies (National Science Foundation, 2003, 2004, 2005) have compiled many reports that show the leaks in the math and science pipeline of talent from 6th grade onwards. Nevertheless, there are increasing numbers of smart girls who navigate the barriers to their success, who find their voices, and who go on to become accomplished women. This chapter, in the true spirit of positive psychology, focuses upon the strengths that allow women to overcome internal resistance to growth and the behaviors they manifest in order to transcend the limitations of traditional gender roles.

WHO ARE GIFTED GIRLS?

Where once the upper percentiles of intelligence tests narrowly defined giftedness, it has now been redefined in such a way that it is more inclusive, more culturally sensitive, and more carefully linked to the neuroscience of intelligence. While this has often led to some confusion and to needless complexity of definitions, the result has been the identification of a far more diverse and promising group of young women. The first studies of gifted girls were Terman and his colleagues' longitudinal investigations of 1,528 gifted children identified as those who scored over 140 on Terman's Stanford-Binet intelligence tests (Terman, 1925; Terman & Oden, 1935,

1947, 1959). Using this definition, and sampling from school districts in large cities in California, the Terman sample of gifted girls was largely middle class, with an underrepresentation of students of color and an overrepresentation of Jewish students.

The gifted girls were described by Terman (1925) as larger, stronger, and healthier than average girls. In addition, Terman took pains to describe how these girls, while having many masculine interests, still retained gender role appropriate behaviors such as playing with dolls and reading girls' magazines. The *Genetic Studies of Genius* is characterized throughout by an ambivalence about gender role noncompliance. Nevertheless, the conclusion was inescapable from the descriptions of their adventurous play, their broad-ranging interests, and their unusually high career aspirations that these gifted girls were more similar in many ways to gifted boys than to average girls.

As the girls grew up, they became more feminine in their interests while retaining high achievement throughout high school. Many more of them went on to college than other women of their generation (Terman & Oden, 1935). However, after college, the gifted women began to fall away from their original career dreams. Fewer gifted women than gifted men went on to graduate school and an even smaller proportion entered careers. (Terman & Oden, 1947).

Although half of the Terman women became homemakers, and a large number of the others entered traditionally feminine careers, there was a handful that overcame the considerable barriers to women's entry into the professions and became accomplished in nontraditional careers. In addition, the Terman sample of women remained psychologically well adjusted throughout their lives, although in terms of overall life satisfaction, those who had chosen to be single, childless, and career oriented were more likely to be happy with their choices. (Terman & Oden, 1959; Sears & Barbee, 1977).

For 50 years, the Terman definition of giftedness dominated gifted education, and therefore, little progress was made in understanding gifted girls who did not fit the white, middle-class profile of talent. Because the Terman girls were, for the most part, privileged children, a blind eye was often turned by researchers to the impact of sexism, racism, and poverty in the development of talent, so that gifted girls who did not achieve their potential were considered to have a "fear of success" (Horner, 1972) or to be suffering from "Imposter Phenomenon" (Clance & Imes, 1978). The role of resilience in the internal lives of bright girls was virtually unexplored. In addition, because intelligence tests predict academic, but not creative achievement, the accomplishments of women who pursue occupations that do not require academic degrees were deemphasized in the first decades of research.

All of this changed in the 1970s as increased criticism of intelligence testing and academic "tracking" reached a crescendo. Concerns about equal opportunity led to a search for broader definitions of giftedness. Torrance (1977) broadened the definition of giftedness by persuasively showing that creatively gifted children were unlikely to be identified through intelligence or achievement testing alone and made a case for the use of creativity tests to identify ideational fluency, flexibility, and originality. The U.S. Office of Gifted Education, following the Marland Report (1972), added creativity, leadership, and artistic ability to academic ability as signs of giftedness. What this meant for girls was that giftedness now included many abilities that girls have encouragement in developing, such as aesthetic and interpersonal skills.

A new emphasis on equity also encouraged research on "culture-fair" intelligence testing, and although the goal proved elusive, a plethora of new measures and adaptations of old measures appeared in the 1980s, such as the Culture Fair Intelligence Tests based on Cattell's Culture Free Intelligence Test (1963) and the Raven Standard Progressive Matrices (Raven, 2000), which claimed to measure fluid intelligence, or abstract reasoning, rather than crystallized intelligence, which was assumed to be based more on achievement and experience within one culture. Although these tests were never in wide use of the identification of gifted students, they signaled a change in attitudes toward children of non-White, lower socioeconomic status backgrounds so that educators were more aware and more motivated to search for talent among these populations. This, too, was a step forward for bright girls.

The creation of university-based talent search programs, however, was somewhat of a mixed blessing for gifted girls. These programs, begun at the Johns Hopkins University (The Study for Mathematically Precocious Youth) and spreading to seven talent search regions, promoted the use of the SAT college admissions tests among 7th graders to identify youth who were already performing at the level of high school seniors. Although both the Verbal and the Mathematics tests were given, most of the emphasis was upon the high scoring students in math, for whom the creation of linear, highly accelerated math curricula was simpler than the creation of accelerated verbal programs.

Sadly, for gifted girls, the majority of the research publications as well as the popular media took up the observed predominance of males at the upper end of math scores as evidence of a possible male superiority in mathematics. This is a finding that to this day has been misinterpreted and overgeneralized to create barriers for females in math achievement. It took 2 decades of research and meta-analyses of mathematics achievement tests to overturn the idea among scholars of hereditary superiority of males in mathematics (Spelke, 2005); yet the popular notion of male superiority in math remains.

Nevertheless, the talent search programs did open up a new method of identification of specific talents rather than general intelligence, and thousands of girls who otherwise might never have come to the attention of educators were provided with summer programs, camps, and out-of-school opportunities to enhance their academic abilities and to learn with their intellectual peers.

An emphasis on specific abilities brought gifted identification into a closer predictive relationship with actual adult accomplishment, because although eminent people across professions indeed have high general intelligence, they tend to have particular interests, passion, and motivation to develop their talents in just one, focused area of strength. Gardner's (1983) publication of *Frames of Mind: The Theory of Multiple Intelligences* further expanded the possibilities of identification of talent, because he made a case for the existence of not one, but seven intelligences (later expanded further to eight). Curiously, although feminist psychologists had long lamented the failure of psychology to recognize interpersonal skills as being as valuable enough to be considered an aspect of intelligence; it took male authors to provide the convincing argument. The advent of research on emotional intelligence (Bar-On, 1997; Goleman, 1997) and social intelligence (Goleman, 2006) has opened the way for a discussion of those strengths that have long been considered the domains in which women express their giftedness. Whether this is because, as cultural feminists such as Gilligan claim, women truly think, reason, and express themselves with a "different voice," or because women, as lower status people in most societies have had to cultivate emotional and social abilities to gain and preserve power, does not matter. What matters is that such capacities as understanding and managing the emotions of oneself and others (emotional intelligence) and understanding and using intuition to make decisions (social intelligence) are now part of the discussion about what makes it possible for gifted girls to become accomplished women.

GENERALIZATION FROM STUDIES OF EMINENT INDIVIDUALS

Besides a few studies of eminent women, there are few studies of eminent individuals that point to gender differences in the development of eminence. In fact, Lubinski and Benbow (2006) have made a convincing case that the conditions for attaining eminence are similar for males and females. Many authors of studies of eminent individuals have pointed out the difficulties in studying the lives of eminent women. Terman and Oden (1935) noted that by midlife, it was necessary to limit their study of adult accomplishment to males, because by this point in life, most of the gifted women in their study listed their occupation as "homemaker." Because there was a "lack of a yardstick" to measure eminence in homemaking, and the number of women who had attained eminence was small, no conclusions could be drawn about women's path to eminence. Even though the number of women attaining eminence in all field grew steadily from the early 1970s onward, most authors of studies of eminence continued to avoid the topic; for example, Simonton's (1988) study of genius; Gardner's (1994; 1996) studies of creatively eminent people and leaders have had little to say about eminent women. One must read between the lines of all of these studies to make generalizations about the lives of eminent women, and these statements must be made with caution. Only Csikszentmihalyi (1996) was careful in his study to include proportionate representation of women. There are, however, some findings about eminent people that are so robust across studies that they should be considered in determining the strengths of eminent women.

Loss of a Parent

The most common finding across all studies of eminent individuals is the finding of parent loss. This strange and disturbing fact has led to much speculation about how parental loss can engender creativity, drive, and achievement. For males, the loss of a father seems more common than loss of a mother; for females, it is unclear whether it is the loss of a father or mother that is most significant. Yewchuk, Aysto, and Schlosser's (2001) data would suggest that the presence of a strong father figure is very important to the development of eminence for women. Kerr (1997) suggested that psychological or physical separation from a mother might allow girls to diverge from traditional paths of marriage and motherhood. In studies of eminent people, the loss of a parent has been considered to be important in promoting early emotional and financial independence (Csikszentmihalyi, 1996); in producing a more creative, less linear approach to career development (Albert, 1994) and in creating the psychological tension necessary for creativity (Runco & Richards, 1997). For many of the talented at-risk girls in the NSF gender equity studies (Kurpius & Kerr, 2005), the absence of a father meant that they took additional responsibility for themselves as well as for siblings. Many of the girls spoke proudly of their role as their mother's ally and of their desire to achieve their career goals for the sake of their mother and siblings. The absence of a mother, according to Edelman's (2006) theory, if worked through, can lead to a strong and independent identity if a daughter is not required to take on too many of her mother's responsibilities.

In sum, the loss of a parent, although devastating for any child, may lead to greater creativity and autonomy in the long run. The strengths that are a part of eminent women's lives that can be related to early loss include resilience in the face of setbacks, individuation and independent identity formation, and early assumption of adult responsibilities with the attendant life skills.

Early Engagement and Time Spent Learning

Across studies of eminent individuals is the finding of early engagement with a specific domain of talent. Most creatively eminent individuals show an early passion for a specific intellectual activity. Future artists spend many hours as children perfecting their drawing, copying cartoons, and experimenting with designs (Getzels & Csikszentmihalyi, 1976). Future writers read voraciously, write journals and stories, and are fascinated by language at an early age (Piirto, 2002). This specific, powerful interest can get in the way of general school achievement, because many young people destined for eminence show little interest in being well rounded or in stellar achievement outside of their areas of interest (Csikszentmihalyi, 1996). Nevertheless, early engagement is critical in some fields such as music where few achieve eminence that have not begun their career as children (Sloane & Sosniak, 1985) and important even in later developing talents such as writing.

In addition, great accomplishment in any field is directly related to the number of hours spent working toward expertise and the number of hours spent while on the job (Lubinski & Benbow, 2006). Although there is a tendency for women to want to spend less time working than men prefer, it is clear that part-time commitment to a passion will not result in great achievement in a field. Therefore, early engagement with a domain of talent, including working toward excellence and expertise, gives gifted girls a head start in gathering the sheer amount of knowledge and skills needed to make a difference.

Therefore, it is likely that preoccupation with a specific talent domain is a strength for gifted girls that can translate to adult accomplishment. For girls, an early passion not only builds important skills but also may provide resilience in the face societal pressures to redirect interests to prettiness and popularity (Kerr, 1997).

Making Connection to a Master Teacher

Although proximity to and access to a master teacher is characteristic of the eminent person's environment, the capacity to make connection with a master teacher is a psychological strength. All people who achieve eminence in their fields are people who have come in contact with at least one teacher who challenged the student to achieve his or her full potential; who held extremely high expectations; who developed the student's technical skills and knowledge base; and who provided access to the student's future profession (Bloom, 1985; Csikszentmihalyi, 1996). Master teachers can be difficult and demanding, and it takes a special set of strengths to be able to profit from their instruction. Students who can persist with only minimal reinforcement and who can weather intense criticism are those who respond best to master teachers. These students are primarily interested in gaining skills and knowledge rather than in garnering approval. In most studies of eminent individuals, the future artist, musician, scientist, or inventor went to great lengths to find the right teacher, to find the resources to pay for instruction, and to engage the teacher in mentoring and guidance beyond the usual expectations.

The strengths that are necessary for the gifted girl to obtain such rigorous instruction and mentoring are persistence and resourcefulness. The strengths necessary for a continuing bond with the master teacher are a "thick skin;" a desire to prove oneself worthy; and willingness to show consistent and sustained effort.

CONDITIONS OF EMINENCE FOR WOMEN

What are the characteristics of gifted girls that are most predictive of adult accomplishment? In the analysis of themes in the lives of eminent women, Kerr (1997) suggested that voracious reading and learning; ability to be alone; willingness to be different and acceptance of being special; and high aspirations set gifted girls who had potential for eminence apart.

Yewchuk et al.'s (2001) studies of Canadian and Finnish eminent women placed a strong emphasis on the role of being "special" and showed how supportive, loving parents (particularly fathers) who encouraged girls' identities as brainy, smart, and capable were critical to the origins of eminence. Interestingly, however, in Yewchuk's studies, the eminent women gave primary importance to their own abilities and personal characteristics in childhood as the source of their accomplishments. This is in keeping with research showing the importance of self-efficacy (Betz & Hackett, 2006) and self-esteem (American Association of University Women, 1991) in the development of talent. Kerr and Kurpius (2005) suggested that ability and personal characteristics such as self-esteem and self-efficacy might be necessary but not sufficient for the development of talent. Rather, they said, the childhoods of eminent women were marked by loss, stress, and adversities that had to be endured or overcome. In their NSF studies of girls gifted in math and science, they tested the idea that being an "at risk" gifted girl might actually build the resilience that would be necessary in adolescence and adulthood. Their samples of talented at-risk girls did indeed match the profiles of scientific interest and curiosity, self-efficacy, and resilience that are characteristic of accomplished women scientists.

Freeman and Walberg (1999) study of eminent African American women showed that although they shared many traits with eminent women and men in general, their eminence also appears fostered by psychological traits and conditions generally similar to those that benefit other eminent men and women, they were significantly more often advantaged with respect to several psychological traits, including independence, perseverance, single-mindedness, and alertness to novelty.

A LOVE OF SOLITUDE

Eminent women remember girlhoods full of exploration, adventure, and voracious reading. Although both eminent women and men spent a great deal of time in solitary activities as children, solitariness is not as strong a theme in eminent men's lives as it is in those of eminent women. Alone time seems critical to the development of girls' talents (Kerr, 1997).

Why is it that aloneness is so much more important to the achievement of goals for women? Perhaps it is because society places so much more emphasis on social achievement for girls and women than for boys or men. Girls are expected to participate in extracurricular activities, informal social groups, and a wide network of friendships. From a human capital perspective (Bryant, 1992), girls have less time available for intellectual pursuits because of their investment in social activities, particularly after adolescence. Therefore, girls who spend time alone in childhood, by choice or chance, are likely to have more time for reading, reflection, and skill building.

Another possibility is that aloneness in childhood develops the habit of solitude, a condition that is critical to adult productivity. People who have difficulty spending time alone may never develop the capacity to spend long hours solving a problem or experimenting with a new design. Girls who are able to be alone are less likely to be caught up in the "culture of romance" (Holland & Eisenhart, 1991) that persuades them that their career goals are less important than their relationships with men. Solitude to these girls becomes not a source of social embarrassment but a source of strength.

DEVELOPED IDENTITY

One of the major differences between gifted young women and gifted young men seems to be the ways in which career identity is developed. Talented females are either slower or less willing to claim an identity in their chosen vocation. For example, while male students at the Art Institute of Chicago claimed the identity of "artist," female students were more likely to say that they were "students" (Kerr, 1991). In the Holland and Eisenhart (1991) study of the "culture of romance" on college campuses, the authors observed that bright women subverted their career identities to the development of their romantic relationships. In general, there may be gender differences in how women form their identity.

Early research showing sex differences yielded to studies showing similarities, with the current consensus being that there are differences in how women and men develop their identities in particular domains such as occupational and sex role domains, but overall, they are similar to one another. Women seem to develop their relationship and career identities simultaneously, while men may delay exploration of their relationship identity until after achieving their career identity.

Nevertheless, it is clear from the studies of lives of eminent women that the development of a strong, clear vocational identity is critical to adult accomplishment in all domains. The identity of the gifted girl must be as a "musician" or "scientist," for example to advance in these fields.

BOUNDARIES

For many eminent women, childhood isolation prevented them from exposure to pressures to conform to feminine norms. Many gifted girls today experience social isolation, merely because these girls do not fill the traditional mold. They also may try to hide and deny their abilities in order to become socially accepted. As a result of others reactions to their giftedness, talented girls often develop "thorns and shells" in their personalities in order to protect themselves from social scrutiny (Kerr, 1997). Thorns can manifest themselves by way of sarcasm, intolerance, self-righteousness, brusqueness, or simply having a sharp tongue. On the other hand, a gifted girl can alternately form shells by wrapping herself in shyness, timidity, and modesty. In this way, girls can protect themselves from the social persecution they experience. Kurpius and Kerr (2005) found that the strongest need and characteristic of talented at-risk girls with career goals in science was defendence, the need to defend oneself from interpersonal attacks and threats. Kerr, McKay, and Hammond (2007) also found defendence to be one of the strongest needs of creatively gifted girls. Although defendence is often seen as a negative personality trait by psychologists, it may be a necessary protective factor for gifted girls who are focused on accomplishment.

Another trait seen among eminent women is their resistance to confluence (Kerr, 1997). Many females tend to view themselves as part of someone else—they may have borrowed values and interests from their romantic partners and friends and tend to say "we" instead of "I." Although the capacity to connect to another in intimacy is a basic human need, the tendency to overidentify with another's needs can cause women lose their identities. However, eminent women have the ability to still feel connected with others without relinquishing their sense of self, which is perhaps a testament to their strong personalities.

RESISTANCE TO STEREOTYPE THREAT

A common belief held by many is that boys naturally perform better than girls in math and science. This belief affects the mentality and efficacy for girls in school. However, a meta-analysis by Hyde (2005) found that male and female students are alike in terms of personality, cognitive ability, and leadership. Differences arise when comparing male and female performance in mathematics and the sciences not because of an inherent biological difference but because of the existence of stereotype threat (Steele, 1997), which can cause women to underperform in these areas. Stereotype threat works by lowering expectations for women in the areas of science and math. When women are aware of a stereotype, according to this research, they will not only suffer damage to their intellectual identity but will also unconsciously underachieve. So not only does society disadvantage women by expecting them not to achieve in these areas, but it also harms them by making them believe that they simply cannot do it, because of being female.

How then, can young women protect themselves from stereotype threat? An intervention designed by Johns, Schmader, and Martnes (2005) found that simply by teaching women about stereotype threat and the anxiety that it rends boosted performance in stereotype-relevant tasks. This worked because it allowed women to not base their performance on unchangeable internal factors—such as being female—and allowed them to attribute their performance to external factors instead. So women gifted in areas of math and science must be educated about the existence of these stereotypes and how they relate to the widespread belief that boys are better than girls in some areas.

In addition, women can show a general resiliency to societal expectations by using positive emotionality to cope with stress and negative experiences. Tugade and Fredrickson (2004) found that positive emotions may contribute to efficient emotion regulation, which leads to quicker recovery from negative events and finding meaning even under negative circumstances. They found that highly resilient people expressed more positive emotions in the face of frustration. Letzring, Block, and Funder (2004) additionally found that people with high ego-resiliency could exert emotional control over life events, resulting in higher levels of self-confidence and better psychological adjustment. The results of these studies should not be discounted when examining the processes that eminent women use to overcome barriers.

RESISTANCE TO THE CULTURE OF ROMANCE

Young women, particularly upon their entrance to college, are at risk to become entangled in the "culture of romance," which revolves around the pressure for young women to become heavily involved in the romantic world (Holland & Eisenhart, 1991). Rather than focusing on academic goals and career development, women often find themselves being pressured to make themselves attractive, participate in parties and dances, and go to places like bars and clubs all with the sole purpose of meeting men. These female students are pressured both subtly and overtly to participate in romantic pursuits, which requires them to devote most of their time and energy into making themselves attractive and finding men to date who will boost their status and prestige. By dating men of high status, such as athletes, women thereby prove that they are highly attractive, thereby boosting their prestige among their peers. Evidence from the nationwide freshman survey (Sax, Lindholm, Astin, Korn, & Mahoney, 2003) shows that college women spend more time taking care of family and household responsibilities than do college men, even to the extent of doing their boyfriend's laundry. College women are essentially being socialized to take on conventional marriage roles. Conventional marriage arrangements in which women take primary responsibility for home and family are a benefit to male scientists but are a liability to the success of female scientists. It may be that the culture of romance encourages conventional relationships, preventing women from seeking and finding the more equitable marriages that will support their career goals.

A strong personality as well as a resistance to confluence may protect talented young women from becoming enmeshed in the culture of romance (Kerr, 1997). In addition, Kerr and Kurpius (2005) developed counseling and mentoring interventions designed to strengthen scientifically talented young women's resistance to the culture of romance. These interventions included career exploration and career counseling that encouraged young womens' science interests and retreats with women scientists that focused on modeling equitable gender relations. Recent evidence from the NSF studies of women in science, technology, engineering, and math fields shows that the nature of relationships, marriage, and family is the strongest predictor of women's tenure and promotion in the sciences.

COURAGE

An important way of understanding how gifted women overcome the barriers is the concept of courage and how it shapes a person's perceptions of life's obstacles. Courage may be defined as having three basic domains—physical, moral, and vital. Moral courage is defined as standing up for one's beliefs in the face of adversity (Snyder & Lopez, 2007). Particularly in relation to eminent women, moral courage is needed to stand up against the social pressure and sexism they may face so that they might achieve their true potential.

Courageous people are more likely to perceive problems as challenges, rather than impassible obstacles. So, for women to surpass the obstacles they must face throughout their lives, a certain measure of courage is important for them to realize their dreams and aspirations.

EGALITARIAN RELATIONSHIPS AND FLEXIBLE CHILDREARING

There is increasing evidence that accomplished women tend to create their own models of marriage, family, and mothering that are independent of societal ideals and stereotypes. Kerr (1997) found that eminent women found their love through their work; that is, they chose partners who either shared the same career interests or were respectful of the chosen work of the gifted women and equally devoted to a cause or purpose. Recent NSF studies show that women scholars are more likely to persist toward the highest levels of achievement in their fields when they are in dual career couples rather than more conventional marriages (NSF, 2005). Kerr found that eminent women tended to find ways to have children on their own terms, taking their children with them to work and in the field, making creative use of extended family and friendship networks for childcare, and seeking high quality childcare. In addition, Yewchuk et al. (2001) found that eminent women had more egalitarian partnerships and flexible childrearing arrangements.

FALLING IN LOVE WITH AN IDEA

Of all of the characteristics of eminent women, the capacity to fall in love with an idea may be the most powerful determinant of success. Torrance (1995) named this as the major characteristic of creatively gifted adults. Csikszentimihalyi (1990) described the sense of flow that was experienced by eminent individuals in participation in their chosen domain; whether art, science, or leadership, these creative people felt at one with their work, felt a sense of challenge and mastery, and experienced a timelessness and joy in the practice of their discipline. Falling in love with an idea strengthens gifted young women's resolve in almost every other area of her life, giving her the courage to overcome obstacles, to ignore gender barriers and stereotypes and to spend intensive time alone in pursuit of mastery of her field. In addition, falling in love with an idea may encourage even a shy, isolated gifted girl to seek master teachers and mentors and to insist on the educational opportunities she needs to fulfill her potential (Kerr, 1997).

LESSONS FROM EMINENT WOMEN FOR GIFTED GIRLS

Not all gifted girls will become, or want to become eminent women. However, most gifted girls do want to realize their potential and fulfill their dreams, and most teachers, counselors, and parents want to assist them in achieving their goals. Many of the experiences of eminent women are not those that one would wish for any child, such as parental loss and early, unchosen isolation. In addition, a good many of the conditions of eminence are almost the opposite of the conditions of contemporary girlhood. For example, girls are encouraged to be socially active and to have busy lives; seldom are today's girls encouraged to be reflective and solitary. Most media that are oriented toward girls and young women concerns grooming, weight loss, and relationship skills rather than self-exploration or career development. Nevertheless, it seems that some of the conditions of eminence could be moderated in such a way as to suggest strengths that can be encouraged. Even if eminence is not the goal, optimal development of gifted girls may sometimes require guiding them away from unchallenging education, media stereotypes of girls, and negative peer relationships.

PERSONAL MINI-EXPERIMENTS

Going from Smart Girl to Talented Woman

In this chapter, we have explored the strengths that allow women to overcome internal resistance to growth and the behaviors they manifest to transcend the limitations of traditional gender roles. We encourage you to discover your own strengths and the barriers that sit between you and your goals.

An Exercise in Noticing: Take one day to notice all the ways that popular Web sites, television, magazines, and music give messages that women should be pretty and popular, thin and sweet, and oriented toward relationships with men. How much have you believed these stereotypes and acted on them by dieting, talking exclusively with friends about relationships, and avoiding thinking about your long-term goals? Now, the next day, become your own positive psychologist, and notice every time you see an example in the media of women being strong and healthy, goal-oriented and achieving, and supportive of other women's goals? How can you become more like these women?

A Female Family Tree of Strengths: Build a family tree of the women in your family. Ask your mom, your grandmother, your aunts, and your sisters what their dreams were for themselves, and why they did to achieve those dreams. Now, think about your own dreams for yourself. How will your life be different from that of the women in your family? If you have daughters some day, what will you dream for them?

Using Your Strengths to Change the World: Open the newspaper and look through the headlines. Which headlines upset you the most? What is the problem behind those headlines—conflict among people, disrespect of the environment, injustice? Now, make a list of your interests, abilities, and strengths. How can your interests, abilities, and strengths be brought to bear upon the problem? How can you make a difference in the world given your unique capacities?

> ***Let's Hear It from the Boys:*** Guys, take one day to notice how the girls or women in your life sell themselves short, compromise their goals, or try to be something they're not to please a man in their lives. Just for today, challenge every girl and woman you know to see herself as a strong and capable person and to go for her goals.

REFERENCES

Albert, R. S. (1994). The achievement of eminence: A longitudinal study of exceptionally gifted boys and their families. In R. Subotnik & K. D. Arnold (Eds.), *Beyond Terman: Contemporary longitudinal studies of giftedness and talent.* Newark, NJ: Ablex.

American Association of University Women. (1991). Shortchanging girls, shortchanging America. Washington, DC: American Association of University Women.

Bar-On, R. (1997). The Emotional Intelligence Inventory (EQ-I): Technical manual. Toronto, Canada: Multi-Health Systems.

Betz, N. E., & Hackett, G. (2006). Career self-efficacy theory: Back to the future. *Journal of Career Assessment, 14*(1), 3–11.

Bloom, B. S. (1985). *Developing talent in young people.* Chicago: University of Chicago Press.

Brown, L. M., & Gilligan, C. (1993). *Meeting at the crossroads: Women's psychology and girls' development.* New York: Ballantine.

Bryant, W. K. (1992). Human capital, time use, and other family behavior. *Journal of Family and Economic Issues, 13*(4), 395–405.

Cattell, R. B. (1963). *Culture Free Intelligence Test, Scale 1, Handbook.* Champaign, IL: Institute of Personality and Ability.

Clance, P. R., & Imes, S. A. (1978). The impostor phenomenon in high achieving women: Dynamics and therapeutic intervention. *Psychotherapy: Theory, Research, and Practice, 15,* 241–245.

Csikszentmihalyi, M. (1990). *Flow: The psychology of optimal experience.* New York: Harper and Row.

Csikszentmihalyi, M. (1996). *Creativity: Flow and the psychology of discovery and invention.* New York: HarperCollins.

Edelman, H. (2006). *Motherless daughters: The legacy of loss.* New York: Random House/Delta.

Freeman, K. A., & Walberg, H. J. (1999). Childhood traits and conditions of eminent African American women. *Journal for the Education of the Gifted, 22,* 402–419.

Gardner, H. (1983). *Frames of mind: The theory of multiple intelligences.* New York: Basic Books.

Gardner, H. (1994). *Creating minds: An anatomy of creativity seen through the lives of Freud, Einstein, Picasso, Stravinsky, Eliot, Graham, and Gandhi.* New York: Basic Books.

Gardner, H. (1996). *Leading minds: An anatomy of leadership.* New York: HarperCollins.

Getzels, J. W., & Csikszentmihalyi, M. (1976). *The creative vision: A study of problem finding in art.* New York: Wiley.

Goleman, D. (1997). *Emotional intelligence: Why it can matter more than I.Q.* New York: Bantam.

Goleman, D. (2006). *Social intelligence: The new science of human relationships.* New York: Bantam.

Holland, D. C., & Eisenhart, M. A. (1990). *Educated in romance: Women, achievement, and college culture.* Chicago: University of Chicago Press.

Horner, M. S. (1972). Toward and understanding of achievement related conflicts in women. *Journal of Social Issues, 28*(2), 157–176.

Hyde, J. S. (2005). The gender similarities hypothesis. *American Psychologist, 60*(6), 581–92.

Johns, M., Schmader, T., & Martens, A. (2005). Knowing is half the battle: Teaching stereotype threat as a means of improving women's math performance. *American Psychological Society, 16,* 175–179.

Kerr, B. A. (1985). *Smart girls, gifted women.* Dayton, OH: Gifted Psychology Press.

Kerr, B. A. (1991). *Handbook for counseling the gifted and talented.* Alexandria, VA: American Association for Counseling and Development.

Kerr, B. A. (1997). *Smart girls: A new psychology of girls, women, and giftedness.* Scottsdale, AZ: Great Potential Press.

Kerr, B. A., & Kurpius, S. R. (Eds.) (2005) *Counseling girls and women: Ten years of NSF gender equity studies. Volume 2: Talent development.* Arlington, VA: National Science Foundation.

Kerr, B. A., McKay, R. A., & Hammond, D. (2007, November). The CLEOS Project: FirstFindings. Paper presented at National Association for Gifted Children Annual Meeting, Minneapolis, MN.

Kurpius, S. R., & Kerr, B. A. (Eds.) (2005) *Counseling girls and women: Ten years of NSF gender equity studies. Volume 1: Talent, risk, and resiliency.* Arlington, VA: National Science Foundation.

Letzring, T., Block, J., and Funder, D. (2004). Ego-control and ego-resiliency: Generalization of self-report scales based on personality descriptions from acquaintances, clinicians, and the self. *Journal of Research in Personality, 39,* 395–422.

Lubinski, D., & Benbow, C. (2006). Study of mathematically precocious youth after 35 years: Uncovering the antecedents for the development of math-science expertise. *Perspectives in Psychological Science, 1*(4), 316–344.

Marland. S. P. (1972). Education of the gifted and talented. *Report to the Congress of the United States by the U.S. Commissioner of Education.* Washington, DC: U.S. Government Printing Office.

National Science Foundation. (2003, 2004, 2005). *New formulas for America's workforce: Girls in science and engineering.* Reston, VA: Author.

Piirto, J. (2002). *"My teeming brain": Understanding creative writers.* Cresskill, NJ: Hampton.

Raven, J. C. (2000). *Raven standard progressive matrices.* San Antonio, TX: Harcourt Assessments.

Runco, M. A., & Richards, R. (1997). *Eminent creativity, everyday creativity, and health.* Greenwich, CT: Ablex.

Sax, L. J., Lindholm, J. A., Astin, A. W., Korn, W. S., & Mahoney, K. M. (2003). *Gender differences in time use of college freshman 1987 to 2002, 133,* 1–16.

Sears, P. S., & Barbee, A. H. (1977). Career and life satisfaction among Terman's gifted women. In J. Stanley, W. C. George, & C. H. Solano (Eds.), *The gifted and creative: A fifty year perspective.* Baltimore: Johns Hopkins University Press.

Simonton, D. (1988). Age and outstanding achievement: What do we know after a century of research? *Psychological Bulletin, 104,* 251–267.

Sloane, K. D., & Sosniak, L. A. (1985). The development of accomplished sculptors. In B. Broom (Ed.), *The development of talent in young people* (pp. 90–138). New York: Ballantine.

Snyder, C. R., & Lopez, S. J. (2007). Wisdom and courage. In C. R. Snyder & S. J. Lopez, *Positive psychology: The scientific and practical explorations of human strengths.* Thousand Oaks, CA: Sage Publications.

Spelke, E. S. (2005). Sex differences in intrinsic aptitude for mathematics and science: A critical review. *American Psychologist, 60,* 950–958.

Steele, C. (1997). A threat in the air: How stereotypes shape intellectual identity and performance. *American Psychologist, 52,* 301–311.

Subotnik, R. F. (1988). The motivation to experiment: A study of gifted adolescents' attitudes towards scientific research. *Journal for the Education of the Gifted, 11,* 19–35.

Terman, L. M. (1925). *Genetic studies of genius: Mental and physical traits of a thousand gifted children.* Palo Alto, CA: Stanford University Press.

Terman, L. M., & Oden, M. H. (1935). *Genetic studies of genius: Vol. 3. The promise of youth.* Palo Alto, CA: Stanford University Press.

Terman, L. M., & Oden, M. H. (1947). *The gifted child grows up: Twenty-five years' follow-up of a superior group.* Palo Alto, CA: Stanford University Press.

Terman, L. M., & Oden, M. H. (1959). *Genetic studies of genius: Vol. V. The gifted group at mid-life.* Palo Alto, CA: Stanford University Press.

Torrance, E. P. (1977). *Creativity in the classroom.* Washington, DC: National Education Association.

Torrance, E. P. (1995). Insights about creativity: Questioned, rejected, ridiculed, ignored. *Educational Psychology Review, 7*(3), 336–339.

Tugade, M., & Fredrickson, B. L. (2004). Resilient individuals use positive emotions to bounce back from negative emotional experiences. *Journal of Personality and Social Psychology, 86,* 320–333.

Yewchuk, C., Aysto, S., & Schlosser, G. (2001). Attribution of career facilitators of eminent women. *High ability studies, 12*(1), 201–205.

CHAPTER 9

Practicing Authentic Leadership

Bruce J. Avolio and Tara S. Wernsing

In today's world, there is a strong chorus of calls for more authentic leadership. Maybe these calls abound because of the growing level of cynicism that many people have expressed regarding leaders around the globe who seem to pad their own pockets at the expense of their people and the organizations they serve. Many examples exist, including the leader of North Korea who lives in opulence while the majority of his population is starving, contractors working in Iraq who are supposed to be there to support the multi-national war effort but incurring scores of accusations concerning overcharges and special bonuses, and prominent members of the U.S. Congress found guilty of taking bribes and misusing public funds. It is somewhat staggering to read that recent polls done by the Gallup Organization indicated that a third of the American public believed members of Congress were corrupt!

Nowadays, we know more about everything leaders do in the spotlight and beyond. Their failures are big news, and this publicity sparks the call for more authenticity in leadership. For example, less than a decade ago, we had moment-to-moment coverage on President Clinton's affair while in office, whereas few Americans probably realize that President Franklin D. Roosevelt died ostensibly in the arms of his long-term lover in Warm Springs, Georgia, while his wife Eleanor was in Washington, D.C. (Gerber, 2002).

The enormous availability of information on governments and organizations, the standard of transparency being demanded of organizational leaders, as well as the growing awareness of the general populace that they can access this information online is promoting a call for more authentic leadership. We also suspect that as followers become more challenging of authority because they simply know more, they also would expect more from leaders in positions of authority. So what we have occurring perhaps is a "perfect storm" for promoting authentic leadership whereby more information, smarter citizens and employees, coupled with the ability to quickly connect with others around the world through the Internet to establish a collective voice are contributing to increasing demands on leaders to get it right!

If the perfect storm is upon us, then where are we in our understanding of what constitutes authentic leadership and, perhaps more important, its development? We start with some examples of authentic leadership in practice and then move more into what are its components. The good news is that it has always been around if we look for it and are willing promote it in our organizations.

Forty years ago, Martin Luther King Jr. was interviewed on the *Mike Douglas Show* about his stance on the Vietnam War. Although he offered many eloquent responses on this television show, two comments were particularly relevant to examining the practice of authentic leadership:

MLK: A man of conscience can never be a consensus leader ... he doesn't take a stand in order to search for consensus. He is ultimately a molder of consensus. I've always said a measure of a man is not where he stands in moments of comfort and moments of convenience, but where he stands in moments of challenge and moments of controversy.

Douglas: Do you care if you lost favor with [President] Johnson?

MLK: Well that isn't the most important thing to me. The most important thing is that I not lose favor with truth, and with what conscience tell me is right, and what conscience tells me is just. I'm much more concerned about keeping favor with these principles than keeping favor with a person who may misunderstand a position I take. (Pugliese, 2007)

Through these particular words, Martin Luther King Jr. illustrated authentic leadership. First, he spoke of conscience being his guiding factor. Authentic leaders listen to inner conscience to guide them in decision making and taking a stand on controversial issues. Yet, the truth they listen for from within themselves is how to best serve their constituencies. In this way, authentic leadership is inner-guided yet other-focused. Robert E. Quinn (2004) describes this phenomenon and seeming paradox in his book *Building the Bridge as You Walk on It*. Through deep change, leaders become more authentic in their approach, guided by inner values and desire to serve other people. It follows that Bill George and Peter Sims (2007) place self-awareness at the core of developing authentic leadership. Indeed, leaders must undertake the lifelong journey of self-discovery to lead authentically.

Second, Martin Luther King Jr. (MLK) spoke of being true to certain principles other than concern for what people think or how they might misinterpret his words or intentions. This shows how authentic leaders are guided by principles for the betterment of humankind, not for one group of people at the expense of others. MLK described his core principles as genuine equality and peace; he did not discuss annihilation or punishment of one group of people (e.g., Whites) so that another group (e.g., Blacks) might feel vindicated for the past or more able to thrive in the future. He described a future in which all people are equally thriving. His expression of these ideals became shared goals among many people from both groups and motivated political action on a national and eventually global basis. Ironically, and in contrast to King's philosophy, Hitler had used the U.S. "Jim Crow" laws to justify his differential treatment of the Jews during World War II.

Last, MLK shared his thoughts and feelings about the war regardless of political backlash and physical threats. Moreover, his actions reflected the core values of equality and peace of which he spoke often. The way he interacted and communicated with people over a lifetime reflected these values. The effort he put into creating peaceful marches for equality across the nation required daily commitment to these ideals. For these reasons, MLK modeled authentic leadership by (a) being guided by inner conscience, as to how to (b) be true to core principles of improving well-being (equality and peace) for all people, and (c) taking actions aligned with core principles regardless of external pressures or threats.

Eleanor Roosevelt is an example of another kind of authentic leader. She was told that her husband had died while on vacation in Warm Springs, Georgia. She was asked to come to Georgia to accompany his remains back to Washington, D.C. Unfortunately, when she arrived she was told that her Franklin had continued his long-time affair, and perhaps more devastating, that her daughter had been arranging for her father and his girlfriend to have clandestine meetings over the years.

During the time the president was in Georgia, he was sitting for a portrait for his girlfriend. Months later, Eleanor who had now left the White House, was in Hyde Park, New York, when she discovered the nearly completed portrait of her husband. Of course, one might not fault the former first lady for throwing the portrait in the trash. Yet, instead, she wrote a note to his girlfriend indicating that she did realize how much the girlfriend must have loved her husband and that Eleanor Roosevelt was sure the portrait had great meaning for her. Eleanor Roosevelt was the same person who, as a member of the United Nations, promoted the international code of human rights, while demonstrating in this instance amazing authentic leadership in this most personal challenge of her own (R. Gerber, personal communication, January 26, 2007).

Warren Buffett at this writing is the second richest man in the world behind his close friend Bill Gates. For a number of years, he discussed taking all the money "he borrowed" from the economy and giving it back to a foundation he would create to address some of the most compelling issues of our time, such as nuclear proliferation or world hunger. When asked by a student in a class held at the University of Nebraska–Lincoln what he would like his foundation to focus on, he replied, if the money had been there at the time, he would have funded the Civil Rights Movement in the United States because it had no significant constituency with enough wealth to do so (University of Nebraska–Lincoln, 2006).

In 2007, Mr. Buffett took a step that perhaps solidifies his authenticity as a leader. Rather than taking his 30 or 40 billion dollars and setting up a foundation in his family's name, he is investing his wealth in the Bill & Melinda Gates Foundation, as he believes together they can accomplish much more than each alone. In this one act, he has demonstrated the importance of doing what is good for the collective, even at the expense of his legacy not being tied to a foundation name like his predecessors Ford, Kellogg, Carnegie, and now Gates.

WHAT IS AUTHENTIC LEADERSHIP?

The previous examples offer some interesting insights into what constitutes authentic leadership. The common core is doing what is good for others while being guided by inner conscience, even at great personal sacrifice (such as no legacy foundation, or being kind to your spouse's mistress, or even assault and assassination). This kind of leadership is not blind attention to serving the larger group or one's individual desires, but rather a very high form of altruism that shows how the individual and the group can both achieve their aims, if (a) the leader and group can be aligned in core principles and (b) a leader challenges the notion that it is a zero sum game between them, i.e., that one's gain is the other's loss.

The level of self-awareness at the core of authentic leadership requires substantial time and effort invested over many years into self-discovery to distinguish inner conscience from external programming. In addition, authentic leaders recognize and accept that people in the group are at different levels of developing their self-awareness and authenticity and may not be able to see paradoxical possibilities suggested by the stories of authentic leaders presented thus far.

Authentic leadership clearly depicts a higher level of moral reasoning and capacity to make judgments that goes beyond one's self interest, or said another way, includes one's self-interest to the serve the collective interests of the group. Yet, it doesn't stop there. These leaders go through life continually revisiting their theory of the self that represents the beliefs, views, and evaluations they hold about themselves (Epstein, 1973). This self-awareness and revision process allows them to determine how they can be better so that the collective can be better. It seems many people are incapable of evaluating their own theory of self, often unconscious to the fact that they even have a concept of themselves that is shaping all they do. So they simply execute on a theory they have never fully discovered. In this way, they operate by default on theories that early experiences programmed into them.

Basically, authentic leadership is leading from the core theory of oneself that is tied to high moral values and beliefs. Developing an understanding of those core values is a central component of authentic leadership, and then over time elevating them as new circumstances and challenges are confronted constitutes the practice and development of authentic leadership. As the starting point for authentic leadership development, leaders must question what constitutes their current core values and beliefs. What represents the center or base for their important decisions, actions, and behaviors? Moreover, because this is leadership, these core values and beliefs must include more universal principles than simply one's personal desires and incorporate ideals as to how such individuals come to influence others by raising themselves and others to higher standards of moral conduct. It is also important to consider that authentic leadership is not something that either exists or does not exist; rather, there is more or less authentic leadership in leadership episodes over time.

In this chapter, we explore the development of authentic leadership practices by describing the nature of authenticity, the role of self-awareness, components for practicing authentic leadership, and assessments available.

AUTHENTIC LEADERSHIP DEVELOPMENT THEORY

Inevitably, people will say, "Sure, Martin Luther King Jr., Eleanor Roosevelt, and Warren Buffett are exceptional people who exhibited high moral principles. But what if a leader's values and true self at the root or core are evil? Are they authentic expressing that?" The answer to this commonly asked question is that enacting authentic leadership assumes a positive path toward developing oneself toward higher levels of moral perspective and adult development. At these higher levels of human development, we know from years of accumulated theory and research (Erikson, 1959; Kegan, 1982; Kohlberg, 1976; Loevinger, 1976; Piaget, 1954) that people move to more complex and sophisticated ways of understanding the world and relating to other people. They go through transitions, crises, and transformations, and emerge into each new stage with a broader set of perspectives for interpreting their experiences that is more inclusive than the last.

These perspectives move from primarily individual concerns for personal gain, to relational concerns for support and status, to universal concerns for higher order principles such as genuine freedom, justice, equality, and peace for all members of the human family. The highest levels of development imply a move toward universal consciousness, an awareness of everything being connected (Beck & Cowan, 1996; Debold, 2002; Wilber, 2000). For example, to the extent the leaders of the nations of the world exemplify high moral character and perspective we would expect these individuals to delay judgment in determining the underlying causes for any one country's actions. By delaying judgment they would be signaling they are willing to listen, and hear one country's reasoning and cost–benefit considerations for all constituencies in a balanced way.

Balanced processing is thus another essential component of authentic leadership identified by Gardner, Avolio, Luthans, May, and Walumbwa (2005). Unfortunately, the trend of global opinion about U.S. attention to self-interest compared with collective interests suggests that the world is trending toward seeing this superpower as being much less authentic these days. The tangible impact of this trend is that the United States needs to invest billions more in security and much more time in convincing other nations that the direction chosen will benefit them as well.

Authentic leadership is based in core values and beliefs, but ultimately we judge such leaders by the authentic leadership episodes that are expressed through action, that is, forgoing putting one's name on a foundation to have a more positive and sustainable impact on the world's problems. Avolio and Luthans (2006) argued that authentic leadership represents the root construct or base underlying all positive forms of leadership. This means there can be authentic directive and participative leaders, just as there can be authentic transformational leaders.

An important distinction was made by Bass and Steidlmeier (1999) that there can be authentic forms of ethical or transformational leadership, as well pseudo-authentic expressions of leadership. Additionally, transformational leaders were defined by Bass and Avolio (1990) and earlier by Burns (1978) as being focused on developing followers into leaders themselves. Thus the basic "transformation" was in the follower becoming a leader. They reasoned that a leader that would be so concerned about developing followers into leaders, versus having them remain as "subordinates," evidenced a higher level of moral perspective. Why? Such leaders would be focused on the good of the individuals, not just their own self-interests, and would want to leave behind individuals and organizations more capable of leading into the future. One only has to look at several despot dictators to realize this was clearly not part of their intentions.

The work on transformational leadership in particular led Avolio (2005) to explore where such authentic leadership originates, which we discuss in more detail in the latter part of this chapter. The important point made by Avolio and his colleagues at the Global Leadership Institute is that authentic leadership is the root, and that like the roots of a plant, if it becomes corrupt so does any form of leadership exhibited above the root or base.

So how does such root-based leadership get developed? Authentic leadership is a developmental process that is largely characterized by learning about the self as it evolves toward broader and more complex perspectives, while in turn applying this learning to leadership episodes and practices. The self here is the core concept, mental model, and theory an individual leader holds that addresses the question—Who am I?

DEVELOPING AUTHENTICITY

> To thine own self be true, and it must follow, as the night the day, thou canst not then be false to any man.
> *Hamlet*, act 1, scene 3, lines 564–566, Shakespeare, 1604

Authenticity is defined as being true to the self (Harter, 2002). As Shakespeare wrote above, being true to one's self is the highest level of truth there is. As the theory of authentic leadership describes, the self we are talking about is linked to higher levels of moral development. In the cognitive psychology literature, Lord and Brown (2004) present a way to more clearly understand the theories of the self each person holds. The first theory is the *feared self*, which represents areas that we do not feel adept at engaging, e.g., "I am not able to sway people by standing up and presenting my deep beliefs and opinions." The second theory of the self represents the current view of the self or *actual self*. The actual self represents that which we have come to understand about ourselves and that which guides our action, for example, "I am not an empathetic person, so I don't try to engage people in counseling because I am not good at it." The actual self represents our theory of our self in use day to day. The final self is referred to as the hoped for or *possible self*. This represents the individual I am becoming or could become, e.g., "I know that to be a successful manager in most organizations today, I must develop a global mind-set. With such a mind-set, I will be able to successfully engage my employees and customers across cultural contexts in a way that we each come to understand the other's perspective and develop trust."

At any one point in time, we can consider that we all have a feared self, an actual self, and a possible self that are each evolving in some unique way depending on the challenges we have chosen to confront, or that occur through serendipity and life events. Authentic leadership development focuses on the dynamic between these components with the intent of moving the actual self to a higher level perspective towards the possible self. Thus, authentic leadership development begins by developing this sense of clarity about the self and authenticity through action (Gardner et al., 2005).

Taking actions that go against inner values or inner base represents self-abandonment and a slide into negativity. We suggest that individuals who truly know themselves and are progressing throughout their lives towards higher perspectives are people who are more positive, and we have some evidence to support this assumption. Indeed, in one police study, officers who were rated by their followers as more authentic, and who were higher in psychological capital, over a 6-month period of time had followers who showed higher levels of flourishing, on-the-job performance, and well-being (Peterson, Walumbwa, Avolio, & Fredrickson, 2007; Luthans, Youssef, & Avolio, 2007).

Now contrast the above focus on positivity and think of the officers in the German army in World War II, who were required to dehumanize and eventually put to death approximately six million people in death camps. For many of these officers, there must have been an initial moment when they went against their own inner principles—knowing that killing these human beings was against their moral values. Yet for their own survival (and safety of their families) they bought into, or at least went along with, Nazi policies. It seems that once you abandon your inner values, it becomes easier each time as you become a little more deadened to its voice. These officers may have thought they were surviving, but instead, they experienced the slow death of their moral perspective and well-being.

We see this same pattern occurring for people in organizations, who are selling out their inner values, often for security or status. At first, it may be one difficult choice, and it may not even be noticed. But over time, these people no longer hear their inner conscience, and they make decisions purely based on economic reasoning. This too results in slow death. Inauthentic behavior shows up in leaders and followers who behave as social chameleons, changing who they are according to whatever group or authority figure with whom they are currently interacting.

We suggest one indicator of inauthencity is that people experience polarities of energy: (a) frenetic, hyper, wired energy or (b) low, dull, exhausted energy or (c) a constant swing between both extremes over a short period of time. This is because inauthenticity reflects an imbalance. When someone is not grounded in who they are, they are likely to look outside themselves for answers, validation, or direction. Repeatedly ignoring one's own inner moral base drains a person's energy, and not being aware of inner conscience and instead tuned toward other's people attitudes and opinions leads to more frenetic energy states. We also know that maintaining this sort of psychological and physical imbalance will eventually take a toll on the person's well-being.

In sum, authentic leaders have a better understanding of who they are, as well as more experience and facility in acting in alignment with their true selves under various conditions (Gardner, Avolio, Luthans, May, & Walumbwa, 2005; Luthans & Avolio, 2003). Accordingly, being true to the self, being authentic, involves both a "knowing" and "doing" component. That is, leaders must first *know* who they are, and only then can they choose to *do* things that match their true values and principles. Thus, the first component to developing authenticity in individual leaders and authentic leadership is leader self-awareness.

SELF-AWARENESS IS THE FIRST STEP

Most people tend to overestimate or are more favorable toward themselves compared with ratings they receive from coworkers (Nilsen & Campbell, 1993). So we know from this research that most people really aren't clear about how they are perceived by others. But self-awareness is more than knowing how others see you; also it is being aware of aspects that others don't see, as well as understanding some basic principles common to all people, such as how we all make sense of and derive meaning from our life experiences. It also allows for the possibility that everyone else may be wrong about you!

Although the term self-awareness is often used to refer to a certain state of "enlightenment" that some people attain, in practice self-awareness is a long-term, really a lifetime, learning process without an ultimate destination level of 100%. This is because the actual self is dynamic and changes over time. As noted above, there are multiple components to the self (i.e., actual, feared, and possible) and not everything about the self can be known anyway. In fact, cognitive psychologists suggest there is a "working self-concept" that represents what we are able to access about ourselves at any one point in time, since we cannot access all of it all of the time (Lord, Brown, & Freiberg, 1999; Markus & Wurf, 1987).

In the book titled *Blink: The Power of Thinking without Thinking* by Malcolm Gladwell (2005), a study was described where unsuspecting people were primed to think either young or old, and as a result their subsequent behaviors changed. Priming them involved flashing a word on a screen below the threshold of awareness, so that people were unaware this was happening yet unconsciously processing the words. People who were primed with old words walked more slowly afterwards than those that were not primed with such words.

In another clever experiment, people primed with aggressive words interrupted a meeting after about 5 minutes of waiting, while those who were primed with polite words did not interrupt the meeting at all (Bargh, Chen, & Burrows, 1996). This series of studies provides evidence of how people's thoughts and perspectives of themselves affect their actions, and yet they can be unaware of what is driving their behavior. Developing greater self-awareness is one way to become more conscious of what shapes behavior. Although it probably cannot overcome intentional priming conducted in laboratories by scientific researchers as described here, self-awareness development can bring to consciousness many other aspects of the self that do shape behaviors and that can be adjusted. For instance, leaders who become aware of these common biases in the ways they perceive and process information can intentionally seek more ways to balance their perspectives. Therefore, authentic leaders are likely to engage in a more balanced processing as a result of greater self-awareness.

SELF-AWARENESS BEGINS WITH A TRIGGER MOMENT

So what is a trigger moment? An example of a trigger moment might be: *"Consider that when you are leading every single conversation matters."* A young leader asked her mentor, "What is the one thing that would help me be a better leader?" His reply to her question was the statement above, and she indicated to us that it has guided her very successfully through the past 10 years of work in the public school systems.

Self-awareness means asking central questions about yourself that relate to your theory of yourself. When am I at my best? How can I improve? Where am I being true to myself, and where am I selling out? It can be triggered by receiving feedback. For example, how many of your friends would hide you if your life and theirs depended on it? This kind of question really gets one to think about true and deep friendships and what they mean in life. Thus, self-awareness is a process of learning about the self that includes moments of insight (i.e., an "aha!" moment), self-reflection, and an accumulation of knowledge about the self over time.

Trigger moments cause leaders to pause and reflect on the meaning of the event and implications for their current and future leadership. These moments may be negative, neutral, or positive. One clear indication we have found for authentic leadership development is when leaders stop searching for answers from outside sources and listen to their own wisdom and conscience on key issues. One hospital director remarked that he had read so many books on leadership that were useful to his development, but his real development started to emerge when he set out to understand and address his own model or theory of leadership. When he began to dig deeper into his own model, he was able to see how he wanted to be guided from the inside out. Here is another example we picked up in a class where a student addressed the following question to Warren Buffett.

> STUDENT: But when you need advice and feedback about an idea or a decision, I'd like to know who do you go to?
>
> WARREN BUFFETT: Well, usually I look in the mirror, to be totally honest. The nature of what I do means I have to think pretty much independently because if I take a poll, in effect, I'm gonna do whatever everybody else is doing, and I don't think much of that usually in investments; and so I have to have an environment and I have to have the temperament personally that lets me think for myself (University of Nebraska–Lincoln, 2007).

Mr. Buffett has no doubt sought advice throughout his life from his acquaintances and readings, but there comes a point where such leaders believe they must fully own the decision and its consequences. Given his response, he has apparently reached a level of experience where he knows that he has his own answers. This behavior represents trust in one's self that comes with years of experience and experimentation. Contrast this example with a new leader who doesn't have much experience in his field and decides not to ask for feedback or advice on a key business decision. What we describe here is a leader not willing to be vulnerable, which can be the kiss of death in most careers, particularly those where we observe leaders who are extremely high in exhibiting hubris! Of course, this behavior could be considered arrogance and ignorance. This is why we refer to authentic leadership *development* ... because it is a long-term process of moving toward more complex ways of understanding yourself, others, and the effective leadership that comes through experience and deep reflection. For leaders, this happens while they are on the job in leadership episodes, as well as through separate reflective practices, like journaling or meditation. Self-reflection is critical thinking usually performed after some event has occurred deemed relevant to oneself. Feedback from other people (such as performance reviews at work or after-action reviews and debriefing) is a common trigger for self-reflection.

This kind of leader self-awareness is more than just surface level thinking and learning; it includes, yet moves beyond, knowing your own strengths and weaknesses. It is knowing one's self on many levels and also knowing certain aspects of the self in much greater depth and detail. First, consider how people always are interpreting their circumstances, situations, and interactions with other people. They are assessing, judging, evaluating, trying to understand and make meaning of each event, while determining if action is needed. This process is referred to as meaning making or sense making. So at one level of self-awareness a leader comes to the realization that all people are meaning makers. In fact, leadership itself is considered a meaning-making function. It involves creating meaning through describing a vision and engaging people in sharing the vision and taking action towards specific goals that fulfill the vision. Leader self-awareness contributes to ensuring that leaders responsibly shape the meaning and sense-making that goes on in their teams, organizations, and communities.

Gaining greater self-awareness is a choice, and for some it is uncomfortable to discover new things about themselves. Thus, one of the ways to facilitate leader self-awareness is through self-observation and mindfulness. Mindfulness allows a leader to observe him or her self with a minimum amount of judgment, as a witness or as a third-party observer. Practicing mindfulness is one way to turn off or slow the meaning-making process for a time. This nonjudgmental self-observation contributes to self-acceptance, which is also important to authentic leadership development (Gardner, Avolio, et al., 2005). Gaining more awareness of the self without accompanying self-acceptance can be painful. Thus, combining a variety of self-awareness practices (i.e., self-reflection, journaling, mindfulness) to develop authentic leadership works best.

ALIGNING ACTIONS WITH INNER VALUES IS THE SECOND STEP TO AUTHENTICITY

Clif Bar is a private company with estimated annual revenues of about $150 million and employs about 170 employees. Yet, there was a moment when they almost became another product line of a large conglomerate corporation. It was a "moment" of authentic leadership that changed the course of this company's future.

After key competitors were bought up by large corporations, an offer was made by another large corporation to purchase the company in the year 2000. It was a great offer, sure to make both owners of Clif Bar very wealthy so they would never have to work another day in their lives. On the day of signing the contract, one owner felt a sense of panic, so he took a walk outside and in that moment realized he did not want to sell the company. He decided he was not going to give in to the rational reasons people gave him for selling the business, primarily that the key competitive products recently were bought by corporations with large marketing budgets and Clif Bar would never be able to compete at that level and would wither away under the attack. But on that day, he listened to his conscience and he made a decision that went against all the experts including the other owner of Clif Bar, who he would now have to buy out.

Gary Erickson decided to buy out the other owner for over $60 million, even though he only had $10,000 in his bank account that day. The company has since grown from about $40 million in sales to $150 million in just 6 years, even while competing with those other large companies. Most recently Clif Bar became a leader in business sustainability by offering the nation's first incentive program to pay cash to employees who purchase clean-burning biodiesel cars, also helping employees buy high-mileage hybrids, and offering a variety of rewards to those who leave their cars at home altogether (Burlingham, 2005; Erickson, 2007).

Gary Erickson demonstrated authentic leadership by aligning his actions with his conscience, when he chose to back out of the sale at the last minute and follow through on his inner voice and values. He honored and trusted his own wisdom over the advice of the other highly experienced business people involved, and he not only succeeded in sustaining the revenue growth of the company over time, but he continues to create innovative ways to be a company that values and takes actions towards sustaining the planet. In retrospect, he could have been wrong about the future potential, but he would have still been right about himself.

AUTHENTIC LEADERSHIP DEVELOPMENT PRACTICES

As noted above, we witness authentic leadership in the episodes of leading that occur in everyday decisions and in moments of great challenge and change. Martin Luther King Jr. practiced a high level of authentic leadership through the clarity and transparency with which he shared his dreams for equality and peace, and through his daily choices to adopt a nonviolent approach to leading political and social change. Gary Erickson practiced authentic leadership through making an important and expensive decision based on his inner conscience, values and concern for his employees.

Authentic leadership development (ALD) theory suggests there are several specific core practices involved in practicing authentic leadership: namely self-awareness, transparency, balanced processing, and moral perspective and actions. We discussed leader self-awareness and its development through trigger moments and self-reflection above. Now we explore specific practices associated with self-awareness and the other components of authentic leadership below.

Self-Awareness Practices

Authentic leaders choose a path of self-discovery. They invite feedback and insights about the self, choosing to engage in practices that enhance leader self-awareness. These practices include three main types: (a) seeking feedback regularly, thereby creating trigger moments, (b) engaging in self-reflection to understand the meaning of triggers to the actual self and emotional responses, and (c) spending time in self-observation, or mindfulness mode, which makes one aware of immediate thoughts and feelings. These three practices contribute to heightened self-awareness. When the focus of feedback, reflection, and self-observation are on leadership episodes, and leaders intend to learn about implicit theories they hold regarding themselves, effective leadership, and worldviews, we call this process leader self-awareness.

Receiving feedback from a variety of sources is a way to gain perspective on how a leader is perceived across a range of people. Hence, 360-degree performance feedback instruments are very popular in organizations as a tool for leader development (see Atwater, Brett, & Waldman, 2003). Although these instruments are useful for triggering self-reflection via feedback, it is also important to point out that they are only one mechanism for enhancing self-awareness. Moreover, a leader may know herself very well and still differ in her ratings of leadership from followers, and in our view, this does not necessarily mean the leader is not self-aware.

In terms of learning one's strengths and receiving feedback on them, Roberts, Dutton, Spreitzer, Heaphy, and Quinn (2005) have developed an exercise called the "Reflected Best Self." In this exercise, people seek feedback on when they have been at their best, what characteristics they display, and under what circumstances. Authentic leaders invest time in understanding their own strengths and best possible self, as well as helping those around them learn the same. Leveraging strengths and being at your best affects well-being positively (i.e., feels better), and it also is likely to lead to better individual and ultimately group performance, since everyone is encouraged to rely on knowing their strengths and blending them into a more effective course for execution.

A second practice for heightening self-awareness is self-reflection. Making time to consider trigger moments and learn from leadership experiences is practicing reflection. Adaptive self-reflection is a form of critical thinking, involving examination and evaluation that results in insights (aha! moments) and learning about the self. Maladaptive self-reflection is spending time renumerating what and why things went wrong and never deriving positive lessons learned. Authentic leaders seek out trigger moments for learning from their own actions as well as those of others. They actively engage in self-reflection on a regular basis, whether asking for feedback on which they can reflect, or by performing a "debrief" or after-action review on a weekly leadership episode or experience.

Thirdly, practicing mindfulness and self-observation is another component practice of self-awareness. This practice involves observing your thoughts, feelings, and behaviors as they are happening. Mindfulness involves being attentive to what is happening in the present moment without judgment (Baer, 2003; Brown & Ryan, 2003). Although this sounds simple, practicing mindfulness can be quite a challenge. Most people use meditation or reflective exercise techniques to learn how to observe their inner thoughts, emotions, and visceral reactions from a nonjudgmental, witness-like perspective. This kind of self-observation is distinct from thinking about whether your thoughts and behaviors are aligned with your goals. This latter practice represents an example of self-reflection, and both practices are central to self-awareness development.

Mindfulness helps leaders become more self-aware of the current flow of thoughts and feelings they are having in the present moment. This metacognitive (thinking about the way one thinks) capacity for this kind of awareness allows for greater immediate adjustments and adaptive flexibility. Mindfulness allows leaders to interrupt automatic or habitual reactions and to select alternative pathways of thinking and responses based on insights gleaned from self-reflection. For example, Martin Luther King Jr. may have felt at many times an automatic reaction of anger or a desire to aggressively push back or defend against attacks as his contemporary Malcolm X did. Yet, it is likely his ability to practice peaceful responses in a variety of challenging and even violent situations was due at least in part to his capacity to observe his automatic reactions in the moment and choose to respond differently.

Thus, authentic leaders are those who have built the capacity to choose to act true to their core values, even when they have more automatic human emotional reactions to perceived threatening situations. There may be leaders who reach a state of transcending emotional triggers and remain disciplined in linking their positive core values to positive growth strategies for resolving dilemmas. How easy it would have been for Nelson Mandela to come out of 27 years in prison and seek revenge on his captors. What made this authentic leader so different in that "moment"?

Practicing Balanced Processing

Based in the process of leader self-awareness just described, authentic leaders come to understand that all people are biased processors of information. Just like the people in the Bargh's experiments who responded to nonconscious priming from words related to being young or old or to aggression (Bargh et al., 1996), authentic self-aware leaders realize that all humans filter what they perceive, interpret their environment according to past experiences, and are nonconsciously influenced by a variety of phenomena around them, including other's people emotions. Thus, authentic leaders seek out alternative, often competing perspectives on important issues. They know that any one person is a biased processor of information. Therefore, this core component of practicing authentic leadership encourages leaders to create the conditions for adaptive conflict (Avolio, 2005). Adaptive conflict occurs when a diversity of views from people of different backgrounds are considered in decision making. Healthy debate and fair consideration of competing ideas result in more creative, emergent, and adaptive solutions.

It stands to reason that if leaders aren't aware of the inherent biases in their own meaning-making processes, and that of their teams, they will not set up their organizations to benefit from the diversity and innovative solutions that come from adaptive conflict. At the other extreme, stereotyping, prejudice, and righteousness set up the conditions for maladaptive conflict. Thus, people need education and training about these inherent cognitive biases and automatic sense-making processes, so they can begin to decipher their own implicit theories and to learn how to constructively interact with others who are operating from their own personal filters and biases at all times. Realizing these processes are in place is a huge step toward more balanced processing.

Practicing Transparency

Authentic leadership development recognizes the relational nature of leadership: that leadership is built on social interactions and influence. As such, a key component of authentic leadership is relational or interactional transparency, defined here as sharing relevant information, being open to giving and receiving feedback, being forthright regarding motives and the reasoning behind decisions, and displaying alignment between words and actions (Vogelgesang, 2007).

Transparency is central to building trust between people. Withholding information, saying one thing but doing another, and not being willing to receive or give feedback all erode transparency in relationships and reduce trust. Although we do know in practice, people wonder how much information is necessary to share. Avolio and Luthans (2006) reason that that the more certain you are about your values and beliefs, the more clear you will become about how transparent to act with others. Being transparent may cause feelings of vulnerability at times but should not make you so vulnerable as to invoke anxiety or invite exploitation from others. If you know your core values, and your core is based on high moral principles, why would you not want to be transparent in your interactions with others?

Practicing Moral Actions

ALD ultimately is about leaders being true to themselves in their leadership practices. The "self" to which we refer has been described in many ways (i.e., the possible self, the best self, or one's conscience and core values). All these terms imply a higher level of awareness than might be average for most people. To practice ALD means regularly identifying with your best self, checking in with your core values concerning your leadership agendas and operating practices, and verifying that indeed your actions are aligned with the highest ethical and moral principles you hold. In this way, practicing authentic leadership becomes taking actions that serve high moral principles concerning relationships, social responsibilities, and performance standards. Practicing ALD means continual engagement in self-discovery and awareness opportunities, and learning which values and principles are the highest form of conscience and possible self for each leader at the current stage in his or her life stream.

In sum, authentic leadership development involves several practices, including self-awareness, balanced processing, transparency, and moral actions. Together these practices put a leader on a path to becoming more authentic and to serving as a role model in their leadership relationships, and it follows that the leadership experience for all exemplifies higher levels of trust, engagement, and performance.

CONCLUSION

Returning to our example of Martin Luther King Jr., he challenged all of us in the United States to find a way to create a nation that viewed all people as equal and demonstrated true equal opportunities for all. He challenged our nation and indeed the world to practice authentic leadership and to hold ourselves true to the principles upon which the nation, and now the United Nations, was founded—equal liberties for all. Forty years later, we are challenging ourselves in a similar way to practice authentic leadership on a global scale. This does not imply a right way, but rather implicates a process of transforming perspectives to become broader, more inclusive and integrated than before.

For example, many Americans would be surprised to find out from a Gallup Muslim poll, that a majority of Muslims have a tremendous respect for our innovativeness and liberties (Esposito, 2006). However, the majority of Muslims believe that Americans have little respect for their culture and what Muslims stand for. One Muslim professor in Singapore illustrated this latter point by showing clips of the myriad of American movies that had "Arab" characters in them. In every movie over the last 3 decades the Arabs were depicted as being gang members, terrorists, or extravagantly wealthy, corrupt business men.

Reflecting back on the findings above, we can think about every world leader today, and ask: how self-aware are those leaders and how does that affect their ability to be authentic leaders? How does the current global context affect the development of authentic leadership in our world today? If we could take those leaders and simply enhance their self-awareness, their level of transparency, balanced processing, and moral perspective-taking concerning their actions, could we change the path of human history? Absolutely! Indeed, we believe that inauthentic leadership is at the root of what is causing many of the dilemmas facing current and future generations. Leadership has been a significant force in the course of human history with both good and bad results. Shifting our focus to developing more authentic leadership could actually help drive humanity to a much higher and more positive level of development.

The question is: how can each of us commit to a new level of authentic leadership in our lives, relationships, and leadership opportunities? How can we become more aware of our biases, blind spots, and filters? How can we up the level of transparency in our interactions with those we want to instill trust? How can we learn to act more in alignment with our highest moral principles and inner conscience everyday? Provided below are some initial suggestions for engaging this developmental path.

PERSONAL MINI-EXPERIMENTS

Everyday Practices

Life is a series of quasi-experiments where you choose one thing over another in pursuing learning or a course of action. Here are some actions you can choose or not choose to pursue, and the experimental outcomes, so to speak, are up to you.

Discovering Your Authentic Leadership: Assess your Authentic Leadership Development online using a short well-validated survey that assesses the components of authentic leadership described above. Go to www.gli.unl.edu and take the survey.

Personal Reflections to Develop Self-Awareness: Learn what your implicit theories are about yourself and your beliefs about good leaders and effective leadership. Start by listing what you feel are the top positive attributes of leaders and compare your list with a colleague's list. What was the first one you put on the list "top of mind" versus your colleague's list?

Personal Reflections on Your Worldview: Discover your "worldview." Learn how it differs from other people close to you, and how this "filter" impacts your behavior. What is your worldview regarding the responsibilities of leaders to develop followers into leaders? What is your worldview regarding how other cultures perceive exemplary leadership in your own culture? What is your worldview on leadership legacies?

Asking Others About Your Strengths: Try a "reflected best self" exercise (Roberts, Spreitzer, Dutton, Quinn, Heaphy, & Barker, 2005). Ask the key people you work with and live with: what are your strengths, when are you at your best at work or at home, and what circumstances bring out your best?

Getting to Know How You Make Fair Decisions: Seek out conflicting perspectives when making important decisions. Uncover and understand the assumptions underlying your decisions.

Create diverse teams by ensuring diversity of backgrounds and beliefs. Be sure to obtain training for these team members in understanding cognitive biases and learning to thrive from adaptive conflict. Pick a topic that might be controversial and have each member describe their core belief and discover differences.

Getting to Know Your Level of Transparency: Develop transparency in your interactions and trust in your relationships: What information are you most and least comfortable in sharing? Why? Try to share relevant information freely. Regularly seek out feedback and be willing to give feedback, especially positive feedback often. Ask people what they don't know and how you can better inform them. Share your motives and reasoning behind decisions. Make sure that you align your words and actions by debriefing important events to see if you were in alignment. Ask others to give you feedback on how aligned you were from their point of view.

Getting to Know Your Level of Moral Perspective: Align your actions with your highest principles and inner conscience. Of course, you must first engage in some self-reflection and self-awareness activities to understand who you are at your best, and what are your core values and principles. Take a difficult moral dilemma and explore the principles you use to guide the decision that should be taken. Ask your colleagues to do the same and compare your moral principles. Read about world class leaders who you consider the highest in exhibiting moral values and principles. Describe how those values align with your own.

Compile What You Have Learned About Authentic Leadership: Now that you have looked at the components of authentic leadership, consider how they may be applied in terms of your development each and every day. What would you now choose to work on to become a more effective authentic leader? What would you stop doing? What would be your leadership goal and how would you measure success?

REFERENCES

Atwater, L. E., Brett, J. F., & Waldman, D. A. (2003). Understanding the benefits and risks of multi-source feedback within the leadership development process. In S. E. Murphy & R. Riggio (Eds.), *The future of leadership development* (pp. 89–106). Mahwah, NJ: Erlbaum.

Avolio, B. J. (2005). *Leadership development in balance: Made/born.* Mahwah, NJ: Erlbaum.

Avolio, B. J. & Luthans, F. (2006). *The high impact leader: Moments matter in accelerating authentic leadership development.* New York: McGraw-Hill.

Baer, R. A. (2003). Mindfulness training as a clinical intervention: A conceptual and empirical review. *Clinical Psychology: Science & Practice, 10*(2), 125–143.

Bargh, J. A., Chen, M. & Burrows, L. (1996). Automaticity of social behavior: direct effects of trait construct and stereotype activation on action. *Journal of Personality and Social Psychology, 71*(2), 230–244.

Bass, B. M., & Steidlmeier, P. (1999). Ethics, character and authentic transformational leadership. *Leadership Quarterly, 10,* 181–217.

Beck, D. E. & Cowan, C. C. (1996). *Spiral dynamics: Mastering values, leadership, and change.* Malden, MA: Blackwell Publishers.

Brown, K. W., & Ryan, R. M. (2003). The benefits of being present: Mindfulness and its role in psychological well-being. *Journal of Personality & Social Psychology, 84*(4), 822–848.

Burlingham, B. (2005). *Small giants.* New York: Penguin Books.

Burns, J. M. (1978). *Leadership.* New York: Harper & Row.

Debold, E. (2002). Epistemology, fourth order consciousness, and the subject-object relationship or ... How the self evolves with Robert Kegan. *What is Enlightenment,* 22. Retrieved April 15, 2007, from http://www.wie.org/j22/kegan.asp.

Epstein, S. (1973). The self-concept revisited: Or a theory of a theory. *American Psychologist, 28*(5), 404–416.

Erickson, G. (2007). *The day I almost sold the company.* Retrieved February 2, 2007, from http://www.clifbar.com/ourstory/document.cfm?location=journey&id=137.

Erikson, E. H. (1959). *Identity and the life cycle.* New York: International Universities Press.

Esposito, J. L. (2006). The Muslim world: What executives need to know. *Gallup Management Journal, August,* 1–3.

Gardner, W. L., Avolio, B. J., Luthans, F., May, D. R., & Walumbwa, F. O. (2005). "Can you see the real me?" A self-based model of authentic leader and follower development. *Leadership Quarterly, 16*(3), 343–372.

George, W. & Sims, P. (2007). *True north: Discover your authentic leadership.* San Francisco: Jossey-Bass.

Gerber, R. (2002). *Leadership the Eleanor Roosevelt way.* Englewood Cliffs, NJ: Prentice Hall.

Gladwell, M. (2005). *Blink: The power of thinking without thinking.* New York: Little, Brown.

Harter, N. (2002). Authenticity. In C. R. Snyder & S. J. Lopez (Eds.), *Handbook of positive psychology* (pp. 382–394). Oxford: Oxford University Press.

Kegan, R. (1982). *The evolving self: Problem and process in human development.* Cambridge, MA: Harvard University Press.

Kohlberg, L. (1976). Moral stages and moralization. *Moral Development and Behavior.* New York: Holt, Rinehart and Winston.

Loevinger, J. (1976). *Ego development.* San Francisco: Jossey-Bass.

Lord, R. G., & Brown, D. J. (2004). *Leadership processes and follower self-identity.* Mahwah, NJ: Erlbaum.

Lord, R. G., Brown, D. J., & Freiberg, S. J. (1999). Understanding the dynamics of leadership: The role of follower self-concepts in the leader/follower relationship. *Organizational Behavior and Human Decision Processes, 78*(3), 167–203.

Luthans, F., & Avolio, B. J. (2003). Authentic leadership: A positive developmental approach. In K. S. Cameron, J. E. Dutton & R. E. Quinn (Eds.), *Positive organizational scholarship* (pp. 241–261). San Francisco: Barrett-Koehler.

Luthans, F., Youssef, C. M., & Avolio, B. J. (2007). *Psychological capital: Developing the human competitive edge.* Oxford: Oxford University Press.

Markus, H., & Wurf, E. (1987). The dynamic self-concept: A social psychological perspective. *Annual Review of Psychology, 38,* 299–337.

Nilsen, D., & Campbell, D. P. (1993). Self-observer rating discrepancies: Once an overrater, always an overrater? *Human Resource Management, 32,* 265–281.

Peterson, S. J., Walumbwa, F. O., Avolio, B. J., & Fredrickson, B. L. (2007). *Taking on "Hill Street Blues": Examining a more positive approach to leading in police organizations.* Unpublished manuscript.

Piaget, J. (1954). *The construction of the reality in the child.* Oxford: Basic Books.

Pugliese, D. J. (2007). *King: Man of peace in a time of war* [DVD]. North Hollywood, CA: Passport International Entertainment.

Quinn, R. E. (2004). *Building the bridge as you walk on it.* San Francisco: Jossey-Bass.

Roberts, L. M., Dutton, J. E., Spreitzer, G. M., Heaphy, E. D., & Quinn, R. E. (2005). Composing the reflected best-self portrait: Building pathways for becoming extraordinary in work organizations. *Academy of Management Review, 30*(4), 712–736.

Roberts, L. M., Spreitzer, G., Dutton, J., Quinn, R., Heaphy, E., and Barker, B. (2005). How to play to your strengths. *Harvard Business Review, 83*(1): 75–80.

University of Nebraska–Lincoln, College of Business Administration. (2007). Buffett and Gates go back to school [DVD]. Lincoln, NE: Nebraska Educational Television.

Vogelgesang, G. (2007). *How leader interactional transparency can impact follower psychological safety and role engagement.* Unpublished doctoral dissertation, University of Nebraska, Lincoln.

Wilber, K. (2000). *A brief history of everything.* Boston, MA: Shambhala.

CHAPTER 10

Cultivating Civic Engagement

Lonnie R. Sherrod and James W. Lauckhardt

T he first author has a vivid memory from early adolescence that to this day serves to define his interest in the development of civic engagement. "I grew up in the Southeastern United States. Every fall there was a county fair on the other side of town from where I lived. It had amusement park rides, games, junk food, 4-H animal judging, and other activities. I loved going but my parents hated it. For the first time, my best friend and I were allowed to go on our own. We thought this was fantastic because we could now do whatever we wanted at the fair. I was about 12 years of age. We took public transportation and we had to change city buses in downtown. When we boarded the bus in downtown, the aisles were crowded with people standing even though there were numerous empty seats. We stood because the aisles were so crowded you could not get to an empty seat.

At home that night, I told my mom, and she explained to me about the ongoing civil rights movement. African Americans were protesting having to sit in the back of the bus by sitting one person per seat so that the White people had to sit by a Black person in order to sit down. They chose to stand. What amazed me the most was that I had never noticed that Blacks had to sit at the back of the bus—nor that they had separate water fountains, bathrooms, and all lived in a particular region of the city. I also had never observed that there was not a single Black person in my school— teacher or student. My school did a good job of attending to civic engagement, better than schools do today. We took civics classes, had mock congresses and elections, emphasized school government as politics, and even pledged allegiance to the flag until it was outlawed. The schools did nothing however to attend to issues of social justice nor did they socialize students to recognize their freedom to take action to correct injustices when identified.

Civic engagement was defined as obeying laws, following the rules, and *not* "rocking the boat." I should have noticed the gross injustice being done to African Americans, but nothing served to alert me to it, until I was directly confronted with the civil rights movement. Segregation was part of the natural landscape of the environment in which I had grown up."

Our current research shows that teens today often conceptualize citizenship as obeying laws and not as correcting social injustice (Sherrod, 2003). How do we socialize young people into citizenship in such a way that attention to equity and social justice becomes part of their duties as citizens—part of their natural landscape?

In this chapter we review the current mechanisms U. S. society uses to cultivate civic engagement. Cultivate is a strategically chosen word to emphasize that civic engagement is grown across childhood and adolescence and requires the same kind of attention and care as for nurturing a plant. We first discuss existing social mechanisms that research has shown relates to later civic engagement, including civic education, community service, school activities, youth programs and family influences. We next discuss some influences such as the media for which there is less research so we are not certain of their impact. We conclude by discussing some limitations of current research and by considering where we need further research, especially to understand how to promote development of citizenship so that adult citizens are aware of social justice issues.

THE IMPORTANCE OF ATTENTION TO THE DEVELOPMENT OF CIVIC ENGAGEMENT

Citizenship is as important a domain of adult responsibility as work or family, yet it has been the subject of far less research and program attention. I have referred to this statement as my mandate since I have begun almost every paper and presentation in recent years with it. If we are to maintain a viable democratic civil society, we must attend to the development of citizenship (Lerner, 2004; Sherrod, 2007a). Democracies such as the United States are dependent on the active, engaged, and informed participation of their citizenry. It has been argued that we are facing a crisis in this country in terms of low levels of civic engagement, especially in youth (Putnam, 1996, 2000). This argument is controversial; others argue that civic engagement has changed not declined (Youniss, Bales, Christmas-Best, Diversi, McLaughlin, & Silbereisen, 2002; Youniss & Yates, 1997). Nonetheless, we know that voting rates and the level of civic knowledge in our population are lower than is preferred. As a result, it is imperative that we as a nation attend explicitly to the development of civic engagement. Science is a powerful tool for generating information that can be used to design policies and programs to cultivate citizenship. As a result, we emphasize research on the development of civic engagement in this chapter.

There have been two periods of research attention to the development of citizenship across the past few decades. In the 1950s research emphasized early experience and therefore focused mainly on how the family socialized children into citizenship relevant behaviors. Developmental research then generally emphasized early development so that this approach was consistent with then current trends. The second period of research occurred during the 1970s when a variety of social movements were occurring such as civil rights and the anti-Vietnam War protests. This research therefore involved adolescents and youth but it did not really ask developmental questions; it described civic engagement in young people in the form of their participation in these social movements. However, studies at this time did not try to understand how civic engagement developed nor why individual differences arose (Flanagan & Sherrod, 1998; Sherrod, 2007a). Now a new wave of research is emerging fueled in part by Robert Putnam's book titled *Bowling Alone* (2000). Putnam, a political scientist, argues that we are facing a crisis in regard to low levels of civic participation, and that the crisis is especially serious in youth. As we stated previously, this argument has been contested, but nevertheless, it has captured the attention of researchers and policy makers resulting in increased attention.

CIVIC ENGAGEMENT AS POSITIVE DEVELOPMENT

A new approach to youth research and policy, described as a positive youth development approach, is based on the ideas that all youth have needs, so that youth vary according to whether their needs are met, not by individual qualities such as risk and resilience. This approach shifts the focus of both research and policy to fixing environments such as families, schools, or neighborhoods, not fixing individuals. Positive youth development has three important ideas: (a) Development is promoted by developmental assets, both internal and external; (b) communities vary in the qualities that promote the development of these assets; (c) societies at large vary in the qualities that promote these assets. Forty assets have been identified. And it is clear that the more internal and external assets youth have, the healthier and more successful is their development into adulthood (Scales, Blyth, Berkas, & Kielsmeier, 2000). Yet research indicates that young people have only 16.5–21.6 assets on average (Benson, 2004). Hence, we as a society need to do much more to promote the positive development of our young people, and promoting civic engagement is one way of doing that (Sherrod, 2007b).

"Five Cs" of positive youth development have been described: character, competence, confidence, connection, and caring (or compassion). Youth who exemplify these five Cs are likely to be productive members of their community (Damon, Menon, & Bronk, 2003); that is, they are likely to be civically engaged. Contribution is often referred to as a sixth C, and it most directly represents civic participation (Lerner, 2004). Civic engagement clearly represents positive development, but it also contributes to further positive development. The two go hand in hand.

DEFINING CITIZENSHIP

The Cs indicate that the definition of civic engagement is not quite clear; in fact, it is somewhat controversial. For some, a focus on citizenship is often interpreted to reflect a conservative orientation. The first author prepared a prospectus for a textbook on child development and proposed a major focus on citizenship. Reviewers of the proposal argued that he must be a right-wing fanatic from a Christian university! In fact, this author is quite liberal and does not hold any particular religious affiliation, but a concern for the development of citizenship was seen to reflect a conservative religious interest. Having an active, engaged, and informed citizenry, irrespective of political orientation, party affiliation, or specific civic beliefs is a goal that benefits the many and not the few. Walzer (1989, p. 211) offers the following: "A citizen is, most simply, a member of a political community, entitled to whatever prerogatives and encumbered with whatever responsibilities are attached to membership. The word comes to us from the Latin *civis*; the Greek equivalent is *polites*, member of the polis, from which comes our politics." Borrowing from Walzer's definition Flanagan and Faaison (2001) define civic engagement in terms of both the civic and the political. However, Walzer's definition also includes membership— of a nation. And it involves both rights and responsibilities. One responsibility involves generally taking an interest in and being involved in one's country by obeying laws, voting, following current events, and so on. And in exchange the individual gets certain rights such as freedom of speech and certain benefits such as public education—at least in the United States.

Adolescents do have opinions about the duties and rights they will acquire as adult citizens that map onto this differentiation of civic and political. They see responsibilities to consist of civic ones such as showing tolerance or political ones such as voting (Bogard & Sherrod, in press). They see rights to consist of freedoms that relate to political participation and entitlements that relate to nurturance from their community (Sherrod, 2007c).

The complexities of the definition of "citizen" arise because one can be a member of institutions other than the nation state or the government of the country, and such memberships also carry benefits and duties. As a result, the individual can express some of those same behaviors that constitute citizenship through membership in or allegiance to other institutions. Examples of other allegiances or memberships include one's community, school or church, and research has shown that these other allegiances relate to adolescents' views of citizenship (Bogard & Sherrod, in press). But the controversy in regard to the definition of citizenship is whether the behaviors that result from allegiances to community or family should be viewed to be as important to citizenship as actual political behaviors such as voting. The civic would certainly relate to some of these other allegiances but are they sufficiently related to the political?

Another issue for the definition of citizenship is whether concern for others and altruism should be viewed as a component of citizenship. Working for one's community by doing service is, for example, usually seen to be somewhat altruistic. But, can one be quite selfish and oriented entirely to one's own material or occupational success and still be considered a good citizen? What is your view? Would you answer the same if the person is self-oriented but also involved with and committed to the nation state, in regard to voting, campaigning, following news, and so on? At any rate, citizenship is certainly a quite complex domain of adult behavior (Sherrod, Flanagan, & Youniss, 2002). As a result, the developmental path into citizenship is by no means clear.

THE DEVELOPMENT OF CITIZENSHIP

One does not typically engage in behaviors that we define as active citizenship until adulthood. Eighteen is the legal voting age; formerly it was 21. Yet, younger persons can and should also be informed about political events. And some teens do work in political campaigns or do student government, for example. Nonetheless, most do not so that different behaviors than those that actually constitute citizenship are considered childhood and adolescent precursors of adult citizenship. That is, the developmental progression to the behaviors that are explicitly defined as citizenship must involve earlier behaviors that may be only loosely related to civic engagement in adulthood. In this regard, civic engagement clearly shows what is described as developmental discontinuity. Research has shown earlier influences to include civics education, school activities, youth programs, community service and service learning programs. Most research has however involved adolescents because they are on the threshold of exercising their citizenship. However earlier experiences, even during the preschool period, must underlie the precursors identified during the teen years.

There are also a variety of other influences for which there is less research than for the precursors listed above. In today's world, the media are an important influence (McLeod, 2000). Parents and family, of course, have a role; politically active parents produce politically active children (Niemi & Junn, 2000). Religiosity or spirituality has been shown to relate directly or indirectly through participation in service to civic engagement (Lerner, 2004). Finally research has shown that the macro socio-political context certainly plays a role (Flanagan, Bowes, Jonsson, Csapo, & Sheblanova, 1998). Based on research about the early influences on later civic engagement, a small number of programs have been designed specifically in recent years to influence directly the development of civic engagement.

Hence young people may show involvement in and commitment to institutions such as schools or community organizations before they are able to exercise their rights and responsibilities as citizens. Extracurricular school activities, community service and youth organizations such as 4-H and Boys and Girls Clubs, for example, may offer opportunities for behavior that is a precursor to citizenship behavior. However, we need to be more strategic about using these activities and institutions to influence the development of civic engagement. Citizenship is too important to leave to chance. In the remainder of this chapter we discuss these influences and consider what more we may do as a society to further the development of civic engagement.

THE CIVIC STATUS OF TODAY'S YOUTH

In 2006 the Center for Information and Research for Civic Learning and Engagement completed the National Civic and Political Health Study. This study surveyed 1,700 youth aged 15–25 years. Also 550 adults over 26 years of age were surveyed. The sample was representative of the population in the United States except that various ethnic groups were over-sampled. There were 19 core measures of civic engagement; these measures were based on a scale used by Keeter, Sukin, Andolina, and Jenkins (2002). Hence this study provides a reasonably good glimpse of the civic attitudes and behaviors of today's young people. The report of the study offers both good news, in that some forms of engagement are quite widespread, and bad news in that substantial numbers of young people are not at all involved in either politics or community life. Some notable results follow: (a) 72% say that at least some of the time they follow what's going on in government and public affairs; (b) 36% have volunteered within the last year; (c) 35% participate in political discussions; (d) 30% have boycotted a product because of the conditions under which it was made or the values of the company that made it; (e) 26% of those ages 20 to 25 years say that they "always" vote.

The report suggests that some young people are intensely involved. Thirteen percent engage in at least two different forms of both community engagement and political participation. Seven percent are even more involved and report 10 or more different kinds of civic participation. Those highly involved shows a particular demographic profile: more likely to be Democratic (or leaning toward the Democrats), liberal, urban, from a family with parents who volunteer, a current student (in college or high school), and from college-educated homes. They are also more likely to regularly attend church and to be African American. These findings generally replicate previous research (Bogard & Sherrod, in press; Flanagan & Tucker, 1999).

A lot of young people (58%) are not involved at all, failing to report even two forms of civic or political engagement. The report describes these youth as "disengaged." Of these disengaged young people, 28% report doing not even one of the 19 forms of civic engagement measured in this survey. One reason for their disengagement is that have much less confidence in their ability to make a difference than does the highly engaged group. Demographically they are less likely to have college-educated parents or to have parents who volunteer. They themselves are also less likely to have any college experience. They align with either political party and are more likely to be Latinos or immigrants.

One general summary of these results is that education and politically active parents make a difference, in part because they empower youth to believe that they can have an effect through their involvement.

THE SOCIALIZATION OF CIVIC ENGAGEMENT

Civic Education

Certainly education is an especially important early influence. Both the extent of civic education adolescents receive in school as well as factors such as school climate and teacher behavior have been shown to predict later civic participation (Flanagan & Tucker, 1999; Niemi & Junn, 2000). For example, teachers who treat students fairly promote the development of just behavior in teens. Classes that promote open discussion of issues promote higher levels of understanding of civics materials. A large international study recently examined the civic education of 14,000 14-year-olds across 28 countries (Torney-Purta, Lehmann, Oswald, & Schultz, 2001), asking about the teens' understanding of democracy, of the governments in their country, and of their rights and responsibilities as citizens. There was little variability from nation to nation in teen levels of civic knowledge, and overall civic knowledge was not as high as civic-minded adults would want.

Youth need to understand how their government works, how they can legitimately influence it, when it is important to take action to change things for the better and how to do so. Civic education should be of the same national priority as math and science; it is as important to functioning as an adult in society as are math and science, and it is also as important to the functioning of the country (Sherrod, 2003). Civic knowledge is also important because it is the single most important predictor of voting; students with more knowledge are more likely to vote in political elections. If democracy is to work, citizens need to participate, and voting is one of the most important forms of adult participation (Torney-Purta, 2002). Nonetheless the current No Child Left Behind legislation is being implemented to focus entirely on achievement in reading, math, and science. Although a variety of school-based character education programs have been funded, there has been little attention to civics achievement. In fact a number of schools and school districts are abandoning their social studies curriculum altogether because of the need to focus on achievement in other areas.

School Activities and Youth Programs

School extracurricular activities have been shown to be particularly important early contributors to later civic involvement (Barber & Eccles, 1997; Eccles & Barber, 1999). Participation in school government, clubs, publications, even athletics are in many ways similar to participation in politics later in life. The difference is that they support people's schools rather than their country. It is therefore not surprising that teens who participate in these school activities are more likely to participate in civic and political activities later in life. What we need now is research that connects specific activities to later specific civic behaviors. For example, participation in school government would seem to be more relevant than participation in an arts club.

Youth programs can also serve to prepare young people for citizenship. There are a number of relevant programs today including the 4-H, Boys and Girls Clubs, and Youthbuild. Youthbuild is a particularly interesting program. It is a training and leadership effort that employs out-of-school youth to rehabilitate housing in low-income areas. The youth are connected to meaningful experiences, do something to help their communities, develop relationships with building supervisors and peers, and learn practical as well as social skills. Many of the youth move into more management level positions within the program after completing the initial experience. There is a strong commitment and connection to the program among the participants, just as we hope citizens feel toward their country. Participation in Youthbuild offers clear opportunities for young people to get involved and immediately see the results of their efforts (Stoneman, 2002; Tolan, Sherrod, Gorman-Smith, & Henry, 2003).

The 4-H was created for the educational development of youth and to tap their creativity and energy, but it has been associated with clubs that relate to agricultural activities such as growing corn, tomatoes, and pigs or other livestock. Recently it has redirected its attention to urban youth. It is the first youth organization to add young people as voting members of its Board of Directors.

One example of a new activity with urban youth is the Metro Youth Art Force. This program recognizes youth's need for support for their artistic activities (Tolan et al., 2003). Various activities such as weekend workshops are organized from the perspective of promoting positive youth development, which then relates to civic engagement. It promotes artistic expression as a form of involvement. Commoncents is a New York City based program that collects pennies from individuals, organizations, and businesses. This organization has raised hundreds of thousands of dollars. The funds raised by collecting pennies are used to set up small school-based foundations that are run by youth and offer small grants for youth-designed and run projects. Youth review applications for funding and establish priorities (Tolan et al., 2003). As is true for Youthbuild, participants see how their involvement has an impact. They play a role in their schools by funding projects that can benefit the school and all its students.

After-school programs are increasingly popular with youth. There has been very little research asking how participation in after school relates to later civic engagement. One preliminary study shows that after-school programs do not show a strong relationship to adolescents' views of citizenship (Sherrod & Hoxie, 2007). However, this may result from the fact that many programs emphasize academics and offer activities such as homework help. Programs that attend to civics by discussing political issues do relate to views of citizenship (Sherrod & Hoxie, 2007). Hence after-school programs may represent a vehicle for promoting civic engagement that has yet to be tapped for this purpose.

Community Service and Service Learning

For the second author, a high school service learning class had the most influence of all of his high school courses. The information covered in this class addressed social responsibility issues as well as the importance of being an active member of one's community. The students, regardless of their direction in life, learned skills that could be used to benefit their communities. For example, one class unit consisted of completing grant applications to support a community service project.

This project consisted of applying for a grant to improve the nature trail around the school, including renovating the existing signs that described exercise activities that users could complete throughout the trail. Appling for this grant provided a sense of worth within society—a sense that one could actually make a difference. This type of empowerment provided the motivation to undertake and complete this project, which was difficult for a high school student. The grade received for doing the project and the approval of the teacher offered little motivation; the sense of doing something important and making a contribution was intrinsically motivating. This service learning experience was enjoyed by all participants, so that it did not seem like a class. It is possible to look back on the experience of this class and the lessons learned from it, making it as valuable and salient as the academic education. The difference between this type of learning and more typical academic learning is the incomparable feeling of accomplishment and the ability to see directly the impact on something and someone larger than a subject in an academic class. This service learning experience in high school made the second author the passionate positive youth development researcher that he is today.

In the last 2 decades, there has been a significant increase in attention to youth service. One reason for this attention is that there are reports that volunteerism is at an all-time high (Yates & Youniss, 1996; Youniss et al., 2002). Another is that service has been found to relate to a host of positive outcomes, of which increased civic engagement is only one desirable goal (Andersen, 1998; Myers-Lipton, 1994). Service has been found to increase prosocial skills, to relate to positive self-esteem, to promote identity development, to relate to career choice, and to promote civic engagement (Andersen, 1998; Austin, Vogelgesang, Ikeda, & Yee, 2000; Markus, Howard, & King, 1993; Stukas, Clary & Snyder, 1999; Tierney & Branch, 1992; Youniss & Yates, 1999). Although most research on service is not done with typical psychological experiments, there have been a few experimental studies that have reported similar findings to those from correlational studies (Andersen, 1998). Service also relates to future service (McAdam, 1988) and enhances moral development (Leming, 2001; Lerner, Dowling, & Anderson, 2003).

Service has also been found to relate to academic gains (Markus et al., 1993). As attention to educational gains has increased over the past 10 years, a more pronounced movement to combine service and learning has emerged. The term *service learning* was first coined in 1967 as a result of a credit-based internship program for students working on community-based projects with the Southern Regional Economic Board. The practice of service learning was however limited to a small number of participants until the mid 1980s, but the 1990s saw great growth in service learning initiatives. Service learning is in fact now regarded as an educational movement

(Billig, Root, & Jesse, 2000; Markus et al., 1993; Reinders & Youniss, 2006; Scales et al., 2000; Yates & Youniss, 1996), and it represents a significant component of youth's overall participation in service.

Youniss and Yates (1997) have offered the most detailed description of the importance of community service to adolescents' moral development. Adolescents volunteered in a soup kitchen, which had a major impact on reducing stereotypes about the homeless. The authors argue that views were changed through the adolescents' interactions with the homeless they served. They came to realize that the homeless are similar to them; they have just had a different string of luck.

Leming (2001) presents a study indicating one way to promote moral development. He describes two different types of community service. The first type includes a structured ethical reasoning component. The students are given a chance to ethically reflect on the work they do. The second type incorporates limited reflection on the ethics of the service. Students who participated in the ethical expression form of service had a stronger sense of social responsibility within their school. Also, these students focused less on personal pleasure and more on responsibility and helping others than those that did not have the expression component. That is, both identity formation and ethical consideration was shown to be enhanced by the ethical expression component of the community service.

Community service clearly represents the positive contribution of youth. It both uses adolescents' positive assets and contributes to the development of these assets. That is, there bidirectional relationship between adolescent and community assets; by doing service adolescents become both products and producers of their actions (Lerner et al., 2003). Schools provide an ideal opportunity to foster service in youth.

The Role of the Media

Although civic engagement has dropped as a whole, youth political participation seems to have dropped precipitously (Delli Carpini, 2000). Voter turnout, as one among many criteria of participation, averaged 37%, in the age 18–24 category in the past three presidential elections; this was 21% lower than among all citizens. This level compares unfavorably with three earlier elections, 1972–1980, when the 19–24 age group averaged 44% and was 17% below that of all citizens, respectively (McLeod, 2000). This raises the issue of what, exactly, is causing this change. One possibility could be the salience of issues presented in the media.

The media, in particular entertainment television, have been criticized as one important cause for the decline in civic engagement (Putnam, 2000). There is a public perception that entertainment media rarely addresses serious societal issues and instead may be used as an outlet to escape serious issues as politics or current events, especially among adolescents. However, Pasek, Kenski, Romer, and Jamieson (2006) report that media use is associated with greater involvement in civic activities and higher levels of political awareness. This report was based on an aggregate scale of media use, and as a whole, media use was positively related to civic activities.

However some forms of media might have been negatively related to civic engagement but this specific study did not review specific categories of media use. McLeod (2000) found that with respect to political learning among adolescents, newspaper and news magazine use has positive effects that are stronger than the negative effects of television time. Content makes a difference within television use. Watching news has beneficial effects, whereas watching entertainments has a negative influence on civic knowledge.

The growing availability of the Internet implies that this form of information dissemination should have an impact on society, and this impact may disproportionately involve youth since they are heavy users (McLeod, 2000). It does not seem however that youth between the ages of 18 and 24 years are using the Internet to compensate for their inattention to newspapers and television news sources (Keeter et al., 2002). In fact, the Internet is not a more popular source among 15- to 25year-olds than it is for those 26 and older. The frequency of use of the Internet for news information is comparable across these two age groups; the older group may in fact use the Internet more than the younger one (Keeter et al., 2002).

Meyrowitz (1985) argued that one effect of the electronic media, especially television, is the reduction of trust in formal institutions, such as the government. However, it has also been argued that the more exposure could lead to greater political involvement in the future. For example, McDevitt and Chaffee (2002) found that when children reach adolescence, newspaper use becomes a strong predictor of further progress toward political competence. While this information is important, we also need to figure out how we can get adolescents to become consistent consumers of information. Atkin (1981) regards adolescent media use as a cost–benefit trade-off in which the child weighs various gratifications against expenditures such as mental effort. The implication of this theory is that it is necessary to make news media consumption more gratifying for a child so that they are more willing to put the mental effort across to process the information they are receiving. McDevitt and Chaffee (2002) found that news attention is more likely when children perceive that the media provides useful information for conversations or school assignments. Examples of service learning programs aimed at increasing critical consumption of media as well as fostering civic engagement are provided subsequently.

Programs Designed to Promote Civic Engagement

Because of the association between media use and civic activity (Pasek et al., 2006), a number of school-based interventions devoted to enhancing civic involvement have a media component. For example, the Student Voices project piloted by the Annenberg School of Communication at the University of Pennsylvania suggests that Web-based information gathering and interactions can increase high school students' knowledge of and interest and engagement in local elections (Delli Carpini, 2000). In this program, the main goal was to actively engage students in the learning process through interactive exercises.

> The Student Voices Project encourages the civic engagement of young people by bringing the study of local government, policy issues, and political campaigns into the classroom. Working with school districts throughout the country, Student Voices makes the study of government relevant and exciting for high school students by helping them examine how issues they consider important are played out in their own governments and election campaigns. Each class formulates a Youth Issues Agenda, reflecting the issues that are of most concern to students and their communities. These issues provide the focus for students through the rest of the program, ensuring they research and act on issues that concern them. Students use the interactive Student Voices website to find information on issues and candidates and discuss policy issues online. Through classroom visits and forums, students raise their concerns directly to political candidates and public officials and hear what can be done to address them. Finally, students communicate their concerns to the general public by making their voices heard in the news media. (Annenberg Public Policy Center, 2007)

In an evaluation of this program, Flanagan, Syvertsen, Mitra, Oliver, and Sethuraman (2006) found this to be the case; there was an increased overall use of media to obtain political information as well as an increase in use of specific forms of media such as radio, newspaper, and the Internet to access information about political affairs and current events.

Another school-based intervention called Kids Voting, USA produced similar results to the Student Voices program. Kids Voting, USA gets students involved and ready to be educated, engaged citizens through a combination of classroom activities, an authentic voting experience, and family dialogue. The creators of the program claim that their "high-quality instructional materials provide K–12 teachers with valuable civic learning tools to be used throughout the school year, every year. In addition to classroom activities about voting and elections, students also explore the right to vote, democracy and citizenship" (McDevitt & Chaffee, 2000) In an evaluation of the program, McDevitt and Chaffee (2000) found that this school-based curriculum prompted student–parent discussion at home and that there was an increase in students' newspaper reading, TV news viewing, attention to campaign news, and election knowledge.

Not only do programs like these foster knowledge within the students, but they can also have an impact on the family. McDevitt and Chafee (2000) found that because of the student–parent discussion component of the curriculum, parents were significantly more likely to watch television news and become interested in current events after their students were involved in the curriculum than before they were involved with the program. Hence, school-based curricula show a potential to benefit students involved in the program as well as members of their family.

Social Political Context

There have been a number of studies that have examined the impact of major social political factors (e.g., collapse of communism in Eastern Europe, the fall of apartheid in South Africa, and the off and on religious strife in Northern Ireland) on young people's political attitudes and behaviors. The most ambitious of these studies examined adolescents' civic commitments in seven countries. The countries were divided into three stable democracies and four in the midst of social change. Overall this study examined public interest as a life goal of adolescents and asked how it was influenced by volunteering, by school climate, and by family values. A family ethic that emphasized social responsibility influenced public interest as a life goal across both gender and type of country. In addition, volunteering and developing a sense of solidarity at school related to this life goal. Another major finding was differences between boys and girls in five of the countries; girls' families encouraged more social responsibility and girls volunteered more than did boys (Flanagan et al., 1998).

Another study examined adolescents' perceptions of economic changes occurring in three countries undergoing social change in Eastern Europe—Hungary, Bulgaria, and the Czech Republic. Perceptions of the justice of the newly emerging social contract were also examined. Older adolescents and girls were more likely to observe that economic disparities were increasing as a result of the social change; as a result they were cynical about the value of working hard. There were also differences across countries, with high school students in the Czech Republic being the least cynical and those in Bulgaria being the most cynical (Macek et al., 1998).

South Africa is another country that underwent massive social changes in the 1990s, and because the changes were clearly of a political nature, researchers were keen to examine the influence on youth civic engagement. Racial segregation in the form of apartheid was eliminated, a democratic government was put in place for all citizens, and the first elections were held. A study by Finchilescu and Dawes (1998) examined high school students' reactions to these changes. All had grown up in an era of racially segregated communities not unlike what the first author experienced as a teen in the Southeastern United States. All adolescents were concerned about the future in the midst of this change. However, White adolescents felt alienation whereas Black Africans were generally positive. Indian teens and those of mixed racial descent fell in the middle. Age was not an important influence on views (Finchilescu & Dawes, 1998).

Northern Ireland is a country where politics and religion loom large in citizens' daily lives even though it is not undergoing current social change. A study of adolescents in Belfast, Ireland, found that national identity was important to their perceptions of the fairness of the current political system. Teens who saw themselves as Irish or British were more likely to rate politics higher than those who saw themselves as Catholic or Protestant (Whyte, 1998).

The Need for Greater Specificity

Research examining early childhood and adolescent precursors of adult citizenship participation has certain limitations. First, we need to examine how specific experiences relate to specific later civic behaviors. We know for example that civic knowledge predicts adult voting, but that seems to be its only long-term consequence—although we found that knowledge did protect youth from fearfulness following the 9/11 disaster (Sherrod, Quinones, & Davila, 2004). Similarly in regard to school activities, we would expect working for school government to have different consequences than working for the yearbook but available research does not allow us to make such differentiations. Community service carries the desired consequences only if it has certain qualities and most service programs do not show the necessary qualities. HHHence, much more research is needed to understand what childhood and youth experiences promote the development of citizenship, and such research is of course preliminary to designing policies and programs to promote its development. We especially need research that examines those factors that lead to an activist orientation to youth's ideas of citizenship (Sherrod, Flanagan, Kassimir, & Syvelsten, 2005).

Attention to Diverse Populations

Second, the socialization factors that have been identified by research are not part of the life experience of all youth. Poor, disadvantaged youth may for example not be able to afford to do either school extracurricular activities or community service (Hart, Atkins, & Ford, 1998). Sexual minority youth do not enjoy all the rights of citizenship such as the right to marry, and this is likely to influence their views of citizenship and their participation (Russell, 2002). As a result, we need research examining how the diversity that characterizes today's youth population maps onto the early predictors of later civic engagement (Sherrod, 2007a; Sherrod et al., 2002). Different strategies are likely to be needed to promote citizenship in different youth.

A Developmental Focus

Developmental considerations are also critical to the emergence of citizenship. Concern for others as a component of citizenship shows a particular developmental trajectory. Even quite young children show forms of prosocial behaviors and empathy, which may be precursors of a generalized concern for others, for the welfare of other people. Hence, early behaviors involving cooperation, sharing, and emotions such as empathy may relate rather straightforwardly to later development of concern for social justice and to the development of a concern for others (Eisenberg et al., 1999). Moral development is another area that intersects the development of prosocial behavior. Furthermore, social cognitive development and children's understanding of their rights and responsibilities is also likely to play a role (Ruck, Abramovitch, & Keating, 1998).

So in summary, although research offers quite a bit of information on the childhood and adolescent precursors of adult civic engagement, more studies are needed before we are able to launch programs and policies to promote civic involvement in all youth.

PERSONAL MINI-EXPERIMENTS

Cultivating Civic Engagement

In this chapter, we have explored various factors that influence the development of civic engagement in children. In these mini-experiments, we ask that you examine some of these, such as the media and participating in community service. We also ask that you look into voting, which is considered to be one very important index of civic participation.

Use of the Media: Locate two different newspapers, a national one such as the *New York Times* or *Boston Globe* and a local newspaper, such as the *Knoxville (TN) News Sentinel* or the *Pocono (PA) Record.* Compare three news stories from the cover page of each newspaper. Is there overlap in the news covered? What are the differences? Does coverage of a specific event vary in the amount of detail or the specific details? Would readers of the different newspapers get the same information about current events?

Now do the same thing for TV news coverage. First watch a national news show, such as CNN or one of the network news shows usually on around dinnertime. Then, watch a local news show for the area in which you live. Channel 1 would be an example for New York City, for example. Then, evaluate them the same way you did the newspapers. How does the news coverage vary across the different TV shows? How is it the same?

Finally, look up an Internet news site such as MSN or CNN, as well as a local Internet news site, and do the same comparisons as above. How do these vary from the newspapers or TV? What does this analysis tell you about media coverage of news and how helpful it might be to young people's sense of civic involvement?

Community Service: Talk to some of your friends or relatives about community service. Do they do it, or have they done it? Why or why not? If so, what kind of service did they do—e.g., work in a soup kitchen or tutor young children? Did their program include a time to reflect on their service experience, and if so, what was its value? Have they done service learning? If so, how was it different from or the same as service?

Voting: Talk to three people of different ages about their past and planned voting. Poll an adult your parents' age, a young adult 18–25 years of age, and someone younger than 18. Ask them if they voted in a past national and past local election—or if they would have if they had been old enough. Then ask why or why not. Ask who they voted for or would have voted for, and why. Ask whether they have heard of MTV's Rock the Vote or Nickelodeon's KidsVote. If so, ask what they think of them. Do these interviews offer any information about how we might increase the percentage of voters at different ages?

NOTE

Portions of this chapter were based on the Summer 2005 issue of the newsletter of the Committee on Children, Youth and Families of the American Psychological Association. The newsletter can be found online at www.apa.org/cyf.

REFERENCES

Annenberg Public Policy Center (2007). *About Student Voices*. Retrieved April 25, 2007, from http://student-voices.org/about/index.php?SiteID=10

Andersen, S. (1998). Service learning: A national strategy for youth development. Position paper prepared for Education Policy Task Force, George Washington University. Available from http://www.gwu.edu-ccps/pops/svc.html

Atkin, C. (1981). Communication and political socialization. In D. Nimmo & K. Sanders (Eds.), *Handbook of Political Communication* (pp. 299–328). Beverly Hills, CA: Sage.

Austin, A., Vogelgesang, L., Ikeda, E., & Yee, J. (2000). How service learning affects students. Paper prepared for Higher Education Research Institute, University of California, Los Angeles.

Barber, B., & Eccles, J. (1997, April). Student council, volunteering, basketball, or marching band: What kind of extracurricular involvement matters? Presentation at meeting of Society for Research in Child Development, Washington, DC.

Benson, P. (2004, October). Developmental assets and human development. Paper presented at the International Conference on Applied Developmental Science, University of Jena, Germany.

Billig, S., Root S., & Jesse, D. (2005). The impact of participation in service learning on high school students' civic engagement. Center for Information and Research on Civic Learning & Engagement, Working Paper 33. Available at http://www.civicyouth.org/?page_id=152.

Bogard, K., & Sherrod, L. (in press). The influence of discrimination distress and parent socialization on civic attitudes among youth of color. *Journal of Cultural and Ethnic Minority Psychology.*

Damon, W., Menon, J., & Bronk, K. C. (2003). The development of purpose during adolescence. *Applied Developmental Science, 7,* 119–128.

Delli Carpini, M. X. (2000). Gen.Com: Youth, civic engagement, and the new information environment. *Political Communication, 17,* 341–349.

Eccles, J. & Barber, B. (1999). Student council, volunteering, basketball, or marching band: What kind of extracurricular involvement matters? *Journal of Adolescent Research, 12,* 287–315.

Eisenberg, N., Guthrie, I., Murphy, B., Shepard, S., Cumberland, A., & Carlo, G. (1999). Consistency and development of prosocial dispositions: A longitudinal analysis. *Child Development, 70,* 1360–1372.

Finchilescu, G., & Dawes, A. (1998). Catapulted into democracy: South African adolescents' sociopolitical orientations following rapid social changes. *Journal of Social Issues, 54*(3), 563–584.

Flanagan, C., Bowes, J., Jonsson, B., Csapo, B., & Sheblanova, E. (1998). Ties that bind: Correlates of male and female adolescents' civic commitments in seven countries. *Journal of Social Issues, 54,* 457–476.

Flanagan, C., & Faaison, N. (2001). *Youth civic development: Implications of research for social policy and programs* (Social Policy Reports, No. 1).

Flanagan, C., & Sherrod, L. R. (1998). Youth political development: An introduction. Political development: Growing up in a global community. *Journal of Social Issues, 54*, 447–456.

Flanagan, C., Syvertsen, A., Mitra, D., Oliver, M. B., Sethuraman, S. S. (2006). Evaluation of Student Voices Curriculum for the Annenberg Foundation.

Flanagan, C., & Tucker, C. (1999). Adolescents' explanations for political issues: Concordance with their views of self and society. *Developmental Psychology, 35*, 1198–1209.

Hart, D., Atkins, R., & Ford, D. (1998). Urban America as a context for the development of moral identity in adolescence. *Journal of Social Issues, 54*, 513–530.

Keeter, S., Sukin, C., Andolina, M., & Jenkins, K. (2002). *The civic and political health of the nation: A generational portrait.* New Brunswick, NJ: Center for Information and Research on Civic Learning and Engagement.

Leming, J. (2001). Integrating a structured ethical reflection curriculum into high school community service experiences: Impact on students' sociomoral development. *Journal of Research on Adolescence, 36*(141), 33–45.

Lerner, R. (2004). *Liberty: Thriving and civic engagement among America's youth.* Thousand Oaks, CA: Sage Publications.

Lerner, R., Dowling, E., Anderson, P. (2003). Positive youth development: Thriving as the basis of personhood and civil society. *Applied Developmental Science, 7*(3), 172–180.

Macek, P., Flanagan, C., Gallay, L., Kostron, L., Botcheva, L., & Csapo, B. (1998). Postcommunist societies in times of transition: Perceptions of change among adolescents in central and eastern Europe. *Journal of Social Issues, 54*(3), 547–562.

Markus, G., Howard, J., & King, D. (1993). Integrating community service and classroom instruction enhances learning: Results from an experiment. *Educational Evaluation and Policy Analysis, 15*(4), 410–419.

McAdam, D. (1988). *Freedom summer.* New York: Oxford University Press.

McDevitt, M., & Chaffee, S. (2000). Closing gaps in political communication and knowledge: Effects of a school intervention. *Communication Research, 27*(3), 259–292.

McLeod, J. (2000). Media and civic socialization of youth. *Journal of Adolescent Health, 27*, 45–51.

Meyrowitz, J. (1985). *No sense of place: The impact of electronic media on social behavior.* New York: Oxford University Press.

Myers-Lipton, S. J. (1994). The effects of service-learning on college students' attitudes toward civic responsibility, international understanding and racial prejudice. (Doctoral dissertation, University of Colorado, 1994). *Dissertation Abstracts International, 56*(03), 1133.

Niemi, R., & Junn, J. (2000) *Civic Education: What makes students learn.* New Haven, CT: Yale University Press.

Pasek, J., Kenski, K., Romer, D., &, Hall Jamieson, K. (2006). America's youth and community engagement: How use of mass media is related to civic activity and political awareness in 14 to 22-year-olds. *Communication Research, 33*(3), 115–135.

Putnam, R. (1996). The strange disappearance of civic America. *The American Prospect,* 34–48.

Putnam, R. (2000). *Bowling Alone: The collapse and revival of American community.* New York: Simon and Schuster.

Reinders, H, & Youniss, J. (2006). School-based required community service and civic development in adolescents, *Applied Developmental Science, 10*(1), 2–12.

Ruck, M., Abramovitch, R., & Keating, D. (1998). Children and adolescents' understanding of rights: Balancing nurturance and self-determination. *Child Development, 64,* 404–417.

Russell, S. (2002). Queer in America: Citizenship in sexual minority youth. *Applied Developmental Science,* 6(4), 264–272.

Scales, P., Blyth, D., Berkas, T., & Kielsmeier, J. (2000). The effects of service learning on middle school students' social responsibility and academic success. *Journal of Early Adolescence, 20*(3), 332–358.

Sherrod, L. R. (2003, April). Promoting the development of citizenship in diverse youth. *PS: Political science and politics,* 287–292.

Sherrod, L. R. (2007a). Citizenship and activism in diverse youth. In S. Ginwright, J. Cammarota, & P. Noguera (Eds.), *Social justice, youth and their communities: Building theory for more effective policy.* New York: Rutledge.

Sherrod, L. R. (2007b). Civic engagement as an expression of positive youth development. In R. Silberisen & R. Lerner (Eds.), *Approaches to positive youth development.* Thousand Oaks, CA: Sage Publications.

Sherrod, L. R. (2007c). Youth's perceptions of citizenship. In Ruck, M. & Horn, S. *Young people's perspectives on the rights of the child. Journal of Social Issues.* Manuscript submitted for publication.

Sherrod, L. R., Flanagan, C., Kassimir, R., & Syvelsten, A. (Eds.). (2005). *Youth activism: An international encyclopedia.* Westport, CT: Greenwood Publishing Group.

Sherrod, L. R., Flanagan, C., & Youniss, J. (2002). Dimensions of citizenship and opportunities for youth development. *Applied Developmental Science,* 6(4), 264–272.

Sherrod, L. R., & Hoxie, A. M. (2007, March). *The civic mission of after school.* Paper presented at the biennial meeting of the Society for Research in Child Development, Boston, MA.

Sherrod, L. R., Quinones, O., & Davila, C. (2004). Youth's political views and their experience of September 11, 2001. *Applied Developmental Psychology,* 25, 149–170.

Stoneman, D. (2002).The role of youth programming in the development of civic engagement. L. R. Sherrod, R. Flanagan, & J. Youniss (Eds.), *Applied Developmental Science,* 6(4), 264–272.

Stukas, A., Clary E. G., & Snyder, M. (1999). Service learning: Who benefits and why. *Social Policy Report: Society for Research in Child Development,* 8(4), 1–19.

Tierney, J. P., & Branch, A. Y. (1992). *College students as mentors for at-risk youths.* Philadelphia: Public/Private Ventures.

Tolan, P. H., Sherrod, L. R., Gorman-Smith, D., & Henry, D. (2003). Building protection, support, and opportunity for inner-city children and youth and their families. In K. Maton, C. Schellenbach., & B. Leadbeater. (Eds.), *Fostering resilient children, youth, families and communities: Strength-based research and policy.* Washington, DC: American Psychological Association.

Torney-Purta, J. (2002). The school's role in developing civic engagement: A study of adolescents in twenty-eight countries. *Applied Developmental Science,* 6(4), 202–211.

Torney-Purta, J., Lehmann, R., Oswald, H., & Schultz, W. (2001). *Citizenship and education in 28 countries: Civic knowledge and engagement at age fourteen.* Amsterdam: IEA.

Walzer, M. (1989). *Citizenship.* New York: Cambridge University Press.

Whyte, J. (1998). Young citizens in changing times: Catholics and Protestants in Northern Ireland. *Journal of Social Issues, 54*(3), 603–620.

Yates, M. & Youniss, J. (1996). Community service and political-moral identity in adolescence. *Journal of Research on Adolescence, 6,* 271–284.

Youniss, J., Bales, S., Christmas-Best, V., Diversi, M., McLaughlin, M., & Silbereisen, R. (2002). Youth civic engagement in the twenty-first century. *Journal of Research on Adolescence, 12,* 121–148.

Youniss, J., & Yates, M. (1997). What we know about engendering civic identity. *American Behavioral Scientist, 40,* 620–631.

Youniss, J., & Yates, M. (1999). Youth service and moral-civic identity: A case for everyday morality. *Educational Psychology Review, 11*(4), 361–376.

CHAPTER 11

Positive Psychotherapy

Tayyab Rashid

For more than a century, clients have gone to psychotherapists to discuss their troubles, relying on the largely untested belief that discussing troubles is curative. Every year, hundreds of thousands of people attend workshops, retreats, camps, and courses, engaging in numerous brands of psychotherapy, mostly to repair wounds, deficits, and disorders. In all of these interventions, positives are rarely the focus and never are they systematically so. Therapies that attend explicitly to the strengths of clients are rare. One empirically validated psychotherapy that does attend to patients' strengths is positive psychotherapy (PPT).

PPT is an approach that explicitly builds positive emotions, strengths, and meaning in a client's life to undo psychopathology and promote happiness. In this chapter I argue that psychotherapy needs to go beyond negatives and also should cultivate positives. Notions of well-being and interventions based on these notions are surveyed. Theoretical assumptions, content, potential mechanism of action, and therapeutic process are described, and validation studies of PPT are summarized. Finally, some caveats and future directions are offered.

NEGATIVES—PERVASIVE AND POWERFUL

Negatives fascinate us. They certainly did Machiavelli, Schopenhauer, Hegel, Darwin, Marx, and Freud—all of whom perceived negatives as indispensable to human existence. Freud (1930/1995) even asserted that human civilization is a sublime defense to keep sexual and aggressive impulses at bay. Freudian views are pervasive and have significantly influenced art, literature, and academia. Contemporary media is a vivid illustration. It creatively juxtaposes fear, violence, greed, jealousy, insecurity, and sexual infidelity in news, films, music, dramas, and reality shows. Psychologically, stories of evil arouse our curiosity more than accounts of virtue, integrity, cooperation, altruism, or modesty do. The attraction to negatives is perhaps the courtesy of our Stone-Age brain, which evolved putting out fires, attacking trespassers, and competing for food, shelter, and mates. In evolutionary terms, life until recently has been a Darwinian test of fitness. Research shows that negatives carry more weight and impact (e.g., Cottrell & Neuberg 2005; Wright, 1988), and that our brain is wired to react more strongly to bad than to good (Ito, Larsen, Smith, & Cacioppo, 1998; Luu, Collins, & Tucker, 2000). Fear, sadness, and anger mark the defense lines when we are under threat. Negatives are pervasive as well as potent. By one count, there are twice as many negative emotions than positive ones (Nesse, 1991). We ruminate about negative emotions for months or even years, rather than savoring positive moments and memories (Nolen-Hoeksema, Parker, & Larson, 1994). The pain of losing $100 stings us more than gaining $100 would please (Kahneman & Tversky, 1984). Bad emotions, bad parents, bad feedback—all have more impact than their good counterparts. Negative impressions and stereotypes are quicker to form and more resistant to disconfirmation than are positive ones (Baumeister, Bratslavsky, Finkenauer, & Vohs, 2001).

NEGATIVES IN PSYCHOTHERAPY

By focusing on negatives, psychotherapy has made huge strides. Rigorous studies have demonstrated that psychotherapy helps significantly more than placebos do, and perhaps more long-lastingly than do medications (Lambert et al., 2003; Seligman, 1995; Shadish, Navarro, Matt, & Phillips, 2000). Moreover, in addition to psychotherapies for specific disorders, we now have better understanding of the finer aspects of psychotherapy, such as therapeutic alliance, nuances of therapeutic communication, nonverbal language, therapist effects, treatment process, and the feedback process to and from the client (Wampold, 2001; Weinberger, 1995). While the focus on pathology has effectively eased symptoms, it has not necessarily enhanced happiness, which is still neglected in the therapy process. Despite understanding the evolutionary, philosophical, social, and psychological underpinning of the pervasive impact of negatives, there is little empirical justification for psychology's predominantly negative view of human nature, and this view impacts psychotherapy significantly.

It may be time to re-examine our assumptions regarding psychotherapy. There is a growing awareness that some psychotherapies confound response to treatment with full recovery. Psychotherapy outcome researchers have expressed the view that quality of life needs to be included in the evaluation of treatment outcome (Gladis, Gosch, Dishuk, & Crits-Christoph, 1999), and that psychological well-being needs to be incorporated into the definition of recovery (Fava, 1996). Ryff and Singer (1996) have suggested that the absence of well-being creates vulnerability to possible future adversities, and that the path to lasting recovery lies not exclusively in alleviating symptoms but in engendering the positives. Psychotherapy needs to be a hybrid enterprise—promoting happiness as well as alleviating psychopathology.

HAPPINESS: SOME THEORETICAL NOTIONS

For ages, philosophers, sages, and scientists have pursued happiness, trying to define it and enumerating conditions that lead to it. Aristotle observed that happiness is the meaning and the purpose of life, the whole aim and end of human existence. Benjamin Franklin (1733–1758/1980) emphasized its dependence on industry, temperance, and cleanliness. Bertrand Russell (1930) noted that happiness is accompanied by the fullest exercise of our faculties and the fullest realization of the world in which we live. Before World War II, well-being, optimal functioning, meaning, and happiness featured prominently in the literature. Immediately after the World War II, due largely to economic and political factors the assessment and treatment of psychopathology became virtually the exclusive mission of psychology (Maddux, 2002). However, proponents of humanistic psychology continued to advocate for positives in the therapeutic framework.

Maslow (1968/1999) felt that too little attention is given to topics like creativity, healthy and normal personality, love, play, perspective in life, personal growth, and higher levels of consciousness. He believed that a self-actualizing personality has superior perception of reality, increased acceptance of self, others, and nature, increased spontaneity, increased problem-centering, increased autonomy and resistance to enculturation, higher frequency of peak experiences, increased identification with the human species, more democratic character structure, and increased creativity.

Rogers (1959) proposed that every individual has an inherent tendency to develop all his or her capacities in ways that enhance the person. His contemporary, Marie Jahoda (1958) made a persuasive argument that well-being should be explicitly attended to in its own right. Jahoda extracted six processes that contribute to well-being: acceptance of oneself, growth/development/becoming, integration of personality, autonomy, accurate perception of reality, and environmental mastery. More recently, Ryff and Singer (1996) have identified and empirically examined six components of psychological well-being that markedly overlap those of Jahoda. Ryan, Sheldon, Kasser, and Deci (1996) maintain that well-being is based on three universal psychological needs, namely autonomy, competence, and relatedness, and that the gratification of these needs is a key predictor of psychological well-being. These various shades and flavors of happiness and well-being may give an impression that happiness means many things to many people, with a risk of meaning nothing at all.

However, despite this heterogeneity, recent surge in happiness research has offered two converging insights (e.g., Ben-Shahar, 2007; Haidt, 2006; Lyubomirsky, Sheldon, & Schkade, 2005). First, striving to obtain goods and goals does not bring us more than momentary happiness. We are incredibly adaptable creatures who quickly habituate goods and goal. After achieving one, we pursue the next target and keep on replacing targets. We just don't habituate; we also recalibrate (Haidt, 2006). Second, after the strong influence of genes upon a person's average level of happiness, environmental and demographic factors have little influence on happiness. Gender, climate, age, education, and financial status have little impact on our happiness. Yet, we spend disproportionately large sums of time and effort in pursuit of some of these factors. For example, we believe that more money will make us happier, when in fact, beyond safety net; incremental increases in money have diminishing returns (Diener & Seligman, 2004). Noble laureate Daniel Kahneman and his colleagues (2006) have noted:

> The belief that high income is associated with good mood is widespread but mostly illusory. People with above-average income are relatively satisfied with their lives but are barely happier than others in moment-to-moment experience, tend to be more tense, and do not spend more time in particularly enjoyable activities. Moreover, the effect of income on life satisfaction seems to be transient. (p. 1908)

Because of this illusory belief about money, Ben-Shahar (2007) has observed that we often confuse means with ends and sacrifice happiness (end) for money (means). In demystifying the notion of happiness, Ben-Shahar further notes that money and material goods are not happiness but subordinate to it and have no intrinsic value in themselves. They are desirable, as having them could lead us to experience positive emotions or meaning. Happiness is also not a sacrifice; neither is it a trade-off between present and future benefits. It is not a choice between pursuing meaning or pleasure. Happiness is not about making it to the peak of the mountain nor is it about circling aimlessly around the mountain. Happiness is enjoying the journey itself as well as completing the journey. Most important, it is about synthesis, about creating a life in which all of the elements essential to happiness are in harmony.

INTERVENTIONS TARGETING HAPPINESS

Fordyce (1983) was the first researcher to develop and test a "happiness" intervention, focusing on the characteristics of happy people to extract 14 strategies for increasing happiness. These include being active, socializing more, engaging in meaningful work, forming closer and deeper relationships with loved ones, lowering expectations from oneself, and prioritizing being happy. Fordyce found that students who received detailed instructions were happier and showed fewer depressive symptoms at the end of the term than a control group who did not. These gains were maintained in 9- and 18-month follow-ups.

Well-being therapy, based on Ryff and Singer's (1996) multidimensional model, has been found effective in the residual phase of affective disorders (Fava & Ruini, 2003). Well-being therapy emphasizes building environmental mastery, personal growth, purpose in life, autonomy, self-acceptance, and positive relations with others. Its techniques help clients focus on moments of well-being in their lives, keep a written record of those moments, and encourage self-observation.

Integrating Cognitive Therapy with positive psychology notions, Frisch's quality of life therapy (Frisch, 2006) targets the fulfillment of cherished goals, needs, and wishes in 16 valued areas of life including health, spiritual life, work, play, learning, creativity, helping, love, friendship, and community. The efficacy of quality of life therapy was established in a bibliotherapy outcome study with clinically depressed clients (Grant, Salcedo, Hynan, & Frisch, 1995). Next, PPT is described in detail.

POSITIVE PSYCHOTHERAPY

Positive psychotherapy (PPT) is a therapeutic approach within positive psychology to broaden the scope of traditional psychotherapy. Its central hypothesis is that building positive emotions, strengths, and meaning will not only undo symptoms but also is efficacious in the treatment of psychopathology. Negativity bias and symptomatic stress may not lend positives readily accessible to the consciousness and memory of troubled clients. Therefore, PPT actively elicits from clients positive emotions and memories, in addition to discussing troubles. Because, clients who carry weightiest psychological distress care much more about happiness than simply relieving their misery. In this way, PPT is a "build-what's-strong" supplement the traditional "fix-what's-wrong" approach (Duckworth, Steen, & Seligman (2005, p. 631). Thus the focus in PPT is integration of transgressions and acts of kindness, of insults and compliments, of selfishness and compassion of others, of hubris and humility, of hurry and harmony, of hate and love, of pain of trauma and potential growth from it.

Assumptions

A fundamental assumption of PPT is that clients have an inherent capacity for happiness as well as susceptibility to psychopathology. Clients have good and bad states and traits that influence each other. Psychopathology does not entirely reside inside clients. The interaction between the clients and their environment generates both happiness and psychopathology. This is in sharp contrast to the notion that human behavior is primarily motivated by unconscious sexual and aggressive drives. Seligman (2002) calls this the "rotten-to-the-core" (p. xiv) dogmatic view of human nature, which reduces the client to a mere slave of damaged habits and sexual drives. Governed by this questionable view, the function of psychotherapy would essentially be to restrain aggressive and sexual drives. Before Seligman, Rogers (1959) also questioned this fundamental assumption:

> I have little sympathy with the rather prevalent concept that man is basically irrational, and thus his impulses, if not controlled, would lead to destruction of others and self. Man's behavior is exquisitely rational, moving with subtle

and ordered complexity toward the goals his organism is endeavoring to achieve. (p. 29)

Within the framework of PPT, clients are perceived as autonomous, growth-oriented individuals equipped with a sophisticated executive center in addition to an amygdala. Undoubtedly, clients seeking psychotherapy are prone to attend, perceive, analyze, and internalize negatives more sharply than they do positives. Drawing their attention to positives therefore takes on added importance. Clients have the potential to rise above natural selection and consciously civilize their actions and habits to alter genetic influences. Thus, a client's behavior is best understood in terms of dimensions, not categories. Dividing behavior into categories or pigeon-holes obscures reality. As Alan Watts (1966) said, "however much we divide, count, sort, or classify [the world] into particular things and events, this is no more than a way of thinking about the world. It is never actually divided" (p. 54). In symptom and disorder oriented therapy, clients are often viewed as passive victims of intrapsychic and biological forces, primarily needing help with their disease and disorder *only*—not with their overall well-being.

Clients seeking psychotherapy readily describe how negative emotions, negative actions, bad parents, bad genes, and bad feedback impact their lives. The emotional impact of resentments, traumas, sour interpersonal interactions, and setbacks at work and in love is felt more in the therapy room than the joy of accomplishments, savoring of pleasant experiences, and cheer and laughter of friendships. Clients remember pain much more vividly than pleasure; they share with the therapist the struggle of letting go of grudges and ruminations. In the traditional, pathology-oriented model of psychotherapy, these negatives are perceived, analyzed, and further synthesized into the personality structure, with an underlying assumption that symptoms are authentic and central ingredients of psychotherapy whereas positives are by-products of symptom relief or at most clinical peripheries that do not need exclusive attention. So steeped in this assumption is mainstream psychology that the *Diagnostic Statistical Manual* (*DSM-IV*) labels affiliation, anticipation, altruism, and humor as "defense mechanisms" (American Psychiatric Association, 2000, p. 752). Altruistic behavior is similarly considered a coping mechanism through which defense "depressive people often handle their unconscious dynamics by helping others, by philanthropic activity, or by contributions to social progress that have the effect of counteracting their guilt (McWilliams, 1994, p. 238)." Sharply criticizing this assumption, Seligman (1999) has asked:

> How has it happened that the social sciences view the human strengths and virtues—altruism, courage, honesty, duty, joy, health, responsibility and good cheer—as derivative, defensive or downright illusions, while weakness and negative motivations—anxiety, lust, selfishness, paranoia, anger, disorder and sadness—are viewed as authentic? (p. 559)

In PPT the positive emotions and strengths of clients are considered to be as authentic as their weaknesses are, valued in their own right, contributing to happiness in the same way that weaknesses and symptoms contribute to psychological disorders. Human strengths are as real as human weaknesses, as old as time, and are valued in every culture (Lopez, Snyder, & Rasmussen, 2003; C. Peterson & Seligman, 2004). Some psychotherapists may argue that it is difficult to assess positive emotions because these tend to be fleeting and that strengths naturally do not stand out as much as weaknesses. Furthermore, social desirability may elude a valid assessment of strengths because some clients, in order to seek therapist's attention or from fear of appearing vain, may over- or under-report them. Compared with the assessment of psychopathology, assessment of positive emotions and strengths has seriously lagged behind. Only recently was the first serious classification of strengths *Classification of Character Strengths and Virtues* (C. Peterson & Seligman, 2004) published, whereas four editions of *DSM* have appeared so far. In addition, according to Lopez and colleagues (2003), the unfavorable or favorable self-representation of clients to seek attention or to alter perception is part of the response style and content and should be not statistically controlled. Positive emotions and strengths are authentic and should be valued in their own right.

Without discounting the adaptive value of negatives, human existence is not just about resentment, deception, competition, jealousy, greed, worry, and anxiety. It is also about honesty, co-operation, gratitude, compassion, contentment, and serenity. The function of psychotherapy is not only to help client put out fires, eliminate dangers, reduce hostility, or alleviate moral, social, and emotional malaise—it is also to restore and nurture courage, kindness, modesty, perseverance, and emotional and social intelligence. The former may make life less painful, but the latter are what make it fulfilling. Therefore, psychotherapy—the most visible face of psychology—should explicitly incorporate strengths as they are as real and authentic as weaknesses and misery.

The bulk of traditional therapies, especially before the drug revolution, consisted of talking about troubles such as bad parenting, suppressed emotions and memories, faulty thinking patterns, and resentment in interpersonal relations. Portrayals of psychotherapy in Hollywood films (e.g., *Prince of Tides, Good Will Hunting, A Clockwork Orange, One Flew Over the Cuckoo's Nest*) and television talk shows, mostly anchored by pop therapists, have further reinforced public perception that talking about troubles and ventilation of the "inner child" are cathartic and thereby curative. Clients have been socialized to believe that therapy essentially entails talking about troubles. Some clients at the onset of therapy even tell their therapist, courtesy of a Google search, that their troubles correspond with a specific *DSM* disorder. Most of those seeking treatment view themselves as deeply flawed, fragile, victims of cruel environments or casualties of bad genes. Undoubtedly, talking about troubles with an empathetic, warm, and genuine therapist can be the powerful cathartic experience deemed necessary for any form of psychotherapy. For this reason, all major approaches to psychotherapy emphasize that the therapist–client interaction should be positive and that the psychotherapist should generally be empathetic, genuine, warm, and professional (Luborsky, McLellan, Woody, & O'Brien, 1985). Indeed, psychotherapy outcome research has shown that this is one of the most robust curative factors (Orlinsky, Ronnestad, & Willutzki, 2004; Wampold, 2001).

However, this leads to the assumption, without much empirical evidence, that a strong therapeutic relationship between client and therapist is best built while discussing troubles. So, clients and therapists talk about instances when parents did not meet needs, not when these needs were fulfilled; antecedents of interpersonal conflicts are explored rather than situations when an adaptive compromise resolved a conflict; emphasis is on times when clients were transgressed by others, not when they forgave or were forgiven, on the selfishness of others, not their compassion, on insults hurled, not genuine admiration and appreciation received. It is not that troubles are not worth discussing but this discussion is not the *sine qua non* of building a strong therapeutic relationship. Powerful and healing therapeutic bonds can also be built by discussing deeply felt positive emotions and experiences.

Discussing positives can provide psychotherapists with powerful tools to understand a client's psychological repertoire, which can then be effectively utilized to counter troubles. Considering what strengths a client brings to effectively deal with troubles provokes a very different discussion from a pathology-oriented inquiry asking, "What weaknesses have led to your troubles?" Importantly, in PPT the discussion of psychological pain and distress is not discouraged or undermined. Rather, such an expression is encouraged so that clients can place it in the broader context of positives and strengths.

It is worth noting that curing mental illness through talk therapy and emotional ventilation is largely a Western tradition (Nisbett, 2003). The Western mind applies formal logic to reason through troubling states. This reasoning is verbalized and categorized under labels. The habit of categorizing and labeling may lock us into mechanical reactions, argues Jon Kabat-Zinn (1991). Doing so is beneficial for the analysis of discrete emotions and behaviors. However, emotions and behaviors are rarely completely discrete. Their genesis often involves others, along with a host of contextual features.

Clients seek therapy because of negative feelings and thoughts that are painful and hard to let go. However, if psychotherapy becomes an exercise analyzing the minuscule details of negatives, including tracing down their childhood origins or monitoring every distorted thought, then a vulnerable client will be less motivated to explore anything else. In addition, locating causes of resentments in unsupportive parents and significant others, or attributing problems to environment and bad genes, may be counterproductive for some clients, who may come out of therapy believing that "It wasn't my fault anyway." Blaming others creates sympathy, not happiness.

It is an interesting paradox of the Western tradition of psychotherapy that the therapist is expected to give complete attention and unconditional positive regard to the client, but the client is expected to be more self-indulgent (Rogers, 1951). Contrary to the Western view, the Eastern healing practices of mind emphasize contemplation, reflection, and meditation.

Instead of talking about troubles, healing begins by training attention to observe the flow of thoughts and feelings. The goal is not necessarily to change the content of thoughts and feelings. Rather it is to increase awareness of how one relates to them, and to learn to relate to them from a wider, decentered perspective as "mental events" rather than as aspects of the self or even as necessarily accurate reflections of reality (Teasdale et al., 2000; Wallace & Shapiro, 2006).

The focus of psychotherapy should not be limited to negatives but also include a thorough discussion of positives. For example, reflecting on a positive experience that might initially have received insufficient appreciation, followed by a discussion with the therapist, can uplift a client's depressed mood. Similarly, recalling actions that brought joy, contentment, and satisfaction can undo negative feelings. Rewriting bad events by forgiveness and letting go can loosen the hold of anger and resentment.

Theoretical Background

Positive Psychology, from which PPT evolves, is the scientific study of positive emotions, positive individual traits, and the institutions that facilitate their development (Seligman & Csikszentmihalyi, 2000). PPT is positive psychology's therapeutic arm to broaden the scope of psychotherapy from alleviation of suffering to systematic promotion of happiness. It advocates a more serious consideration of the client's intact faculties, ambitions, positive life experiences, and strengths and asks how these can be marshaled to treat and buffer against psychopathology. It contends that positive emotions, strengths, and meaning serve us best not when life is easy, but when life is difficult.

For example, when one is depressed, having and using such strengths as perspective, integrity, fairness, and loyalty may become more urgent than in good times; the strengths may shore up and enable positive institutions like strong family, peers, and social support to assume an added and immediate importance and may cultivate positive emotions to counteract the negative states. Adversity and trauma may build strengths but they more likely reveal them. Psychotherapy can be a powerful avenue of this revelation. PPT is primarily based on Seligman's (2002) theory of happiness. According to this theory, the vague and fuzzy notion of "happiness" could be decomposed into three more scientifically measurable and manageable components: positive emotion (the pleasant life), engagement (the engaged life), and meaning (the meaningful life).

The Pleasant Life

The pleasant life successfully pursues positive emotions about the present, past, and future. The positive emotions about the past are satisfaction, contentment, and serenity. Optimism, hope, trust, faith, and confidence are future-oriented positive emotions. Positive emotions about the present are divided into two crucially different categories: pleasures and gratifications.

The pleasures are comprised of bodily pleasures and higher pleasures. The bodily pleasures are momentary positive emotions that come through the senses: delicious tastes and smells, sexual feelings, moving your body well, and delightful sights and sounds. The higher pleasures are also momentary, set off by events more complicated and more learned than sensory ones, and are defined by the feelings they bring about: ecstasy, rapture, thrill, gladness, mirth, ebullience, comfort, amusement, relaxation, and the like. These are rock-bottom subjective feelings. The gratifications are the other category of positive emotions about the present. Unlike pleasures, they are not feelings but activities one likes to do, such as reading, rock climbing, dancing, good conversation, baseball, playing chess, and so on.

Positive emotions are not a fleeting luxury but a vital need. They change people's mind-sets, widen the scope of their attention (Chesney, Darbes, Hoerster, Taylor, & Chamber, 2005; Fredrickson & Branigan, 2005), and increase intuition (Bolte, Goschke, & Kuhl, 2003). Positive emotions speed up recovery from the cardiovascular aftereffects of negative affects and alter front brain asymmetry and increase immune system functioning (e.g., Davidson et al., 2003; Fredrickson & Losada, 2005). Positive emotions broaden the thought–action repertoire, leading one to increased well-being, which in turn builds social and psychological resources and, in so doing, increases life satisfaction.

Positive emotions likely buffer against depression and many other psychological problems. Tugade and Fredrickson (2004) also have shown empirically that resilient people use positive emotions to rebound from, and find positive meaning in, stressful encounters. Gratitude and forgiveness exercises enhance positive memories and positive emotions (e.g., Burton & King, 2004; Emmons & McCullough, 2003; Lyubomirsky, Sheldon, & Schkade, 2005).

It appears, then, that lack of positive emotion and pleasure are not just symptoms of psychopathology but may partly cause it. In depression, for example, enhancing the pleasant life could be a goal of psychotherapy for depression, and it should be appealing for patients in a way that exploring the details of childhood traumas, arguing against catastrophic cognitions, or taking medication with potential adverse side-effects are not. It should be noted that cultivation of positive emotions is does not mean ecstasy and excitement. Rather the emphasis is on cultivation of more frequent experiences of moderate positive emotion. Research suggests that people who seek ecstasy much of the time are likely to be disappointed. Even worse, they move from one job or relationship to another, seeking intense levels of pleasure (Diener, Sandvik, & Pavot, 1991).

The Engaged Life

The second "happy" life in Seligman's theory of happiness is the engaged life, a life that pursues engagement, involvement, and absorption in work, intimate relations, and leisure. Engagement is synonymous with Csikszentmihalyi's notion of flow (1990). Flow is a psychological state that accompanies highly engaging activities: time passes quickly; attention is completely focused on the activity; total absorption is experienced; even the sense of self is lost.

A number of psychological symptoms not only correlate with lack of engagement but that very lack of engagement may cause them. Engagement is an important antidote to boredom, anxiety, and depression. Anhedonia, apathy, boredom, and restlessness—hallmarks of many psychological disorders—are largely functions of how attention is structured at a given time. When we are sad or bored, the low level of challenge relative to our skills allows our attention to drift. When we are anxious, the perceived challenges exceed our capacities. Negative states are characterized by disruption of attention, disengagement, and mood instability.

Seligman (2002) proposed that one way to enhance engagement is to identify clients' salient character strengths and then help them to find opportunities to use them more. He calls these *signature strengths*. Every client possesses several signature strengths. These are strengths of character that a client self-consciously owns, celebrates, feels a sense of ownership and authenticity about ("This is the real me"), and feels excited while displaying. The client learns quickly as the signature strength is practiced, continues to learn, feels invigorated rather than exhausted when using it, and pursues projects that revolve around it. In PPT, engagement is created by utilizing a client's signature strengths.

This also allows a client an opportunity for growth around his or her deepest psychological resources (signature strengths). The assumption is that when such growth occurs, happiness will take care of itself. Therapeutic interventions have been designed with the aim of transforming daily negative experiences into more positive ones by increasing engagement (Inghilleri, 1999; Massimini & Delle Fave, 2000; Nakamura & Csikszentmihalyi, 2002).

The use of signature strengths in the pursuit of happiness is illustrated in a thought experiment designed by Robert Nozick (1997). Nozick observes that if our brains could be hooked up to a machine that could give any kind of pleasure desired, most people would find this idea quite unattractive. This is because, in pursuing pleasure, we want to *do* certain things and *be* certain kinds of people. In PPT, the engaging life is promoted by encouraging clients to undertake intentional activities that use their signature strengths to create engagement and happiness.

Unlike hedonic activities, which are short-cuts and rely on modern gadgets, these intentional activities are relatively more time-intensive, including, for example, such things as rock climbing, chess, basketball, dancing, creating or experiencing art, music, and literature, spiritual activities, social interactions, other creative activities like baking, gardening, playing with a child, and so on. Compared to sensory pleasures, which fade quickly, these activities last longer, involve quite a lot of thinking and interpretation, and do not habituate easily. These activities are essentially signature strengths in action. The client is coached that happiness does not simply happen, but is something that they themselves make happen.

Any activity that taps a client's signature strengths can be engaging. For example, a client with the signature strength of creativity is encouraged to take a pottery, photography, or painting class; someone with the signature strength of curiosity might be encouraged to make a list of things they would like to know, identify ways to find them out, and meet someone else who has successfully marshaled curiosity to create engagement.

When individuals are fully engaged, subjective states will provide satisfaction and the motivation to continue. Despite distractions, they will continuously adjust the ongoing relationship with the environment to find the optimal balance. Engagement can replace brooding and rumination. Similarly, instead of indulging in "retail therapy" (Faber, 2004) clients are encouraged to pursue explicit challenges that tap their strengths. As they achieve these challenges, they usually develop greater skills in using their signature strengths, and activity may cease to be as involving as before.

When such roadblocks occur, the therapist can help clients identify increasingly complex challenges. As the process continues, clients realize their potential and see that they are capable of creating their own happiness. The therapist then can discuss long-term engagement goals with the client. If the client reports that present engagement is rewarding, then measures to maintain it are discussed. If it is less rewarding, as it may be in many cases, deployment of other signature strengths or trying out of new pursuits is encouraged to expose the client to new experiences.

The Meaningful Life

The third "happy" life in Seligman's theory of happiness is the pursuit of meaning. This consists of using signature strengths to belong to and to serve something the client believes to be bigger than the self. Victor Frankl (1963), a pioneer in the study of meaning, emphasized that happiness cannot be attainted by wanting to be happy—it must come as the unintended consequence of working for a goal greater than oneself. People who successfully pursue activities that connect them to such larger goals achieve what we call the "meaningful life." There are a number of ways to achieve a meaningful life, including close interpersonal relationships, generativity, social activism or service, careers experienced as callings, and spirituality (e.g., Diener & Seligman, 2004; Larson, 2000; Pargament & Mahoney, 2002; B. E. Peterson & Stewart, 1997; Wrzesniewski, McCauley, Rozin, & Schwartz, 1997). One necessary condition for meaning is the attachment and connection to something larger than is the self. Institutions such as church, synagogue, mosque, temple, a professional or leisure club, or a nonprofit, environmental, or humanitarian organization all offer opportunities to connect with something larger.

Regardless of the particular way in which a person establishes a meaningful life, doing so produces a sense of satisfaction and the belief that one has lived well (Ackerman, Zuroff, & Mosokowitz, 2000; Debats, 1996). Conversely, lack of meaning is linked with physical and psychological problems. A meta-analysis on the efficacy of volunteerism shows that volunteers, on average, are twice as likely to feel happy with themselves as are nonvolunteers. Moreover, volunteering contributes to happiness by decreasing boredom and creating an increased sense of purpose in life (Cris-Houran, 1996). Life satisfaction has been found to improve 24% with the level of altruistic activity (William, Haber, Weaver, & Freeman, 1998). Easterbrook (2004) has observed that most Western societies are undergoing a fundamental shift from "material want" to "meaning want." PPT asserts that lack of meaning is not just a symptom but a cause of depression and a number of other psychological disorders. Through the meaningful life, PPT helps clients to forge connections to deal with psychological problems.

The Full Life

The full life consists of experiencing positive emotions in the past and future, savoring positive feelings from pleasures, deriving abundant gratification through engagement, and creating meaning in the service of something larger than the self. The three lives noted above—pleasant, engaged, and meaningful—are neither exclusive nor exhaustive. Most engagement experiences have the potential for meaningfulness.

Similarly, higher pleasures that require considerable thinking and action can become passions. A passion is usually sufficiently intense to engage an individual. Similarly, when an individual establishes and sustains engagement, it often evolves into a meaningful endeavor. The long-term careers of artists and scientists illustrate a sense of meaning emerging from an extended relationship with an activity that uses their highest abilities. Wrzesniewski and colleagues' (1997) study of individuals' relationships to their work provides an example of pleasure, engagement, and meaning encompassed at work, which translates into a career, and then, for some, into a calling. In short, a full life entails pleasure, engagement, and meaning, through separate activities or through a single activity. In contrast, an empty life lacking these elements, particularly engagement and meaning, is partly causal of psychological problems.

HOW PPT WORKS

Table 11.1 presents an idealized, session-by-session description of PPT. Consistent with the theory discussed, themes of pleasure, engagement, and meaning are integrated throughout the course of therapy. Right from the outset, PPT encourages clients to explore their strengths. It builds a congenial and positive relationship by asking clients to introduce themselves through a real-life story that shows them at their best. This is followed by clients identifying signature strengths and the therapist coaching them to find practical ways of using them more often in work, love, play, friendship, and parenting.

In addition, they are actively encouraged to use their signature strengths to solve problems. Clients set goals of using and enhancing their signature

Table 11.1
Idealized Session-by-Session Description of Positive Psychotherapy

Session & Theme	Description
1 Orientation	**Lack of Positive Resources Maintains Psychopathology** The role played by the absence or lack of positive emotions, character strengths, and meaning in maintaining psychopathology and an empty life is discussed. The framework of PPT, therapist's role, and client's responsibilities are discussed. **HW***: Client writes a one page (roughly 300 words) positive introduction in which a concrete story illustrating his/her character strengths is narrated.
2 Engagement	**Identifying Signature Strengths** Signature strengths are identified from the positive introduction, and situations are discussed in which these signature strengths have helped previously. Three pathways to happiness (pleasure, engagement, and meaning) are discussed in light of PPTI results. **HW:** Client completes VIA-IS questionnaire online, which identifies his/her signature strengths.
3 Engagement/Pleasure	**Cultivation of Signature Strengths and Positive Emotions** Deployment of signature strengths is discussed. Client is coached to formulate specific, concrete, and achievable behaviors to cultivate signature strengths. Role of positive emotions in well-being is discussed. **HW (on-going):** Client starts a Blessings Journal in which three good things that happened during the day (big or small), are written.
4 Pleasure	**Good Versus Bad Memories** Role of good and bad memories is discussed in terms of maintenance of symptoms of depression. Client is encouraged to express feelings of anger and bitterness. Effects on depression and well-being of holding onto anger and bitterness are discussed. **HW:** Client writes about three bad memories, the anger associated with them, and their impact in maintaining depression.

5	Pleasure/Engagement	**Forgiveness** Forgiveness is introduced as a powerful tool that can transform anger and bitterness into feelings of neutrality or even, for some, into positive emotions. **HW:** Client writes a forgiveness letter describing a transgression and related emotions, and pledges to forgive the transgressor (if appropriate), but may not deliver the letter.
6	Pleasure/Engagement	**Gratitude** Gratitude is discussed as enduring thankfulness, and the role of good and bad memories is highlighted again with emphasis on gratitude. **HW:** Client writes and presents a letter of gratitude to someone he/she has never properly thanked.
7	Pleasant/Engagement	**Mid-therapy Check** Both Forgiveness and Gratitude homework are followed up. These homework assignments typically take more than one week. The importance of the cultivation of positive emotions is discussed. Client is encouraged to bring and discuss the effects of Blessing Journal. Goals regarding using signature strengths are reviewed. The process and progress is discussed in detail. Client's feedback about therapeutic gains is elicited and discussed.
8	Meaning/Engagement	**Satisficing instead of Maximizing** Satisficing (good enough; Schwartz, Monterosso, Lyubomirsky, White, & Lehman, 2002) instead of maximizing in the context of the hedonic treadmill is discussed. Satisficing through engagement is encouraged instead of maximizing. **HW:** Client writes ways to increase satisficing and devises a personal satisficing plan.
9	Pleasure	**Optimism and Hope** Client is guided to think of times when she/he lost out on something important, when a big plan collapsed, when he/she was rejected by someone. Then client is asked to consider that when one door closes, another one almost always opens. **HW:** Client identifies three doors that closed and three doors that then opened.

(Continued)

Table 11.1 (*Continued*)

Session & Theme	Description
10 Engagement/Meaning	**Love & Attachment** Active-Constructive responding (Gable et al., 2004) is discussed. Client is invited to recognize the signature strengths of a significant other. **HW1** (on-going): Active-Constructive feedback client is coached how to respond actively and constructively to positive events reported by others. **HW2:** Client arranges a date which celebrates her/his signature strengths and that of her/his significant other.
11 Meaning	**Family Tree of Strengths** Significance of recognizing the signature strengths of family members is discussed. **HW:** Client asks family members to take VIA-IS online and then draws a tree which includes signature strengths of all members of family including children. A family gathering is to be arranged to discuss everyone's signature strengths.
12 Pleasure	**Savoring** Savoring is introduced as awareness of pleasure and a deliberate attempt to make it last. The hedonic treadmill is reiterated as a possible threat to savoring and how to safeguard against it. **HW:** Client plans pleasurable activities and carries them out as planned. Specific savoring techniques are provided.
13 Meaning	**Gift of Time** Ways of using signature strengths to offer the gift of time in serving something much larger than the self are discussed. **HW:** Client is to give the gift of time by doing something that requires a fair amount of time and whose creation calls on signature strengths, such as mentoring a child or doing community service.
14 Integration	**The Full Life** The concept of the full life that integrates pleasure, engagement, and meaning is discussed. Client completes PPTI and other measures before the final session. Therapeutic progress, gains, and maintenance are discussed.

Note. HW = homework; only as serial in the table is based on Rashid (2005) strengths through real-life exercises. Substantial time is spent coaching clients to re-educate their attention and memory to what is good in their lives, with the goal of providing them a more balanced context in which to place their problems. The goal is to keep the positive aspects of clients' lives in the forefront of their mind, to teach behaviors that bring positive feedback from others, and to strengthen already existing positive aspects rather than teaching the reinterpretation of negative aspects.

When clients report negative emotions or troubles, they are empathically attended to and actively coached to deal with their troubles by utilizing their signature strengths. This balanced process enables the therapist to become a witness to the client's deepest positive characteristics rather than just an authority figure who elicits faulty thinking, negative emotions, and maladjusted relationships. Usually, there are already plenty of such critical individuals in a client's life, and this can be the very reason a client seeks therapy. PPT should be custom-tailored to meet a client's immediate clinical needs (e.g., conflict with significant others, romantic break-up, or career related issues), and the length of therapy and order of the exercises can be varied with each client's circumstances and the feasibility of completing the exercises. Likewise, homework assignments are selected from the pool of potential exercises in Table 11.1, and the exercises are tailored to the individual.

PPT, despite the implication of its name, is not just about positives. Neither does it assume that all other psychotherapies are essentially negative. It is utopian to conceive of a life without negative experiences. Therefore, PPT does not deny distressing, unpleasant, or negative states and experiences, nor does it aim to help a client see the world through rose-colored glasses. It fully validates the client's negative experiences originating from physical and psychopathologies, dysfunctional families, and ineffective social institutions (Gable & Haidt, 2005). PPT is a systematic therapeutic effort to treat symptoms by explicitly building positive emotions, character strengths, and meaning. In doing so, it appreciates that human strengths cannot be fully understood without comprehending human weaknesses. Nevertheless, a viable way of undoing negative states is to accentuate positive states and traits. As Folkman and Moskowitz (2000) have shown, positive reappraisal (focusing on the good in what is happening or what has happened) and creating positive events help in dealing with negative emotions and experiences.

PPT draws heavily on clients' signature strengths and suggests undertaking endeavors that best use these strengths. However, in using signature strengths, as suggested by Schwartz and Sharpe (2006), clients are coached about practical wisdom. Specifically, clients are taught three considerations: *relevance* (does a particular situation require a signature strength or some other one?); *conflict* (should one be honest or kind?); and *specificity* (translating one's signature strengths into concrete actions, as real-life situations rarely come labeled with instructions for using a particular signature strength).

By drawing attention to positives, PPT also helps clients find potential positives in traumatic situations. Doing so has been documented to yield health benefits as well as growth (Calhoun & Tedeschi, 2006; King & Miner, 2000). In PPT, through systematic and sustained efforts, potential ways of growing from trauma, adversity and loss are explored. However, the therapist must be careful and avoid mechanistically offering empty platitudes, for example, pointing out what wonderful opportunities for growth trauma, loss, or adversity have brought.

Amidst the warmth, understanding, and goodwill created in the therapeutic milieu, listening mindfully allows the therapist to notice and help the client label experiences in positive terms and learn ways to encounter negative states and traits by keeping genuine positives in the foreground. Working diligently and deeply to articulate the genuine and authentic positives of the client, the PPT therapist does not create a Pollyannaish or Panglossian epitome of happiness or caricature of positive thinking. The therapist neither minimizes nor masks under positives unavoidable negative events and experiences such as abuse, neglect, and suffering, and such issues are dealt with under the standard clinical protocols.

Since clients have long been socialized into believing that therapy entails talking about troubles, any perceived failure to take their troubles seriously violates expectations and can undermine good rapport. PPT adopts a flexible approach. While the focus is helping clients explore their positives, it is inevitable that clients will discuss or even, in some cases, display negative emotions and experiences. In PPT, the expression of negative emotions is never dismissed nor superficially replaced with positive ones. Rather, the stance is to explore the role of negative emotions. One PPT exercise explicitly asks clients to write down bitter memories or resentments and then discuss in therapy the effects of holding onto them. This allows the easing of cognitive and emotional constrictions associated with the memory.

Also, in some cases, negative emotions could have unexplored adaptive functions. For example, fear, sadness, or anger might have prompted clients to utilize their support systems. Drawing on the client's personal emotional intelligence, in PPT, clients are coached to allocate emotional resource appropriately. That is, clients are encouraged to undertake activities at the appropriate time and in proper proportion. In doing so, PPT follows Seligman's (2002) advice, "Choose your venue and design your mood to fit the task at hand" (p. 39). Clients are taught that positive emotions are best utilized in seeking out and establishing new social ties, attempting difficult tasks, undertaking tasks that call for creative, generous, and tolerant thinking, finding ways to increase the amount of love in life, thinking about a new career, hobbies or noncompetitive sports, and in creative writing. By contrast, since negative emotions activate critical thinking (Alloy & Abramson, 1979; Norem & Chang, 2002), tasks such as taking important exams, copy-editing, doing income tax, deciding whom to fire or where to move, dealing with repeated romantic rejections, and making important decisions in competitive endeavors are best undertaken when one feels slightly, though not overly, gloomy.

A number of validation studies of PPT have been completed. Individual PPT with severely depressed clients led to more symptomatic improvement and to more remission from depressive disorder than treatment-as-usual and than treatment-as-usual plus antidepressant medication. PPT also measurably enhanced happiness (Seligman, Rashid, & Parks, 2006). Group PPT given to mild to moderately depressed college students led to significantly greater symptom reduction and more increases in life satisfaction than experienced by the no-treatment control group. This improvement, moreover, lasted for at least 1 year after treatment. Group PPT with middle school children increased their well-being, with large effect size (Rashid & Anjum, 2007). Web-based study and studies with mental health professionals and students that initially validated individual PPT exercises yielded reliable changes in strengths and well-being, with medium effect sizes (Seligman, 2004; Seligman, Steen, Park, & Peterson, 2005). Taken together, across samples and settings, PPT demonstrated efficacy, with large to medium effect sizes.

PPT Mechanisms for Change

Psychologically disturbed individuals exaggerate the natural tendency of remembering the negative. They gravitate toward attending to and remembering the most negative aspects of their lives. Several PPT exercises aim to re-educate attention, memory, and expectations away from the negative and the catastrophic and toward the positive and the hopeful. For example, when a client does the three good things exercise ("Before you go to sleep, write down three things that went well today and why they went well"); the bias toward ruminating only about what has gone wrong is counteracted. The client is more likely to end the day remembering positive events and completions, rather than troubles and unfinished business. Similarly, the gratitude visit may shift memory away from the embittering aspects of past relationships to savoring the good things that friends and family have done for the client.

This re-education of attention, memory, and expectation is accomplished verbally as well as through journal writing. As noted previously, cultivation of positive emotions helps individuals flourish. PPT exercises attempt to create positive emotions in a number of domains of life: noticing positive emotions in the present through the savoring and three good things exercises, remembering the good deed of someone in the past, providing constructive and active feedback to a loved one. This allows clients to generalize the role played by positive emotions across situations. In addition, positive emotions stemming from exercises such as the gratitude letter and visit or active-constructive feedback essentially strengthen close interpersonal relations and help clients notice and value the positive things in their lives rather than brooding over negative aspects. Their repertoire of positive emotions is broadened, which can fuel self-transformation and allow them to identify negative thinking and behavioral patterns.

The mechanism of other PPT exercises tends to be more external and behavioral. For example, increasing clients' awareness of their signature strengths likely encourages them to apply themselves more effectively at work by approaching tasks in a way that better uses their abilities. Having more flow at work and doing better work can lead to an upward spiral of engagement and positive emotion. Similarly, teaching clients to respond in an active and constructive manner to good news from coworkers, friends, and family teaches a social skill that will likely improve most relationships (Gable, Reis, Impett, & Asher, 2004).

Another possible mechanism of change in PPT is sustained emphasis on strengths as a way to have more engagement and meaning in life. Throughout therapy, clients are coached in identifying their signature strengths. Near the outset of therapy, clients are asked to introduce themselves through a real-life story about their highest character strength. The Values in Action Inventory of Strengths (VIA-IS; C. Peterson & Seligman, 2004), a well-validated test that identifies clients' signature strengths, is then administered. The therapist and client collaboratively devise new ways of using those signature strengths in work, love, friendship, parenting, and leisure. Clients are also invited to write or articulate detailed narratives about what they are good at. Without ignoring clients' concerns about their "deficiencies," identifying, attending to, remembering, and using more often the core positive traits they already possess is emphasized. This can allow clients to make "end-runs" around their perceived faults.

In addition to increasing their general awareness of strengths, clients are coached to explicitly employ their signature strengths in countering their symptoms. For example, in the individual PPT trial with severely depressed clients (Seligman, Rashid, & Parks, 2006) one client devised several new, specific ways of using her signature strength (appreciation of beauty) to manage negative moods. She rearranged her bedroom in way that she found to be most aesthetically pleasing and decorated her wall with a print by her favorite artist, so that she would wake up to beauty. She had always wanted to write poetry but had never found time; through PPT, she took the time to join a poetry club. She wrote three experiences of beauty in her journal every day for a week, and as she loved hiking, took a hiking trip to climb Mount Washington.

When PPT is effectively delivered with the basic therapeutic essentials of warmth, empathy, and genuineness, exploring and promoting positives establishes an authentic therapeutic relationship. This relationship is as authentic and genuine as the one in which the therapist only attends to the negatives. In PPT, the therapist is asked to care more for the therapeutic alliance than for adherence to the treatment protocol. Tensions and misunderstandings may arise when clients seek only symptom relief but the therapist is convinced that they would benefit from the active promotion of happiness. In addition, a stressed client may be more inclined to complete pleasure-based exercises rather than engagement and meaning-making exercises. In some cases, due to initial emotional distress, clients may not immediately appreciate the benefits of engagement and connecting with others. The therapist should therefore focus on establishing a strong therapeutic alliance at the outset, as from this relationship adherence to the treatment protocol may naturally flow.

In conducting PPT, some caveats are in order. PPT is not prescriptive but descriptive approach based on converging scientific evidence that clearly document the benefits of positives. PPT is not a panacea, nor is it relevant for all clients in all situations. It is not "one size fits all" approach. Moreover, therapists should not expect a linear progression of improvement as motivation to change long-standing behavioral and emotional patterns fluctuates during the course of therapy. Finally, results of pilot studies, although promising, should be viewed cautiously. Rigorous outcome studies are needed to extrapolate generalizability and role of mediating variables.

FUTURE DIRECTIONS

Benjamin Franklin said that wasted strengths are like sundials in the shade. Similarly, traditional psychotherapy has failed to utilize the vital therapeutic assets of clients. PPT taps these resources in a systematic and planned therapy. The potency of positive psychology exercises, the congeniality of the approach for depressed clients, the length of time that benefits last after the end of treatment, and the sheer effect size of PPT when delivered by a skilled therapist are all encouraging. Should these results replicate well, future therapy for depression may combine talking about troubles with understanding and building positive emotions, engagement, and meaning. The effects of PPT appear to be specific to depression, but it is expected that increasing positive emotions, engagement, and meaning can promote highly general ways of buffering against a variety of disorders and troubles.

With the proliferation of research in positive psychology over recent years, happiness, growth, and well-being based therapies are gaining theoretical and applied momentum (e.g., Joseph & Linley, 2005; Lent, 2004). Currently, Lisa Lewis and her colleagues at the Menningers Clinic are comparing PPT with traditional psychotherapy with a larger inpatient sample ($N = 100$). Such endeavors will help to unearth the answers to important questions regarding PPT's generalizability, specificity, and response rate. In order to justify the inclusion of happiness and well-being based interventions in mainstream clinical practice, more rigorous research may be needed to validate that lack of happiness and well-being is a causal factor in psychopathology and that PPT can demonstrate change in outcome measures that are directly related to treatment outcome. To demonstrate potential as an effective preventive strategy, treatment like PPT should be delivered to at-risk populations through longitudinal and prospective studies.

PERSONAL MINI-EXPERIMENT

Enhancing Pleasure, Engagement, and Meaning: In Pursuit of Happiness

This chapter discussed positive psychotherapy (PPT). PPT is relevant to those who would like to enhance their happiness by cultivating positive emotions, exploring and using signature strengths, and pursuing meaning in their lives. You are encouraged to conduct a mini-experiment by yourself to enhance your level of happiness.

Personal Reflections: Using Appendix A, complete the Positive Psychotherapy Inventory (PPTI). Determine your scores on the pleasant, engaging, and meaningful lives. Then, on a separate page, write things that are most pleasurable, engaging, and meaningful to you, that make you happiest. For example, eating crème brulée, chocolate pops, meeting your dearest friend after a long while, burying the hatchet, savoring the magic curl of waves, helping a friend, resting under cool tree, bringing smiles on a crying child's face, building a train model, reading your favorite author, and so on. Also, write how much time you devote weekly or monthly to these activities. Integrate PPTI scores and list to determine if you have appropriate balance of pleasure, engagement, and meaning that makes you happy. If you feel you do not have appropriate balance in your life, write how this manifests, do you feel unhappy, sad, anxious, or listless?

Envision Balance: Next, envision this balance. Initially you will struggle, but keep in mind that envisioning concrete material things (e.g., income, appliances, impressive status, tangible goals) is easier than envisioning deeply emotional experiences such as fun, glee, ebullience, relaxation, engagement or helping others, which genuinely enhance our happiness. Also remind yourself of research findings that clearly suggest that after sacrificing and negating pleasures, when we attain material goals, we become happy—but only momentarily. Recall and write a couple of such personal pursuits. Then write a clear and vivid description of your optimal balance in which you would enjoy the journey as well as the destination. Recall and write one such pursuit from your past.

Eliminate and Manage Barriers: Make a list of uninspiring internal and external barriers that prevent you from achieving your optimal imagined balance. Next to each of these barriers, write ways of eliminating them. If some of these are your own deeply ingrained habits and patterns, do not expect dramatic overnight changes. Rather, focus on what you can realistically do and write at least two practical ways of gradually eliminating or managing these barriers more effectively. If these barriers involve others, elicit their cooperation and reciprocate them in similar endeavors.

Enhancing Pleasure, Engagement, and Meaning: Review your envisioned balance. Write ways of translating this balance into concrete actions, for example, working 5 hours less or working more efficiently, spending more pleasant time with your loved ones by engaging in activities that tap your and their signature strengths such as cooking, exploring gardening, playing board games, solving problems together, volunteering for local community organization at least once a week. Keep the list short, one or two activities in each domain and for each activity, create a ritual. Your ritual may include a small set of specific behaviors, performed regularly at specific times. Make a sincere commitment of continuing these rituals weekly, bi-weekly, monthly, if not daily. Gradual and regular change is better than ambitious failure. Remember what Aristotle said, we are what we do regularly. To avoid habituation, modify and increase skill and challenge level.

Create a Circle of Support: Create a circle of support, which should include two or more individuals who care about your happiness. Share your vision of optimal balance, your rituals, and your commitment of performing them regularly. Elicit their cooperation to keep you on course and ensure that you follow through on them on your commitments. Discuss your progress with your circle regularly. Reciprocate by encouraging at least one member of your circle of support to conduct similar experiment.

APPENDIX A

Positive Psychotherapy Inventory

Please read each group of statements carefully. Then, pick the one statement in each group that best describes you. Be sure to read all of the statements in each group before making your choice.

Some questions are regarding strengths. Strength in PPTI refers to a stable trait which manifests through thoughts, feelings and actions, is morally valued and is beneficial to self and others. Examples of strength include but not limited to optimism, zest, spirituality, fairness, modesty, social intelligence, perseverance, curiosity, creativity, teamwork … etc.

1. **Joy**
    0. I rarely feel joyful.
    1. I occasionally feel joyful.
    2. I feel more joyful than joyless.
    3. I usually feel joyful.

2. **Knowing strengths**
    0. I do not know my strengths*.
    1. I have some idea about my strengths.
    2. I know my strengths.
    3. I am very well aware of my strengths.

3. **Impact on society**
    0. What I do usually does not matter to society.
    1. What I do occasionally matters to society.
    2. What I do often matters to society.
    3. What I do usually matters to society.

4. **Positive mood observed by others**
    0. Others say I usually do not look happy.
    1. Others say I occasionally look happy.
    2. Others say I usually look happy.
    3. Others say I look happy most of the time.

5. **Pursuing strength activities**
    0. I usually do not pursue activities which use my strengths.
    1. I occasionally pursue activities which use my strengths.
    2. I often pursue activities which use my strengths.
    3. I usually pursue activities which use my strengths.

6. **Sense of connection**
    0. I do not feel connected to people with whom I regularly interact.
    1. I occasionally feel connected to people with whom I regularly interact.
    2. I often feel connected to people with whom I regularly interact.
    3. I usually feel connected to people with whom I regularly interact.

7. **Gratitude**
    0. I usually do not take time to think about the good things in my life.
    1. I occasionally notice good things in my life and feel thankful.

2. I often notice good things in my life and feel thankful.
3. I feel grateful for many good things in my life almost every day.

8. **Solving problem using strengths**
   0. I rarely use my strengths to solve problems.
   1. I occasionally use my strengths to solve problems.
   2. I often use my strengths to solve problems.
   3. I usually use my strengths to solve problems.

9. **Sense of meaning**
   0. I rarely feel like my life has a purpose.
   1. I occasionally feel like my life has a purpose.
   2. I often feel like my life has a purpose.
   3. I usually feel like my life has a purpose.

10. **Relaxation**
    0. I rarely feel relaxed.
    1. I occasionally feel relaxed.
    2. I often feel relaxed.
    3. I usually feel relaxed.

11. **Concentration during strength activities**
    0. My concentration is poor during activities which use my strengths.
    1. My concentration is sometimes good and sometimes poor during activities which use my strengths.
    2. My concentration is usually good during activities which use my strengths.
    3. My concentration is excellent during activities which use my strengths.

12. **Religious or spiritual activities**
    0. I usually do not engage in religious or spiritual activities.
    1. I occasionally spend some time in religious or spiritual activities.
    2. I often spend some time in religious or spiritual activities.
    3. I usually spend some time every day in religious or spiritual activities.

13. **Savoring**
    0. I usually rush through things and don't slow down to enjoy them.
    1. I occasionally savor at things that bring me pleasure.
    2. I savor at least one thing that brings me pleasure every day.
    3. I usually let myself get immersed in pleasant experiences so that I can savor them fully.

14. **Time during strength activities**
    0. Time passes slowly when I am engaged in activities that use my strengths.
    1. Time passes ordinarily when I am engaged in activities that use my strengths.
    2. Time passes quickly when I am engaged in activities that use my strengths.
    3. I lose the sense of time when I am engaged in activities that use my strengths.

15. **Closeness with loved ones**
    0. I usually do not feel close to my loved ones.
    1. I occasionally feel close to my loved ones.
    2. I often feel close to my loved ones.
    3. I usually feel close to my loved ones.

16. **Laughing/smiling**
    0. I usually do not laugh much.
    1. I occasionally laugh heartily.
    2. I often laugh heartily.
    3. I usually laugh heartily several times each day.

17. **Managing strength activities**
    0. It is usually hard for me to manage activities which use my strengths.
    1. I can occasionally manage activities which use my strengths.
    2. I often can manage well activities which use my strengths.
    3. Managing activities which use my strengths comes almost natural to me.

18. **Contributing to something larger**
    0. I rarely do things that contribute to a larger cause.
    1. I occasionally do things that contribute to a larger cause.
    2. I often do things that contribute to a larger cause.
    3. I usually do things that contribute to a larger cause.

19. **Zest**
    0. I usually have little or no energy.
    1. I occasionally feel energized.
    2. I often feel energized.
    3. I usually feel energized.

20. **Accomplishment in strength activities**
    0. I do not feel a sense of accomplishment when I spend time in activities which use my strengths.
    1. I occasionally feel a sense of accomplishment when I spend time in activities which use my strengths.
    2. I often feel a sense of accomplishment when I spend time in activities which use my strengths.
    3. I usually feel a sense of accomplishment when I spend time in activities which use my strengths.

21. **Using strengths to help others**
    0. I rarely use my strengths to help others.
    1. I occasionally use my strengths to help others, mostly when they ask.
    2. I often use my strengths to help others.
    3. I regularly use my strengths to help others.

Please add scores to compute:

Pleasant Life

1. Joy —
4. Positive mood observed by others —

7. Gratitude —
10. Relaxation —
13. Savoring —
16. Laughing/smiling —
19. Zest —
Total _____

Engaged Life

2. Knowing strengths —
5. Pursuing strength activities —
8. Solving problems using strengths —
11. Concentration during strength activities —
14. Time during strength activities —
17. Managing strength activities —
20. Accomplishment in strength activities —
Total _____

Meaningful Life

3. Impact on society —
6. Sense of connection —
9. Sense of meaning —
12. Religious or spiritual activities —
15. Closeness with loved ones —
18. Contributing to something larger —
21. Using strengths to help others —
Total _____

Overall Happiness Score*

Life (range)	Depressed Adults	Non-depressed Adults	*Your Score*
Pleasant Life (0–21)	8	13	
Engaged Life (0–21)	10	14	
Meaningful Life (0–21)	9	12	
Total (0–63)	27	39	

*Scores based on a normative study of 302 adults. For psychometric details please email (tayyab@psych.upenn.edu)

Copyright by Tayyab Rashid. This inventory can be used for research or clinical purposes without contacting the author.

REFERENCES

Ackerman, S., Zuroff, D. C., & Moskowitz, D. S. (2000). Generativity in midlife and young adults: Links to agency, communion, and subjective well-being. *International Journal of Aging & Human Development, 50*, 17–41.

Alloy, L. B., & Abramson, L. Y. (1979). Judgment of contingency in depressed and nondepressed students: Sadder but wiser. *Journal of Experimental Psychology: General, 108,* 441–485.

American Psychiatric Association. (2000). *Diagnostic and statistical manual of mental disorders* (4th ed., text rev.). Washington, DC: Author.

Baumeister, R. F., Bratslavsky, E., Finkenauer, C., & Vohs, K. D. (2001). Bad is stronger than good. *Review of General Psychology, 5,* 323–370.

Ben-Shahar, T. (2007). *Happier.* New York: McGraw-Hill.

Bolte, A., Goschke, T., & Kuhl, J. (2003). Emotion and intuition: Effects of positive and negative mood on implicit judgments of semantic coherence. *Psychological Science, 14,* 416–421.

Burton, C. M., & King, L. A. (2004). The health benefits of writing about intensely positive experiences. *Journal of Research in Personality, 38,* 150–163.

Calhoun, L., & Tedeschi, R. (2006). *The handbook of posttraumatic growth: Research and practice.* Mahwah, NJ: Erlbaum.

Chesney, M. A., Darbes, L. A., Hoerster, K., Taylor, J. M., & Chamber, D. B. (2005). Positive emotions: Exploring the other hemisphere in behavioral medicine. *International Journal of Behavioral Medicine, 12,* 50–58.

Cottrell, C. A., & Neuberg, S. L. (2005). Different emotional reactions to different groups: A sociofunctional threat-based approach to "prejudice." *Journal of Personality and Social Psychology, 88,* 770–789.

Cris-Houran, M. (1996). Efficacy of volunteerism. *Psychological Reports, 79,* 736–738.

Csikszentmihalyi, M. (1990). *Flow: The psychology of optimal experience.* New York: HarperCollins.

Davidson, R. J., Kabat-Zinn, J., Schumacher, J., Rosenkranz, M., Muller, D., Santorelli, S. F., et al. (2003). Alterations in brain and immune function produced by mindfulness meditation. *Psychosomatic Medicine, 65,* 564–570.

Debats, D. L. (1996). Meaning in life: Clinical relevance and predictive power. *British Journal of Clinical Psychology, 35,* 503–516.

Diener, E., Sandvik, E., & Pavot, W. (1991). Happiness is the frequency, not the intensity of positive versus negative affects. In F. Strack, M. Argyle, & N. Schwarz (Eds.), *Subjective well-being: An interdisciplinary perspective* (pp. 119–139). New York: Pergamon Press.

Diener, E., & Seligman, M. E. P. (2004). Beyond money: Towards an economy of well-being, *Psychological Science in Public Interest, 5,* 31–62.

Duckworth, A. L., Steen, T. A., & Seligman, M. E. P. (2005). Positive psychology in clinical practice. *Annual Review of Clinical Psychology, 1,* 629–651.

Easterbrook, G. (2004). *The progress paradox: How life gets better while people feel worse.* New York: Random House.

Emmons, R. A., & McCullough, M. E. (2003). Counting blessings versus burdens: Experimental studies of gratitude and subjective well-being in daily life. *Journal of Personality and Social Psychology, 84,* 377–389.

Faber, R. J. (2004). Self-control and compulsive buying. In T. Kasser & A. D. Kanner (Eds.), *Psychology and consumer culture: The struggle for a good life in a materialistic world* (pp. 169–187). Washington, DC: American Psychological Association.

Fava, G. A. (1996). The concept of recovery in affective disorders. *Psychotherapy and Psychosomatics, 65,* 2–13.

Fava, G. A., & Ruini, C. (2003). Development and characteristics of a well-being enhancing psychotherapeutic strategy: Well-being therapy. *Journal of Behavior Therapy and Experimental Psychiatry, 34,* 45–63.

Folkman, S., & Moskowitz, J. T. (2000). Stress, positive emotion, and coping. *Current Directions in Psychological Science, 9,* 115–118.

Fordyce, M. W. (1983). A program to increase happiness: Further studies. *Journal of Consulting Psychology, 30,* 483–498.

Frankl, V. E. (1963). *Man's search for meaning: An introduction to logotherapy.* New York: Washington Square Press.

Franklin, B. (1980). *Poor Richard's almanac.* Mount Vernon, NY: Peter Pauper Press. (Originally published 1733–1758)

Fredrickson, B. L., & Branigan, C. (2005). Positive emotions broaden the scope of attention and thought-action repertoires. *Cognition and Emotion, 19,* 313–332.

Fredrickson, B. L, & Losada, M. (2005). Positive affect and the complex dynamics of human flourishing. *American Psychologist, 60,* 678–686.

Freud, S. (1995). Civilization and its discontent. In P. Gay (Ed.), *The Freud reader.* London: Vintage. (Originally published 1930)

Frisch, M. B. (2006). *Quality of life therapy: Applying a life satisfaction approach to positive psychology and cognitive therapy.* Hoboken, NJ: Wiley.

Gable, S. L., & Haidt, J. (2005). What (and why) is positive psychology? *Review of General Psychology, 9,* 103–110.

Gable, S. L, Reis, H. T., Impett, E. A., & Asher, E. R. (2004). What do you do when things go right? The intrapersonal and interpersonal benefits of sharing positive events. *Journal of Personality and Social Psychology. 87,* 228–245.

Gladis, M. M., Gosch, E. A., Dishuk, N. M., & Crits-Christoph, P. (1999). Quality of life: expanding the scope of clinical significance. *Journal of Consulting & Clinical Psychology, 67,* 320–331.

Grant, G., Salcedo, V., Hynan, L., & Frisch, M. B. (1995). Effectiveness of quality of life therapy for depression. *Psychological Reports, 76,* 1203–1208.

Haidt, J. (2006). *The happiness hypothesis: Finding modern truth in ancient wisdom.* New York: Basic Books.

Inghilleri, P. (1999). *From subjective experience to cultural change.* Cambridge and New York: Cambridge University Press.

Ito, T. A., Larsen, J. T., Smith, N. K., & Cacioppo, J. T. (1998). Negative information weighs more heavily on the brain: The negativity bias in evaluative categorizations. *Journal of Personality & Social Psychology, 75,* 887–900.

Jahoda, M. (1958). *Current concepts of positive mental health.* New York: Basic Books.

Joseph, S., & Linley, A. P. (2005). Positive psychological approaches to therapy. *Counseling and Psychotherapy Research, 5,* 5–10.

Kabat-Zinn, J. (1991). *Full catastrophe living: Using the wisdom of your body and mind to face stress, pain, and illness.* New York: Dell Publishing.

Kahneman, D., Krueger, A. B., Schkade, D., Schwartz, N., & Stone, A. A. (2006). Would you be happier if you were richer? A focusing illusion. *Science, 312,* 1908–1910.

Kahneman, D., & Tversky, A. (1984). Choices, values, and frames. *American Psychologist, 39,* 341–350.

King, L., & Miner, K. (2000). Writing about the perceived benefits of traumatic events: Implications for physical health. *Personality and Social Psychology Bulletin, 26,* 220–230.

Lambert, M. J., Whipple, J. L., Hawkins, E. J., Vermeersch, D. A., Nielsen, S. L., & Smart, D. W. (2003). Is it time for clinicians to routinely track patient outcome? A meta-analysis. *Clinical Psychology: Science and Practice, 10,* 288–301.

Larson, R. W. (2000). Toward a psychology of positive youth development. *American Psychologist, 55,* 170–183.

Lent, R. W. (2004). Towards a unifying theoretical and practical perspective on well-being and psychosocial adjustment. *Journal of Counseling Psychology, 5,* 482–509.

Lopez, S. J., Synder, C. R., & Rasmussen, N. H. (2003). Striking a vital balance: Developing a complementary focus on human weakness and strength through positive psychological assessment. In S. J. Lopez & C. R. Snyder (Eds.), *Positive psychological assessment: A handbook of models and measures.* (pp. 3–20). Washington, DC: American Psychological Association.

Luborsky, L., McLellan, A. T., Woody, G., & O'Brien, C. (1985). Therapist success and its determinants, *Archives of General Psychiatry, 42,* 602–611.

Luu, P., Collins, P., & Tucker, D. M. (2000). Mood, personality, and self-monitoring: Negative affect and emotionality in relation to frontal lobe mechanisms of error monitoring. *Journal of Experimental Psychology, 129,* 43–60.

Lyubomirsky, S., Sheldon, K. M., & Schkade, D. (2005). Pursuing happiness: The architecture of sustainable change. *Review of General Psychology, 9,* 111–131.

Maddux, J. E. (2002). Stopping the "madness": Positive psychology and the deconstruction of illness ideology and the *DSM.* In C. R. Snyder & S. J. Lopez (Eds.), *Handbook of positive psychology* (pp. 13–25). New York and Oxford: Oxford University Press.

Maslow, A. H. (1999). *Towards a psychology of being* (3rd ed.). New York: Wiley. (Originally published 1968).

Massimini, F., & Delle Fave, A. (2000). Individual development in a bio-cultural perspective. *American Psychologist, 55,* 24–33.

McWilliams, N. (1994). *Psychoanalytic diagnosis.* New York: Guilford.

Nakamura, J., & Csikszentmihalyi, M. (2002). The concept of flow. In C. R. Snyder & S. J. Lopez (Eds.), *Handbook of positive psychology* (pp. 89–105). New York and Oxford: Oxford University Press.

Nesse, R. M. (1991). What good is feeling bad? *The Sciences, 31,* 30–37.

Nisbett, R. E. (2003). *The geography of thought: How Asians and Westerners think differently ... and why?* New York: The Free Press.

Nolen-Hoeksema, S., Parker, L. E., & Larson, J. (1994). Ruminative coping with depressed mood following loss. *Journal of Personality and Social Psychology, 67,* 92–104.

Norem, J., & Chang, E. (2002). The positive psychology of negative thinking. *Journal of Clinical Psychology, 58,* 993–1001.

Nozick, R. (1997). Value and pleasure. In T. L. Carson & P. L. Moser (Eds.), *Morality and the good life* (pp. 135–144). New York and Oxford: Oxford University Press.

Orlinsky, D. E., Ronnestad, M. H., & Willutzki, U. (2004). Fifty years of psychotherapy process-outcome research: Continuity and change. In M. J. Lambert (Ed.), *Bergin and Garfield's handbook of psychotherapy and behavior change,* (5th ed., pp. 307–389), New York: Wiley.

Pargament, K. I., & Mahoney, A. (2002). Spirituality: Discovering and conserving the sacred. In C. R. Snyder & S. J. Lopez (Eds.), *Handbook of positive psychology* (pp. 646–659). New York and Oxford: Oxford University Press.

Peterson, B. E., & Stewart, A. J. (1993). Generativity and social motives in young adults. *Journal of Personality and Social Psychology, 65,* 186–198.

Peterson, C., & Seligman, M. E. P. (2004). *Character strengths and virtues: A handbook and classification.* New York and Oxford: Oxford University Press and Washington, DC: American Psychological Association.

Rashid, T. (2005). *Positive psychotherapy inventory.* Unpublished manuscript. University of Pennsylvania. Philadelphia, PA.

Rashid, T., & Anjum. A (2007). Positive psychotherapy for children and adolescents. In J. R. Z. Abela & B. L. Hankin (Eds.), *Depression in children and adolescents: Causes, treatment and prevention.* New York: Guilford Press.

Rogers, C. R. (1951). *Client-centered therapy: Its current practice, implications, and theory.* Boston: Houghton Mifflin.

Rogers, C. R. (1959). A theory of therapy, personality and interpersonal relationships, as developed in the client-centered framework. In S. Koch (Ed.), *Psychology: A study of a science: Vol. 3. Foundations of the person and the social context* (pp. 184–256). New York: McGraw-Hill.

Russell, B. (1930). *The conquest of happiness.* New York: Liveright.

Ryan, R. M., Sheldon, K. M., Kasser, T., & Deci, E. L. (1996). All goals are not created equal: An organismic perspective on the nature of goals and their regulation. In P. M. Gollwitzer & J. A. Bargh (Eds.), *The psychology of action: Linking cognition and motivation to behavior* (pp. 7–47). New York: Guilford Press.

Ryff, C. D., & Singer, B. (1996). Psychological well-being: Meaning, measurement, and implications for psychotherapy research. *Psychotherapy and Psychosomatics, 65,* 14–23.

Schwartz, B., Monterosso, J., Lyubomirsky, S., White, K., & Lehman, D. R. (2002). Maximizing versus satisficing: Happiness is a matter of choice. *Journal of Personality and Social Psychology, 83,* 1178–1197.

Schwartz, B., & Sharpe, K. E. (2006). Practical wisdom: Aristotle meets positive psychology. *Journal of Happiness Studies, 7,* 377–395.

Seligman, M. E. P. (1995). The effectiveness of psychotherapy: The Consumer Reports study. *American Psychologist, 50,* 965–974.

Seligman, M. E. P. (1999). The president's address. *American Psychologist, 54,* 559–562.

Seligman, M. E. P. (2002). *Authentic happiness: Using the new Positive Psychology to realize your potential for lasting fulfillment.* New York: Free Press.

Seligman, M. E. P. (2004, September). Positive interventions: More evidence of effectiveness. *Authentic Happiness Newsletter,* Retrieved January 9, 2007, from http://www.authentichappiness.sas.upenn.edu/newsletter.aspx?id=45

Seligman, M. E. P., & Csikszentmihalyi, M. (2000). Positive psychology: An introduction. *American Psychologist, 55,* 5–14.

Seligman, M. E. P., Rashid, T., & Parks, A. C. (2006). Positive psychotherapy. *American Psychologist, 61,* 774–788.

Seligman, M. E. P., Steen, T. A., Park, N., & Peterson, C. (2005). Positive psychology progress: Empirical validation of interventions. *American Psychologist, 60,* 410–421.

Shadish, W. R., Navarro, A. M., Matt, G. E., & Phillips, G. (2000). The effects of psychological therapies under clinically representative conditions: A meta-analysis. *Psychological Bulletin, 126,* 512–529.

Teasdale, J. D., Segal, Z. V., & William, J. M., Ridgeway, V. A., Soulsby, J. M., & Lou, M. A. (2000). Prevention of relapse/recurrence in major depression by mindfulness-based cognitive therapy. *Journal of Consulting and Clinical Psychology, 68,* 615–623.

Tugade, M. M., & Fredrickson, B. L. (2004). Resilient individuals use positive emotions to bounce back from negative emotional experiences. *Journal of Personality and Social Psychology, 86,* 320–333.

Wallace, A. B., & Shapiro, S. L. (2006). Mental balance and well-being :Building bridges between Buddhism and western psychology. *American Psychologist, 61,* 690–701.

Wampold, B. E. (2001). *The great psychotherapy debate: Models, methods, and findings.* Mahwah, NJ: Erlbaum.

Watts, A. (1966). *The book: On the taboo against knowing who you are.* New York: Vintage.

Weinberger, J. (1995). Common factors aren't so common: The common factors dilemma. *Clinical Psychology: Science and Practice, 2,* 45–69.

William, A., Haber, D., Weaver, G., & Freeman, J. (1998). Altruistic activity. *Activities, Adaptation and Aging, 22,* 31–43.

Wright, B. A. (1988). Attitudes and the fundamental negative bias. In H. E. Yuker (Ed.), *Attitudes toward persons with disabilities* (pp. 3–21). New York: Springer.

Wrzesniewski, A., McCauley, C., Rozin, P., & Schwartz, B. (1997). Jobs, careers, and callings: People's relations to their work. *Journal of Research in Personality, 31,* 21–33.

Index

About the Editor and Contributors

Shane J. Lopez is research director of the Clifton Strengths Institute and a Gallup senior scientist. He serves on the editorial board of the *Journal of Positive Psychology* and on the advisory board for Ready, Set, Learn, The Discovery Channel's preschool educational television programming. He is examining the effectiveness of hope training programs in the schools, refining a model of psychological courage, and exploring the link between soft life skills and hard outcomes in education, work, health, and family functioning. His books include *The Handbook of Positive Psychology, Positive Psychological Assessment: A Handbook of Models and Measures*, and *Positive Psychology: Scientific and Practical Explorations of Human Strengths*, all with C. R. Snyder.

Virginia Miller Ambler is assistant vice president for student affairs at the College of William and Mary in Virginia, where she earned her Ph.D. in Educational Planning, Policy, and Leadership. A member of Phi Beta Kappa, she also received the National Association of Student Personnel Administrators' 2007 Melvene D. Hardee Dissertation of the Year Award for her doctoral research titled *Who Flourishes in College? Using Positive Psychology and Student Involvement Theory to Explore Mental Health among Traditionally Aged Undergraduates.*

Bruce J. Avolio holds the Clifton Chair in Leadership at the University of Nebraska and is the director of the Global Leadership Institute. He has published nine books and more than a hundred articles on leadership and related areas. His most recent books are *Leadership Development in Balance: Made/ Born, The High Impact Leader: Moments Matter in Authentic Leadership Development*, and *Psychological Capital: Developing the Human Competitive Edge* (with Fred Luthans and Carolyn Youssef).

Matthew Buckman is a graduate student in the school psychology program at the University of Kentucky. His research interests include investigating differences in perceived bullying by teachers and students, and peer victimization. His research has been presented at various national conferences, including the American Psychological Association and the National Association of School Psychologists.

Bart Duriez is a postdoctoral researcher at the Center for Developmental Psychology of the Catholic University of Leuven, Belgium. His main research interests are the development of prejudice dispositions during adolescence and the interplay of prejudice dispositions with group processes and other environmental characteristics in the development of negative outgroup attitudes.

John Eagle is an assistant professor in the School Psychology Program at Rhode Island College. He has published and presented extensively in the areas of parent involvement in education, home-school-community partnerships, and school-based consultation. In 2006, he was selected as an Early Career Scholar by the Society for the Study of School Psychology.

Richard Gilman is an associate professor and coordinator of the Psychology and Special Education Program in the Division of Developmental and Behavioral Pediatrics at Children's Hospital Medical Center in Cincinnati, Ohio. He is also an affiliated faculty member in the Department of Pediatrics at the University of Cincinnati. He has written extensively about factors contributing to the positive development of children and adolescents. His research has been recognized by Division 16 of the American Psychological Association for early career contributions. He is the co-editor (with Michael Furlong and E. Scott Huebner) of the *Handbook of Positive Psychology in Schools.*

James K. Harter is a principal and the chief scientist for Workplace Management and Well-Being research at the Gallup Organization. Since 1985 he has authored or coauthored studies that focus on individual strengths, workplace productivity, and well-being. He is coauthor of the New York Times bestseller *12: The Elements of Great Managing.* In 2002, he coauthored a paper that was awarded "outstanding publication" in Organizational Behavior for the Academy of Management.

E. Scott Huebner is a professor and the director of the School Psychology Program at the University of South Carolina. His research interests focus on the conceptualization, measurement, and application of positive psychology constructs with children and youth in the school setting. He is a fellow of the American Psychological Association (Division 16) and International Society for Quality of Life Studies and an elected member of the Society for the Study of School Psychology.

Barbara A. Kerr is the Williamson Family Distinguished Professor of Counseling Psychology at the University of Kansas. Her research has concerned the nature and nurture of giftedness, creativity, and specific talents. She is the author of *Smart Girls: A New Psychology of Girls, Women, and Giftedness* and *Smart Boys: Talent, Masculinity and the Search for Meaning.* She has been the principal investigator for many National Science Foundation projects for the encouragement of scientific talent and has won both the APA Presidential Citation and the APS Esther Katz Rosen award for research in the psychology of giftedness.

Jaime L. Kurtz is a visiting assistant professor of psychology at Pomona College. She received her B.A. from Millersville University of Pennsylvania and her Ph.D. from the University of Virginia, where her dissertation research on savoring was funded by a National Research Service Award from NIMH. She has created and taught a seminar on the psychology of happiness and is the recipient of the University of Virginia Psychology Department's Distinguished Teaching Fellowship, the Graduate Teaching Award, and the Rebecca Boone Teaching Award.

Amber Lynn Larson is a master's student in counseling psychology at the University of Kansas. Her research interests include multiculturalism and diversity, positive psychology and prosocial behavior, and creativity.

James W. Lauckhardt is currently a second year Ph.D. student in the Applied Developmental Psychology Program at Fordham University. His area of research is Positive Youth Development, particularly in the areas of Civic and Community Engagement.

Sonja Lyubomirsky is a professor of psychology at the University of California, Riverside. She received her Ph.D. in Social/Personality Psychology from Stanford University. In 2002, Lyubomirsky's research was recognized with a Templeton Positive Psychology Prize. Currently, she is an associate editor of the *Journal of Positive Psychology* and (with co-PI Ken Sheldon) holds a 5-year million-dollar grant from the National Institute of Mental Health to conduct research on the possibility of permanently increasing happiness. Her teaching and mentoring of students have been recognized with the Faculty of the Year and Faculty Mentor of the Year Awards. Lyubomirsky's research and her recent book, *The How of Happiness*, have received a great deal of media attention.

David G. Myers is a professor of psychology at Hope College. He communicates psychological science to students and the public through his textbooks for introductory and social psychology and through general audience trade books, including *The Pursuit of Happiness* and related magazine articles.

Tayyab Rashid is a clinical consultant with the Positive Psychology Center at the University of Pennsylvania and also works for the Toronto District School Board, Ontario, Canada. He received his Ph.D. in clinical psychology from the Fairleigh Dickinson University, Teaneck, New Jersey. He completed his predoctoral internship and postdoctoral research fellowship at the University of Pennsylvania, where he worked with Martin Seligman on devising a new psychotherapy for depression called Positive Psychotherapy (PPT). Dr. Rashid teaches and researches active exploration of the proverbial half-full glass.

Lonnie R. Sherrod is the executive director of the Society for Research in Child Development and Professor of Psychology in Fordham University's Applied Developmental Psychology Program (ADP). He received his Ph.D. in Psychology from Yale University in 1978. He edits *The Social Policy Reports*. He is a Fellow in both the American Psychological Association and American Psychological Society. His area of research is Youth Political Development.

Bart Soenens is a postdoctoral researcher at the Department of Developmental, Social, and Personality Psychology at Ghent University, Belgium. His main research interests are processes of parenting and parent-child relationships during adolescence with a focus on dysfunctional and controlling styles of parenting.

Maarten Vansteenkiste is a professor at Ghent University, Belgium. Through his research, he tries to expand the Self-Determination Theory in various ways. He is especially interested in theoretically and empirically linking the Self-determination Theory with other well-established motivation theories, and in studying the effect of pursuing intrinsic relative to extrinsic goals on well-being, performance, and social functioning.

Tara S. Wernsing is an assistant professor at the Instituto de Empresa in Madrid. She earned her Ph.D. at the Global Leadership Institute at University of Nebraska. Her research focuses on self-awareness and leadership development.